Jacquie and Charlie

Happiness, always
JoAnne and Lou
March 20, 1998

Compliments
of the
Chef

The Friends of the Library of Collier County, Inc.
Naples, Florida

Additional copies of **Compliments of the Chef** may be obtained by calling
the Friends of the Library of Collier County, Inc., at 941/262-8135.

First printing: 10,000 Copies September 1996
ISBN 0-9652146-0-5
Library of Congress Card Catalog Number 96-084591

Painting on cover by Barrett Edwards.

Printed in the USA by

WIMMER

The Wimmer Companies, Inc.

Memphis

Table of Contents

Working with Chef's Recipes

Chefs are hardworking, creative people who are always striving to improve their skill of combining ingredients for new taste sensations. They, unlike many of us today, use real butter, heavy cream, and eggs freely, creating the best, purest combinations for the enjoyment of the palate. The cost of an item, like truffle oil, is of little consequence to a professional and, while it may be used sparingly, is added whenever it is thought to be necessary for the right balance of flavor.

The process of obtaining recipes from busy professionals is not always easy. Quantities, specific details and qualifying advice are hard to write down when the most significant ingredient to such recipes is inspiration.

We have worked with the chefs, have tested each recipe for taste, have looked at each one for clarification and present them to you proudly as a work of art to be enjoyed. As with any other work of art, the interpretation of its color, its flavor and its meaning is left to the audience. We suggest that you feel comfortable making substitutions, using lighter, low-fat ingredients if you so wish, adding spices of your own, if you choose, understanding that the chef who has presented you with his recipe has done so with experience and pride.

Of course, the real test of such recipes is going to the establishment and experiencing it for yourself. In Florida, beautiful, lush, tropical Naples and Marco Island offer you endless opportunities to do so.

Whether you come in person or visit these establishments through the recipes in our book, we extend **Compliments of the Chef!**

Chefs Included in the Cookbook

James Alarie
Dean Allen
Douglas Amarn
Brian Annapolen
Löic Auril
Bob Aylwin
Shane Bedford
Giovanni Belsito
Keith Benoit
Frenchie Benoist
Seth Berman
Alex Bernard
Ginna Berry
Anthony Biagetti
Butch Bittle
George Bleem
Dave Bobay
Paul Bradley
Philip Branan
Dee Dee Brown
John Calella
David Cassidy
Mike Conroy
Steve Corio
John B. Craft
José Duran
Richard Elias
Kelly Ellis
Michael Etienne
John R. Farmosa

Parker L. Fausnight
Luis Fernandez
Chaz Franks
Wilhelm Gahabka
Gilbert Gonzales
Joe Gross
Ron Harton
Darek Haupt
Peter Hess
Bill Hoever
Jesse Housman
George Huang
Joe Huang
Steve Joynt
Drew Kasley
Gunter Kilian
Daniel Kniola
Bruce Kretchmer
Hilde Kumpia
Nicholas Kunzli
Ron Landry
Kurt Ledbetter
John Liebels
Norman Love
Richard MacDonald
Jamie MacLarty
Chuck Mahoney
Sol Malo
Ed Marchese
Steve Martin

Bryan Matson
Robert Merriman
Marvin Messenger
Lothar Moese
Wallo Myer
Aaron Newberry
Ken Pace
Keith Parker
Tom Peterson
Alain Pettibon
Richard Perry
Russell Powers
Skip Quillen
Ron Rickaby
Joel Ricobene
Tony Ridgway
Tony Romeo
James Ross
Felix Roux
Felipe Schifano
Justin Schoyder
Vince Serpa
Frank Setera
Fernando Silviero
Bret Siska
Charles Sogness
John Stoker
Joe Szlachetka
Peter Thorpe
Chris Tomboni

Hats Off to the Chefs!

At the present time, when dress is very informal, hats, for the most part, have disappeared. It is interesting to note, therefore, that chefs still wear their hats (or toques) with great pride. And they should! The tall, white pristine toque of an executive chef is an honored symbol of haute cuisine, a badge of honor and authority.

In early times, the toque was a sign of office for the head man in the kitchen. It was the royal headdress of the Assyrian kings that inspired the toque's shape and ribbed sides. Why did the kings allow their crown to be copied in such a manner? Because a loyal chef was the best protection a king could have against being poisoned by traitors in his midst. Chefs were paid lavishly and ranked with members of the court. These bountiful gestures assured loyalty in the face of attempted bribery by any enemy.

Great emphasis was placed on the value of eggs in days of yore. They were regarded by Persians, Greeks and Romans as not only an excellent food item, but a symbol of the universe. Eggs later became a symbol of Easter and a sign of the resurrection. We are told chefs took this information into consideration when designing their hats. Toques are made with 100 pleats, representing 100 ways to prepare an egg, the measuring stick of a really creative cook.

The chef's place of work is a beehive of activity. The executive chef is known as the *chef de cuisine*. The second in command is the *sous-chef*. Under them are various *chefs de partie*. The roast chef is the *chef rotisseur;* the fish cook is the *chef poissonnier;* the sauce cook is the *chef saucier;* the pastry chef is the *chef patissier* and so on.

No matter what the position, the formality or informality of the setting, good chefs put their hearts and soul into their work and, as lovers of good cooking, our hats are off to them! *Merci!*

About the Friends of the Library...

From the time a small room which divided the boy's and girl's restrooms in the local schoolhouse was used as a library, a record room and the principal's office, library facilities in Collier county have grown significantly. Presently there are seven library branches throughout the county.

To get it to this point, it took a lot of cooperation from the local citizens. Since the residents of Naples lacked a library, the school library was open to the general public. The Friends of the Library was established in 1957 to start the first public library. Everyone donated second-hand books and a few new ones were purchased. The only practical place to install this new library was in the powder room of the Naples Woman's Club because that room had a large closet. The honor system was used for checking out books and if one became overdue, payment was dropped into a coin box.

Today, the Friends of the Library operate on a large scale. They own the land upon which the main library sits, leasing it back to the county for $1 a year. Last year, the Friends pledged $100,000 to the library to assist with the purchase of books, videos, the funding of a volunteer coordinator, helping the library system get up and running on the Free-Net and other such things. With the county growing as fast as it is, the library system is hard-pressed to keep pace. The Friends are needed to help where we can.

Recently an Endowment Fund was established so that the Friends will be able to continue to enhance library services for years to come. The proceeds from the sale of this book will benefit this fund. What better way for the Friends to raise money than by producing a beautiful book!

The Friends of the Library of Collier County thank you for your support.

PLEASE NOTE:

 The **key** is a symbol placed beside the name of a private club.

 Look through the book for the symbol of the Pelican, offering tasty historical tidbits.

From Raw Wilderness
to Polished Jewel

Way down on the southwest coast of Florida, the little Town of Naples was literally carved out of a wilderness in 1886, incorporated in 1923, and became the City of Naples in 1949. One year later it had a population of 1,450 – including the suburban areas. By 1970 those figures had shot up to 12,045 and the journey of "discovery" by the world was off and running. Currently, the city population has almost doubled that number and apparently the only way to find city ground for a newer/bigger house is to buy and tear down an older one. But Collier County (one of the biggest in the State) is still going strong, with handsome new developments constantly under construction to add to its present population of well over 216,000 people.

To be sure, there are many long–time residents who are not pleased with this spectacular growth and fondly recall the "old days when we all knew everyone in town." But it was bound to happen! When a superb jewel is removed from the darkness of its velvet case, its shining beauty captures the attention of all who behold it – and so it is with Naples, whose special ambience is no longer a secret.

Historical records for this area go back to 1200 B. C., when an estimated 10,000 Calusa Indians were based here but ruled the roost from Tampa to Cape Sable. Tall, handsome and fearless, they lived on fish and shellfish from the warm Gulf waters; berries, nut, roots and a wide variety of game from the dense forest. Their peaceful existence ended when Ponce de Leon tried to claim the territory for Spain in a series of fierce, cruel attacks that started in 1517 and continued until the Calusas finally drove the Spanish troops back to their St. Augustine settlement, where they stayed until surrendering to the British in 1764. Unfortunately, the Calusas had no natural immunity against the Spaniards' diseases, and by the late 1700s they were almost decimated. The 16 remaining families eventually emigrated to Cuba.

With zero inhabitants through the next century, the area reverted to a wilderness of subtropical vegetation. This time it grew over the huge shell mounds the Indians left on Marco Island, creating small hills on otherwise flat terrain which, in turn, concealed a wealth of artifacts. Most of these artifacts have since been painstakingly unearthed and put on display or stored in various museums.

When Florida became a part of the United States in 1821 the white settlers, who coveted the Indian settlements' choice grounds, demanded their removal. The ensuing ferocious battles took place primarily in north Florida, but many of the Seminoles retreated southward, including some of the Mikasuki tribe. Excellent farmers, hunters and ranchers, the Miccosukees (current spelling)

eventually settled deep in the Everglades where they could conceal their homes and live in peace. Their descendants still live and work in Collier County.

For the next 25 years, only intermittent traders, intrepid loners, and squatters seeking a new and better life, tramped through the dense woods, leaving nothing behind but old campsites. However, a prominent Kentucky politician, General John Williams, had heard of the area's beauty and fine climate and in 1885 he convinced his friend, Walter N. Haldeman, owner–publisher of the *Louisville Courier Journal*, to join him in a long–cherished venture. The idea was to sail down the coast until they found the perfect spot to build houses that wealthy Midwestern families would buy as an escape from their long cold winters.

With a hired engineer aboard a schooner they chartered in Tampa, the men set off on their odyssey...and almost bought 5,000 acres of ground in present–day Venice from a cattle–raiser. They plied him with charm and Kentucky bourbon and thought they had a good deal; but when he didn't return the next morning as promised, they tracked down his wife. Apparently she had chewed him out for allowing the men to get him drunk so they could cheat him out of a fair price – and he promptly took off on his mule for a long ride in the woods.

Back on the schooner they again headed south. Arriving at Gordon Pass late one afternoon, the friends settled down to enjoy a gorgeous sunset. Suddenly inspired, Williams stood up and excitedly announced: "Walter, this is IT! THIS is the ideal spot." According to lore, the name was derived from another gorgeous sunset they recalled having seen in Naples, Italy.

As the saying goes: "If you build it, they will come." But it wasn't easy.

In 1887 Haldeman, Williams and several other partners, established the Naples Town Improvement Company and bought 8,700 acres from the Florida Land Development Company. Lots were sold for $1.50 each; but it was whispered that a shotgun had been traded for three lots that later sold for $5,000 and there was a little fudging on the price of larger blocks. A promotional booklet states that "three months after the survey was commenced, over 1,000 lots were sold 'to many people of prominence and wealth.' "

Plans included a small hotel for tourists, a general store to sell supplies, and a 600' pier to serve as a freight and passenger dock. Without roads, all building materials arrived by boat, and a small tram on narrow gauge iron rails operated between the pier and hotel. The workers slept in tents and ate their meals in "the largest outdoor dining room in Florida" – the beach. Early buyers grouped their houses around the hotel, which could house 20–30 people and was the primary setting for social activity; others lived in tents or fishing shacks. A small steamer made regular stops, which increased during "the season" to twice a week on a bigger steamer.

However, by 1889 the Naples Company was in deep financial trouble and three major newspapers advertised a public sale, to be held in Naples at 1 p. m. January 1st. At the appointed time, Haldeman was the only bidder present and the sale was postponed until the arrival of the next boat at 5 p. m. Haldeman, still the only bidder, bought the entire company for $50,000, which included all town lots and property of the company, the hotel, its fixtures, office equipment, furniture, docks, machinery, the sloop *Edith*, the steamer *Fearless*, all small boats and lighters, and about 8,000 acres of land outside the town.

After Haldeman's death, his sons ran the business until 1914, when they sold it to Ed Crayton. A very successful Ohio real estate executive, Crayton is credited with guiding Naples to the beautiful city it is today. As quickly as possible he added 40 rooms to the hotel and a 10–passenger bus to transport guests to and from the train station in Fort Myers. The hotel, which housed many famous guests over the years and was the setting for many business transactions, closed its doors in 1962 and was torn down 10 years later.

The city of Naples was incorporated on August 13, 1925 and two years later railway service arrived with two separate lines within 10 days of each other. The Atlantic Coast Line, primarily a freight line for shipping fruits and vegetables to northern markets was first; the Seaboard Air Line Railway transported passengers and arrived at 6 p. m. every day – an event that drew half the town to the depot. Both railways are long gone, but the Naples Depot still stands – a treasured landmark.

Barron G. Collier, Sr., for whom the county was named, owned 90% of it at one point and left his clear imprint in many areas, but is probably best known for his gigantic role in the completion of Tamiami Trail, which connects the west and east coasts. A huge undertaking financially and physically, it was also fraught with such dangers as 31 miles of solid rock that had to be blasted out. Construction started in October 1923; the State Roads Department took over in August, 1926 to finish the last 12 most difficult miles, and Tamiami Trail officially opened on April 25, 1928 with an enormous gala celebration at Everglades City.

Growth and improvements continued. Each winter the northern guests returned; each summer most of the stores closed as their owners went north. A serene, pleasant lifestyle – until disaster named Donna, a Category IV hurricane, arrived on September 30, 1960. She was a furious lady that struck hard for an hour,

followed by a surge of water that sent bay, river and gulf waters crashing and churning over the mainland, crumbling buildings under the force of 9 1/2 feet of water. Rain continued to pour down for another six hours and, when morning finally arrived, it was evident that very little remained unscathed. Miraculously, there wasn't a single death and, over the long haul, there was a silver lining.

Faced with the necessity of rebuilding, the city fathers seized the opportunity to rewrite zoning laws that would establish strict regulations for all aspects of building and development. These laws underlie today's beauty.

Accelerated growth started in 1970 and increased in the 80's when newer, bigger homes and communities drew more and more buyers. In the 90's the population explosion brought more commercial enterprises: places to go, to see, to dine in, sleep in, vacation in, play in and to purchase almost anything. In August, 1995, as the result of an annual magazine survey, Naples was selected as one of the 10 best places to live in the United States.

It's really mind–boggling to realize that in just a little over 100 years, the infant Naples has grown from one small hotel with a dining room, nestled in a wilderness, to the status of a city increasingly well–known in foreign countries. Literally, from catching your own fish for dinner to dining in your choice of fine restaurants – or to reproducing the recipes in this book – each of which was contributed with the "Compliments of the Chef."

Dual Creativity

Consider delights – both culinary and visual – you will find an abundance of both in Collier County. Visually, we are bombarded with images of sparkling multi-hued water, of exotic birds proudly flaunting their elegant plumage, of striking tropical foliage, of rare fruits, of smiling flowers and awesome sunsets proclaiming the end of another day in paradise. Nature has showered our region with its brightest colors and most charming creatures. Mankind has cooperated by surrounding its local architectures with an array of groomed and colorful horticulture.

Several Florida artists have captured these elements and recorded them in oils, watercolors, acrylics and pastels. We applaud their talents and appreciate their cooperation in providing the "visual paprika" in this book.

Paul Arsenault — was graduated from the Art Institute of Boston in 1973 and the following year began his professional painting career in Naples, Florida. His fascination with the tropics led him to periodically leave his home base and record in oil the beauty of various islands in the Caribbean and Central and South America. Other artistic forays led him to the Chesapeake area, New England and the Maritimes of Canada.
In addition to annual shows and commissions, he has taught on-location painting classes and completed five murals.
Paul has established galleries in Newport, RI, Gloucester, MA and, of course, Naples, FL.

Judith Blain — specializes in water color paintings, for which she has won several awards, and has been concentrating recently on exotic and colorful tropical themes in her work. Born in Pittsburgh, PA, she received a B.S. and M.A. degrees from Western Reserve University, completed graduate study at Carnegie-Mellon and Pennsylvania State University. Several of her watercolors have been selected for exhibition posters. She is also represented in such corporate collections as Minnesota Mining and Manufacturing, Pillsbury, General Mills, Pittsburgh Plate Glass, Westinghouse, Radisson Suite Beach Resort and others.
Her work may be seen at the Shaw Gallery in Naples, FL.

Gerry Brynjulson — received a BFA degree from the University of Denver and taught art in Denver Public schools, as well as in evening art classes at the University of Denver. At that time he also had several one-man and two-man shows in the area. Moving to Tobago in the West Indies, he continued painting for twenty-three years. The summers of 1970 through 1982 were spent in Florence, Italy, painting and studying print making. Today Gerry lives and works on Marco Island where his oils and watercolors can be seen in his studio.
This artist is represented at the Naples Art Association Gallery in Naples, FL.

David Coolidge — received his BFA degree from Drake University and studied at the Tyler School of Art in Rome, as well as the Pennsylvania Academy of Fine Arts. He is a member of the Philadelphia Watercolor Club and has been included in the annual exhibit of the American Watercolor Society in New York. David has done commissioned work for the Colonial Williamsburg Foundation; the Hershey Foundation; the J. M. Smucker Company, Arthur Anderson & Company and others. His emphasis is upon rural scenes, street scenes, horticulture and documenting in watercolor the beauty of scenes throughout America, plus those of his world-wide travels.
He maintains a studio in Old Naples and is represented by the Naples Art Gallery, the Newman Galleries of Philadelphia and Bryn Mawr, and the Windjammer Gallery of Hamilton, Bermuda.

Barrett Edwards — studied art while living in Paris for several years. Her paintings were twice accepted by the Salon d'Automme at the Grand Palais there. The Gallerie Jean Lammelin selected her work for its Franco-American Exhibition. In Naples she teaches art, does portrait work, as well as still lifes and scenes. Barrett painted the custom art work on our cover.
She is represented by the Naples Art Association Gallery, by Local Color Gallery, by McLarin-Barnes Gallery in Ontario, Canada and by Prism Gallery also in Ontario, Canada.

Dorothy Greene — is a private studio instructor as well as a public and private workshop teacher. She received a Bachelor of Art Education from the University of Miami and a Bachelor of Fine Arts from Florida International University. Her works have appeared in over a dozen shows and have earned several Best in Show, First and/or Second Place awards. Dorothy's paintings are included in several corporate collections, such as Florida Power & Light Corp., The Bascom Palmer Eye Institute, the Center for Fine Arts (Vero Beach, FL), the Tropicana Fruit Company (Bradenton, FL), Florida International University, and Senator Bob Graham's office in the U.S. Senate Office Building, Washington, D.C. Her medium is watercolor and her subject matter is Florida's horticulture enhanced by the effects of natural light.
She is represented at Naples Art Gallery, Inc.

Robert C. Gruppé — is living proof of the strength of genes. He studied for twenty years under the guidance of his father, Emile Gruppé and is the grandson of artist Charles Gruppé. A product of the Gloucester School of Painting, he also studied drawing under the tutelage of sculptor George Demetrios. Robert Gruppé has won more than twenty awards and has had exhibitions at the Shawmut Bank in Boston, MA, the Collectors Gallery in Camden, ME and the Sawyer Library and Seaport Gallery of Gloucester, MA. Working in the oil medium he stresses use of impasto brushwork and vibrant pastels. Many of his works depict marine scenes in both New England and Florida.
Robert is represented by the Gruppé Gallery, Rocky Neck, East Gloucester, MA and by the deBruyne Gallery in Naples, FL.

Don Kettleborough — earned a B.S. in Education from Northern Illinois University, plus a Masters of Art from Bradley University. Early in his career he was an art instructor in Wisconsin and Northern Illinois. Don's commissions include a Portrait of Nancy Reagan, the Eureka College Collection, the Westinghouse Communities Collection, President George Bush Family, the Moorings Country Club, the Quail Creek Country Club and the Bay Colony Club. He has exhibited in the Group Show, Bradley University, Art Expo 1992 and One Man Shows 1990-1996 in Naples, FL. Murals, portraits and nature's striking birds, fish and flowers are part of Don's repertoire.
His works are represented at the Rick Moore Galleries in Naples, FL.

Paula Malone — found her 'niche' after completing several art classes. Her move to Florida in 1986 introduced her to the exquisite bird life in our area and she was immediately captivated by their variety and beauty. Her intricate artistic style focuses into the most minute details of her bird and wildlife studies. An avid wildlife photographer, Paula spends hours in the field photographing and sketching her subjects. This process is followed by an in-depth reference study of the birds' characteristics and habits. The results are rendered in a detailed pencil sketch and then completed in the difficult medium of pastels. Paula's work has been featured at the Collier County Museum and may be found in collections in the United States and abroad.

Carl E. Schwartz — was born in Detroit, MI and received his BFA degree from the Art Institute of Chicago and the University of Chicago. As a well known artist and print maker, he has received several awards, he has participated in juried and international shows, as well as one and two person shows. His work appears in major permanent collections throughout the United States. Carl is listed in *Who's Who in American Art, Who's Who in the Midwest* and *The Dictionary of International Biography*, among others. A realistic painter, Carl moved to Ft. Myers, FL in 1984 from the Chicago area where he had taught and painted for many years. He is represented by the Neapolitan Art Gallery in Old Naples.

The dual creativity of artist and chef is combined
and celebrated in the following pages for your pleasure.

Artwork Shown in This Book

Appetizers

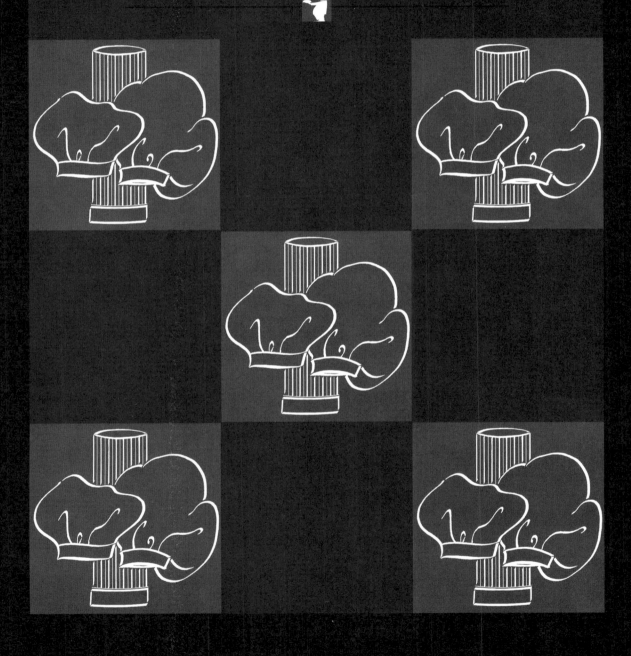

Appetizers

Jezebel Sauce

The Island Club of Naples Inc.

1 10–ounce jar pineapple jam or preserves
1 10–ounce jar apple jelly
1 5–ounce jar horseradish
1 to 2 Tablespoons dry mustard, to taste

Put all ingredients into blender or food processor and blend until combined. To serve, pour over large block of cream cheese. Serve with crackers.

Preparation: 5 minutes   Easy   Yield: 3 cups

Swiss Lorraine Spinach Dip

Kretch's Garden Restaurant

2 10–ounce bags fresh spinach, washed, coarsely chopped
1 medium onion, chopped
1 Tablespoon oil
½ pound Swiss Lorraine cheese, shredded
1 teaspoon salt (optional)
½ cup mayonnaise

Simmer spinach in one cup of water until barely cooked. Drain, chop and cool in refrigerator. Sauté onion in 1 Tablespoon oil until brown. Squeeze excess water out of chilled spinach and place spinach in a mixing bowl. Add cheese, sautéed onion, salt and mayonnaise, mix well. Place in a shallow quiche–type pan. Bake at 350°F. 15–20 minutes until light brown on top. Serve with French bread, chips or crackers.

Preparation: 15 minutes   Serves: 10
Cooking: 20 minutes   Moderately Easy
      Serve warm

Miccosukee (Mikasuki) Indians

Indians from the Mikasuki tribe played an important role in the many battles of the Seminole wars. Although they had come to north Florida from other states and never abandoned their own culture or language, they eventually became generally classified as Seminoles because they freely associated with them. They fought the wars side by side to preserve the Seminole property and way of life.

The most dominant and militant Indians, the Mikasukis determined to stay in Florida. Primarily hunters and farmers, they gradually reduced the deer herds and, after 1750, shifted more and more to cattle raising from herds that were running wild from abandoned Spanish ranches. Some had vast herds individually, not communally.

When the federal government sought to move all Indians to reservations west of the Mississippi, about 200 of them refused and settled deep in the Everglades where they had undisputed possession of a huge area well into this century. Eventually the Seminoles moved closer to the east coast. The Miccosukees (modern spelling) still live and work in Collier County.

HOW-TO: *Blanch Bacon—put the bacon into boiling water and cook for a couple of minutes and then immediately into cold water to halt the cooking process. Blanching the bacon helps to keep it from curling and removes some of the grease before you use it to wrap the shrimp.*

Oysters

Over 70 million pounds of oysters are ingested each year, which would seem to qualify this vitamin–charged bivalve as a national habit. Reputedly, Casanova ate 50 or more every evening. (The source of its legendary power as an aphrodisiac?)

All oysters are edible during their spawning season (the months with an "r" in them). Northern bivalves are at their best in the fall and winter months, while the Gulf oysters are firm and ripe from December on. In its natural state an oyster may grow large or small with the shell flat or deep and rounded. Lovers of oysters–on–the–halfshell believe that is not only the best but the ONLY way to eat them!

The oyster beds that once surrounded Florida on a vast scale have now narrowed the commercial harvest to the Apalachicola region of the Gulf Coast due to habitation, destruction, and pollution. But that doesn't mean oysters have disappeared – you just have to be patient or try harder to find them.

Shrimp Dijonnaise
Apollo's Oceanview Restaurant

2 pounds shrimp (21–25 large shrimp)
24 strips blanched bacon, cut in half
¼ cup lemon juice
¼ cup white wine
2 Tablespoons olive oil
½ cup Dijon mustard
2 teaspoons Worcestershire sauce
2 large cloves garlic, chopped

Clean shrimp and devein; set aside. Blanch bacon in boiling water; set aside. In a shallow pan mix all ingredients except shrimp and bacon. Add shrimp to mustard mixture and mix to coat; refrigerate for 3 hours. Remove shrimp from the marinade and wrap each shrimp with the half strips of bacon from tip of tail to wide part. Place shrimp on baking sheet and bake at 350°F. until shrimp turns pink (about 15 minutes). Serve on fresh sautéed spinach.

Preparation: 30 minutes	Easy	Serves: 8
Baking: 15 minutes	Serve immediately	

Oysters Supreme
Konrad's Seafood & Grille Room

1 slice bacon, diced
2 Tablespoons chopped onion
4 leaves basil, chopped
¼ teaspoon fresh chopped garlic
1 tomato, chopped
¼ cup white wine
8 fresh spinach leaves
6 raw oysters
2 Tablespoons Feta cheese

In a skillet, over medium heat, sauté bacon and onions until onions become translucent. Stir in basil, garlic and chopped tomato. Cook until tomato is soft. Add white wine, and reduce mixture by half. Add spinach leaves and cook just until soft. Place oysters in an ovenproof plate and spoon mixture over. Bake at 375°F. for 5 minutes. Remove from oven, top with crumbled Feta cheese and return to oven for 3 minutes. Season to taste and serve.

Preparation: 15 minutes	Easy	Yield: 6 oysters
Cooking: 8 minutes		

Cajun Tasso Ham Grits Cakes
Savannah a Fine Traditional Restaurant

2 pounds grits (ground instant may be used)
8 ounces Cajun Tasso Ham* (dried), minced
8 ounces Monterey Jack cheese, grated
8 ounces mixed wild mushrooms, sliced thin
1½ cups half–and–half
salt and pepper to taste
2 Tablespoons (mixture) chopped herbs (parsley,
    thyme, basil)
butter for frying

In a large pot bring 3 quarts of water to a boil. Add grits, turn down heat, and let mixture simmer for 30–40 minutes, stirring so mixture doesn't stick to bottom of pan. (Can also make grits in a double boiler.) Add ham, cheese and mushrooms, mix together. Grits should be very thick. Add more water and some of the half–and–half to consistency where wooden spoon still stands in mixture. Season to taste with salt and pepper and herbs for color and flavor. Pour mixture onto a greased baking tray; refrigerate until firm. Using round cutter, cut into half moon shapes. Sauté grits cakes in hot buttered frying pan to golden brown. Serve on roasted tomato sauce.

NOTE: Tasso ham is available at speciality stores or by mail–order.

Preparation: 15 minutes   Moderately Difficult   Serves: 6
Cooking: 30–40 minutes

Roasted Tomato Sauce

12 fresh plum tomatoes
2 cloves garlic, chopped
1 Tablespoon oil or butter
2 Tablespoons chopped fresh basil
2 Tablespoons chopped fresh thyme
2 cups chicken stock
salt and pepper to taste
½ cup heavy cream

Place plum tomatoes on a baking sheet tray and roast in 350°– 375°F. oven for 20 minutes. When roasted, remove skin and seeds, chop into chunks. In medium saucepan heat oil or butter and sauté garlic until golden brown. Add tomatoes, basil and thyme. Stir in chicken stock, season with salt and pepper to taste, and simmer for 20 minutes. Add more chicken stock to desired consistency. Finish sauce with heavy cream and heat through. Sauce should be chunky. To serve, place sauce on a plate and top with Tasso Ham Grits Cake.

Preparation: 15 minutes   Moderately Difficult   Serves: 6
Baking: 20 minutes
Cooking: 20 minutes

Getting By

Natives and early settlers had to make the most of what was available. Curlew was a favorite dish. Butter was scarce and did not keep so they used gravies instead. Tomato gravy was very popular. Jelly was made from guavas and sea grapes. Pies were made from native sour oranges. Bananas were plentiful.

Just Enough

A favorite old Florida story concerns Bone Mizell, South Florida's favorite cow hunter, who worked for Ziba King. On one of their cattle drives, they found themselves without a cook. One of the crew was appointed to run the chuck wagon. He grumbled and took to the task, telling all who would listen, "If anybody complains about the food, they're gonna take over the job!"

Nobody complained and the poor guy kept on cooking. One day he decided he'd get rid of the job one way or another. He stirred up a whole passel of salt into the beans and waited. Bone was the first to speak up. "These beans are awfully salty!" Suddenly remembering the cook's bargain, he quickly added. "Just the way I like 'em!"

Salmon Terrine

The Naples Beach Hotel and Golf Club

3 pounds salmon (boneless and skinless)
1 Tablespoon salt
1 cup heavy cream
2½ ounces Vermouth
white pepper to taste
6 ounces fresh spinach leaves

Cube 2 pounds of salmon, season with salt and pepper, purée in a food processor—piece by piece, add heavy cream and Vermouth. *Note: When making this purée, make sure salmon and cream are very cold and work fast so the fat and protein will not separate.* Season 1 pound of salmon with salt and pepper. Blanch the spinach leaves and wrap around salmon. Brush terrine mold (or loaf pans) with butter, fill half full with salmon purée, set the spinach wrapped salmon onto the purée, fill with remaining purée. Cover the tops with heavy duty foil and place pans in a large roasting pan with enough boiling water to come halfway up the sides of the loaf pans. Bake 45 to 50 minutes in a pre–heated oven at 250°F. Chill overnight. At time of serving, unmold Terrines and cut into slices ¼–⅓–inch thick. Serve on toast rounds, crackers, or bread slices.

Preparation: 45 minutes   Moderately Easy   Serves: 16–25
Baking: 45–50 minutes   Must do ahead
Chilling: overnight

Lobster Strudel with Tomato-Armagnac Sauce
The Naples Yacht Club

2 Tablespoons unsalted butter
1 clove garlic, pressed
½ cup dry bread crumbs
1 box phyllo dough
¼ cup clarified butter
1 pound lobster meat, medium dice
½ pound fresh spinach, blanched and squeezed dry
6 ounces chèvre (goat cheese)
1 Tablespoon fresh minced basil
salt and ground white pepper to taste
1 egg beaten with ¼ cup water

Sauté the bread crumbs and garlic in 2 Tablespoons butter until golden brown; set aside. Preheat oven to 350°F. Carefully separate 2 sheets of phyllo dough and place onto center of a clean tea towel. Lightly brush with clarified butter and top with another layer of phyllo, repeating three times, 8 leaves in all. Sprinkle bread crumbs evenly over the dough. Spread lobster, cheese and seasoning in a 4–inch wide strip along the short side of the dough, leaving one inch free on each side of the dough. Carefully roll the dough around the filling into a long cylinder. Pinch or close the ends, then brush the cylinder with the egg wash. Bake 20–30 minutes or until pastry is golden brown. To serve, pool the Tomato Armagnac Sauce in the center of a plate and top with one or two slices of strudel.

Preparation: 30 minutes   Moderately difficult   Serves: 8
Baking: 20–30 minutes

Tomato Armagnac Sauce

2 Tablespoons olive oil
1 shallot, minced
½ cup Armagnac brandy
1 cup seeded, peeled, diced ripe tomatoes
1 teaspoon chopped fresh thyme
1 teaspoon chopped fresh basil
1 cup strong fish stock
2 Tablespoons Armagnac brandy
salt and pepper to taste

Over medium heat, sweat shallot in oil for 5 minutes. Add Armagnac, tomatoes, herbs, fish stock, and simmer until reduced by half. Pour into food processor or blender and purée. Add 2 Tablespoons Armagnac and adjust seasonings to taste. Serve with Lobster Strudel.

Preparation: 10 minutes   Easy   Serves: 8
Cooking: 10 minutes

HOW-TO: *Clarify Butter—slowly melt unsalted butter so that the solids sink to the bottom of the pan. Skim off the top foam and carefully pour off the clear golden liquid butter. This is the clarified butter.*

Sautéed Portobello Mushrooms
Calella's Bistro Inc.

4 medium portobello mushrooms, stemmed and
washed
¼ cup white wine
salt and pepper to taste
2 Tablespoons olive oil
8 cloves garlic, peeled and finely chopped
1 cup white wine
½ cup butter
½ pound spinach, washed and stemmed
16 ¼–inch strips Italian roasted red peppers
¼ pound fresh buffalo mozzarella, sliced thin

In a 2–quart casserole dish, place the cleaned portobello mushrooms. Fill with 1 inch of water, add ¼ cup white wine and salt and pepper to taste. Cover and bake at 350°F. about 15 minutes, until fork tender. Drain mushrooms and keep them warm (do not reserve liquid). In a 12 –inch skillet over medium heat, add olive oil and fresh garlic, sauté until golden. Add 1 cup white wine, mushrooms, salt and pepper to taste. Cover, let reduce to half the liquid. Remove mushrooms (keep warm) reserve liquid in pan. Add butter to reserved liquid, a little at a time, stirring in to emulsify. Stir in spinach and cook for 1 minute, turning to coat and sauté. To serve, place Portobello in center of plate; surround with fresh sautéed spinach. Garnish with peppers and mozzarella. Spoon sauce over.

Preparation: 20 minutes   Moderately Easy   Serves: 4
Baking: 15 minutes
Cooking: 15 minutes

Wild Mushroom Appetizer
Bayside

Polenta Cakes

2 teaspoons olive oil
2 cloves garlic, chopped
2 cups half–and–half
½ cup Polenta
salt and white pepper to taste

Prepare a jelly roll sheet by covering with buttered baking paper or waxed paper sprayed with vegetable oil. Heat oil in a medium – sized saucepan and briefly sauté garlic in the olive oil. Add the half–and–half and bring to a boil. Stir in the Polenta and whisk to prevent lumps. Reduce heat and simmer, stirring with a wooden spoon until Polenta is no longer grainy. Season with salt and white pepper to taste. Spread Polenta on prepared jelly roll sheet to ½ inch thickness and set aside to cool. Prepare mushroom mixture.

Preparation: 45 minutes   Moderately Easy   Serves: 4–6
Cooking: 10 minutes

Mushroom Mixture

1 Tablespoon olive oil
½ pound wild mushrooms (mixture of chanterelle, portobello, shiitake, porcini)
1 Tablespoon chopped shallot
4 cloves garlic, chopped
2 cups escarole leaves, washed and chopped
¼ pound ham, cut into thick strips (¼" x ¼" x 2")
¼ cup brandy
1½ cup demi–glace or brown sauce
1 Tablespoon fine herbs, chopped (basil, thyme, chives, oregano)
½ cup heavy cream

NOTE: If using dried mushrooms, soak in warm water to soften for at least one hour prior to using. (Reserved liquid can be used in sauce).

Cut mushrooms into uniform slices and sauté in hot oil. Add chopped garlic to mushrooms. Add escarole and ham to mixture and deglaze the pan with the brandy. Add the demi–glace or brown sauce and herbs and reduce until the sauce thickens. Stir in the heavy cream.

Preparation: 45 minutes   Moderately Easy   Serves: 4–6
Cooking: 20 minutes

To Combine and Serve: Cut twelve Polenta cakes, squares or rectangles. Dredge each cake in flour and sauté in non–stick pan in a small amount of oil. Place the cakes on edge of each plate, spooning mushroom mixture into the center. Pour remaining sauce over. Garnish with tomato concassé (peeled, seeded, roughly chopped fresh tomato).

Crab Stuffed Mushrooms
The Key Wester Fish & Pasta House

30 mushrooms with stems removed, blanched and
  chilled
¾ cup clarified butter
2 Spanish onions diced (about 2 cups)
4 green bell peppers diced (about 2 cups)
4 red bell peppers diced (about 2 cups)
½ cup white wine
½ pound snow, or similar crab meat, picked over
3 cups bread crumbs

Blanch the mushrooms by plunging them into boiling water just briefly and then into cold water to stop the cooking
process. Heat butter in a deep frying pan, then add onions
and peppers; cook until tender, stirring as needed. Add white
wine and crab meat, cooking 3 minutes. Stir in just enough
bread crumbs to make a consistency that is fairly dry. Set
aside to cool, then stuff mushrooms with crab mixture and
bake at 400°F. 5–8 minutes until hot.

Preparation: 30 minutes   Easy   Serves: 8–10
Cooking: 15 minutes
Baking: 5–8 minutes

An oyster a day keeps the Spaniard away

*The Calusa Indians, occupying
Southwest Florida for some two
thousand years, were unique in
successfully resisting the Spanish
conquistadores. The Calusas had a
sophisticated theology and a
complex society that was based,
unusually, upon hunting and
gathering rather than cultivation.
Eating enough oysters to leave the
huge mounds of shells that still dot
our landscape, they supplemented
their diet with roots, sea grapes,
palmetto berries and the hearts of
the sabal palm. Sadly they were
killed by bullets and were decimated
by the white man's diseases in the
eighteenth century when Spaniards
came to trade and to fight.*

*"He was a bold man who first
swallowed an oyster"*
James I of England

Oysters Rockefeller
The Key Wester Fish & Pasta House

20 medium to large oysters, shucked and washed
½ cup clarified butter
3 Spanish onions diced
2 bags fresh spinach, stemmed, washed and drained,
or 2 packages frozen spinach, thawed and drained
½ cup Pernod (or Anisette)
1 cup heavy whipping cream
2 cups grated Parmesan cheese
salt and pepper to taste

Heat the clarified butter in a deep frying pan; add onions
and cook until tender. Stir in spinach, then remove pan
from heat and add Pernod. Return to heat and flame off
alcohol. Stir in heavy cream and 1½ cups Parmesan cheese;
allow mixture to reduce until it thickens. Season to taste
with salt and pepper; set aside to cool. [Prepare broiler–safe
pan with rock salt to stabilize shells so they don't rock and
spill contents]. Top each oyster in a shell with the spinach
mixture; sprinkle each with remaining Parmesan cheese.
Bake at 475°F. about 10 minutes, until puffed and brown.

Preparation: 40 minutes   Serves: 8–10
Cooking: 30 minutes
Baking: 15 minutes

Stone Crab and Lobster Quesadilla
Edgewater Beach Hotel

4 Tablespoons oil
1 small red onion, diced
½ red bell pepper, diced
½ green bell pepper, diced
½ yellow bell pepper, diced
2 small jalapeño peppers, seeded and diced
2 cloves garlic, chopped
1 teaspoon cumin
1 teaspoon chili powder
¾ cup lobster (6 ounces), cooked
¾ cup stone crab meat (6 ounces), cooked
salt and pepper to taste
2 Tablespoons chopped cilantro
1 cup shredded Monterey Jack cheese
8 flour tortillas

Serve with:

sour cream
fresh avocado
salsa

Sauté onion, peppers, garlic and spices until tender (about 6–8 minutes). Add lobster and stone crab. Season with salt, pepper and cilantro. Remove from heat and cool in refrigerator for 10 minutes. Stir in cheese, spread on 4 flour tortillas and top with another. Place on griddle or large fry pan with 1 Tablespoon oil and fry until brown; remove from heat. Cut into quarters. Serve with sour cream, fresh avocado, and salsa.

Preparation: 20 minutes   Moderately Easy   Serves: 4
Cooking: 15 minutes
Chilling: 10 minutes

Stone Crabs

Rock–hard and having one large and one small claw, stone–crabs are considered to be gourmet food. Their claw meat is rich, sweet and firm. Some gatherers keep the meaty large claw and return the crab to the water to grow another one—a process that takes about 18 months. Called "retreads" they will never grow to their original size.

Usually found among rocks near beaches and inlet waters, stone crabs grow to about five inches between tips of the shell and about 2 inches deep. Catches are restricted and NO females can be taken. Be forewarned.

They are only available "in season"— November to May. They are cooked en route to market and so arrive "ready–to–eat" and enjoy!

Billy Bowlegs

The final phase of the cruel Indian Wars started on December 19, 1855 when a 10–man patrol decided to camp just two miles from Chief Billy Bowlegs' town in the Big Cypress. Just to be ornery, some of the men raided Billy's garden, pulling bananas off the trees and yanking up all kinds of plants. They even admitted it when Billy charged them with the destruction.

Retribution was quick and to the point. At 5:30 the next morning, 35 Seminoles attacked the patrol, killing two men and wounding four others. Other attacks continued for a while, but the final straw came with the destruction of the villages, homes, fields and crops the Indians thought were carefully concealed. Greatly outnumbered and weary, the Indians simply did not have the strength to defend their properties or families.

On March 4, 1858, Chief Billy Bowlegs conceded defeat, accepting $5,000 for himself and $2,500 for cattle he claimed had been stolen from him. Each warrior was given $1,000, each woman and child received $100. On May 8th the war was declared ended and the last contingent of Florida Indians who agreed to go west left in 1859.

Tortuga Shrimp with Chili Mayonnaise
The Naples Beach Hotel and Golf Club

Chili Mayonnaise

1 cup mayonnaise
1 Tablespoon oregano
1½ Tablespoons chili powder
1½ teaspoons Worcestershire sauce
¼ teaspoon Tabasco sauce
1½ teaspoons cumin
1½ teaspoons paprika
¼ teaspoon garlic powder
½ teaspoon onion powder

Thoroughly combine all ingredients and chill. Best when done ahead and flavors blend. Serve with Tortuga Shrimp (recipe follows).

Preparation: 15 minutes   Easy   Yield: 1¼ cups
Chill: 4 hours or more

Tortuga Shrimp

1 pound jumbo (24 count) raw shrimp, peeled and deveined
3 large jalapeño peppers
1 pound bacon
toothpicks
chili mayonnaise (see recipe above)

Roast jalapeño peppers over charcoal fire or under broiler until charred on all sides. Remove and cover with a towel to rest a moment until you can easily handle them; peel and seed them and cut each pepper into 8 strips. Place a piece of pepper in the shrimp where the vein was removed. Wrap shrimp with a strip of bacon and secure with a toothpick. Grill shrimp over charcoal fire or under the broiler until the bacon is done. Serve hot with Chili Mayonnaise for dipping.

Preparation: 20 minutes   Moderately Easy   Serves: 4–6
Grilling: 20 minutes

Cassolette of Escargot Provençal
L'Auberge on Fifth Restaurant Français

1 Tablespoon butter
12 mushroom caps
12 to 16 large escargots
1 teaspoon chopped garlic
1 Tablespoon brandy (optional)
2 Tablespoons tomato sauce
1 teaspoon chopped parsley or cilantro

In a large pan, sauté mushroom caps in the butter over medium high heat. When mushrooms have browned, add the escargots and sauté 2 to 3 minutes. Add garlic, brandy, tomato sauce and parsley. Reduce. Can be served over toasted bread triangles or rounds.

Preparation: 10 minutes   Easy   Serves: 4
Cooking: 10 minutes

Garlic Stuffed Shrimp
Worthington Country Club

4 to 5 cloves garlic, peeled
2 shallots, peeled
¾ cup butter, softened
¼ cup chopped parsley
½ cup dried bread crumbs
8 jumbo shrimp, peeled (tails on), deveined and
    butterflied
lemon and parsley for garnish

Finely chop the garlic and shallots together so they are well blended, almost to a paste. Mix well with the softened butter and blend in the parsley and bread crumbs. Press stuffing on both sides of butterflied shrimp and bake at 350°F. 4–6 minutes. Take care that the shrimp do not dry out. Garnish with a slice or wedge of lemon and some sprigs of fresh parsley.

Preparation: 30 minutes   Moderately easy   Serves: 4
Baking: 4–6 minutes   Serve immediately

Shrimp

Shrimp are known and enjoyed just about everywhere in the world. About 370 million pounds are landed by United States fishermen and another 200 million are imported from other countries. There are hundreds of species in both saltwater and freshwater.

The Rock shrimp is a relative newcomer to the American market, although it has always been caught in abundance in Florida and Mexican waters. Until 1970, it was discarded because of its extremely hard shell but, finally, a peeling machine was designed to handle the problem and the demand has now reached several million pounds a year.

Cilantro Tequila Cured Salmon
The REGISTRY Resort

2 pounds salmon fillet, with skin on
2 pounds salt
¼ cup sugar
juice of 1 lemon
5 black peppercorns, cracked
1 cup Tequila or enough to cover halfway
1 cup chopped fresh cilantro
1 cup chopped fresh dill
¼ cup olive oil

Place salmon fillet in a glass, stainless, or plastic container and rub the salmon with ½ cup salt, the sugar, and lemon juice. Add cracked peppercorns and Tequila. Cover with cilantro and dill. Pour rest of the salt on salmon and cover with flat pan or tray, adding light weight. Let cure for 48 hours. Scrape off salt with spatula. Sprinkle on olive oil and cover with cheesecloth. Let set for 4 hours. Slice very thin and serve with Lime Margarita Sauce.

Preparation: 20 minutes   Moderately Difficult   Serves: 6
Curing: 48 hours + 4 hours

Lime Margarita Sauce

2 egg yolks
1 Tablespoon Dijon mustard
1 cup olive oil
1 cup vegetable oil
juice of 1 lime
¼ cup Sour mix
2 Tablespoons Tequila
2 Tablespoons chopped cilantro
salt and pepper

In a medium bowl whisk together egg yolks and mustard. Slowly whisk in oil and make a smooth mayonnaise. Mix together in a blender the lime juice, Sour Mix, Tequila and cilantro. Slowly add this mixture to the mayonnaise. Season to taste with salt and pepper.

Preparation: 15 minutes   Moderately Difficult   Yield: 2–3 cups

Garlic Stuffed Portobello Mushrooms with Garlic Crème and Angel Hair Pasta
Collier Athletic Club

Garlic Crème Sauce

½ cup white wine
1 Tablespoon chopped shallots
3–4 cloves roasted garlic (to yield 2 teaspoons chopped)
2 teaspoons olive oil
salt and fresh ground black pepper to taste
½ cup heavy cream (may substitute half–and–half)
2 Tablespoons butter

Peel the garlic cloves, toss in olive oil, salt and pepper to taste. Place in a small baking dish, cover and bake at 325°F. about 25– 30 minutes, until soft. Simmer the white wine, chopped shallot, roasted garlic and black pepper until reduced by ¾. Add heavy cream and reduce by ¾. Place sauce in food processor, pulsing on/off, while adding soft butter until fully blended. Keep warm.

Mushroom

1 Portobello mushroom
1 garlic clove, sliced
1 Tablespoon olive oil
salt and pepper to taste

Insert the point of a small knife randomly around the top of the mushroom. Insert slices of garlic in the holes left by the knife. Brush the top and bottom of the mushroom with olive oil, season with salt and pepper, and grill until soft in the center, about 5 minutes, Keep warm. Slice just before serving.

Pasta:

Angel hair pasta for 2
1 Tablespoon Parmesan cheese
1 Tablespoon olive oil
2 Tablespoons fresh basil, julienne

Cook angel hair pasta; drain and rinse with hot water. Toss with Parmesan cheese, olive oil, and basil. To serve: pour sauce on the plate, twirl pasta on top, arranging slices of mushroom in a fan on top. Garnish with slivers of basil.

Preparation: 45 minutes
Baking: 30 minutes
Cooking: 30 minutes

Moderately difficult
Serve immediately

Serves: 2

Baked Havarti En Croûte with Strawberry Sauce
Quail Creek Country Club

2 unbaked Puff pastry sheets 10" x 10" (1 17–ounce pkg.)
6 ounces Havarti cheese, cut into 1½" squares x ½" thick
¼ cup chopped walnuts
½ cup peeled, diced (¼") apple (Granny Smith or Delicious)
1 egg beaten with 1 teaspoon water

Cut pastry into 5–inch squares. Center cheese on pastry and top each with ½ Tablespoon chopped walnuts and 1 Tablespoon diced apples. Brush the edges of the pastry ¼–inch around with beaten egg; fold into "beggars purse" (folding opposite points to the center), pinching each seam that forms. Place on buttered cookie sheet widely spaced apart. Bake at 400°F. 10 minutes or until golden brown. Serve warm on Strawberry Sauce. (Can be made ahead up to the baking, or after baking can reheat beautifully at 350°F. until hot.)

Strawberry Sauce

16–ounce package frozen whole, unsweetened strawberries
1 Tablespoon cornstarch
1 Tablespoon water

Bring strawberries to a boil and remove from the heat. Mix cornstarch with water until smooth and stir quickly into strawberries. Return to heat and boil one minute. To serve, ladle ¼ cup sauce on plate, placing warm Baked Havarti on top.

NOTE: *When reheating sauce do not boil. Unsweetened strawberries make a tart appetizer. Add sugar or honey to taste when you bring sauce to a boil if you want it sweetened, or for leftover sauce for dessert use.*

Preparation: 30 minutes   Easy   Serves: 8
Baking: 10 minutes   Serve immediately
Cooking: 10–15 minutes

Skewered Barbeque Shrimp
Worthington Country Club

Serving for one; make multiples as needed:

4 large shrimp, peeled (tails on), deveined
2 slices bacon, cut in halves or thirds
1 bamboo skewer
Favorite barbeque sauce

Wrap bacon around peeled shrimp and place on skewer. (This can be prepared ahead of time and refrigerated for later cooking and grilling.) Place rack in a pan, or on accordion–pleated aluminum foil set in a pan. Bake at 350°F. 4–6 minutes. Remove, brush with barbeque sauce, and grill over hot coals or under the broiler to crisp the bacon. Depending on the size of the shrimp and skewers, single shrimp may be done on water–soaked toothpicks, or up to 6 shrimp on bamboo skewers. Serve with extra dipping sauce.

Preparation: 15–30 minutes	Easy	Serves: 1
Baking: 4–6 minutes	Make multiples, as needed	
Grilling: 2–3 minutes	Serve immediately	

John's Favorite Barbeque Sauce

2 teaspoons vegetable oil
1 small onion, diced
1 clove garlic, minced
1½ cups ketchup
1 Tablespoon yellow mustard
¼ cup white vinegar
3 Tablespoons Worcestershire sauce
2 Tablespoons brown sugar
2 shakes hot pepper sauce
½ to 1 cup prepared smokey barbeque sauce

Heat oil in a medium saucepan, sweat the onion and garlic. Add the rest of the ingredients except the prepared barbeque sauce, stirring well; bring to a simmer and simmer, uncovered, 35–40 minutes. Stir as needed. Blend in prepared barbeque sauce in the proportion of half the amount of your fresh sauce.

Preparation: 20 minutes	Easy	Yield: 2–3 cups
Cooking: 45–50 minutes		

Blue Crab Cakes

Michael's Cafe

2 cups seasoned croutons
1 pound jumbo lump crab meat
¼ cup diced red bell pepper
1 teaspoon green peppercorns, crushed
cumin to taste
Old Bay Seasoning to taste
3 eggs, slightly beaten
¼ to ½ cup olive oil

Chop the croutons, not too finely, and place in a stainless bowl. Pick over and clean the crab meat of all membrane and shell pieces. Add the crab meat, red pepper, peppercorns, seasonings and eggs to the croutons. Form into 16 cakes (1 to 1½ ounces each). Heat olive oil in a sauté pan and lightly brown the cakes on both sides.

Preparation: 30 minutes   Moderately easy   Serves: 8
Cooking: 30 minutes

The Blue Crab

The Blue Crab, whose name comes from its color, is found all along the Gulf Coast and the South Atlantic and is the third most important crustacean commercially in the United States. They appear inshore during warm weather (in Florida, possibly as early as February) and remain in the shallows until the onset of cold waters. They also prefer brackish water.

Soups

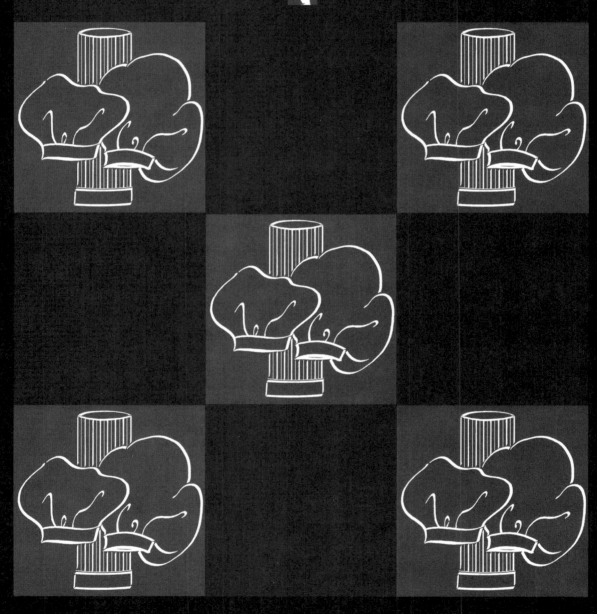

Soups

Beer Cheese Soup

Country Club of Naples

5 strips of bacon, diced
½ cup diced onion
1 quart of milk
5 ounces beer
¼ cup cornstarch
¼ cup water
2 shakes of Tabasco and Worcestershire sauces
1¼ cups Velveeta cheese
salt or chicken bouillon to taste
fresh chives
1 cup croutons, or ½ cup popcorn (optional)

Sauté bacon with onion on medium heat until bacon browns. Drain and set aside. Bring milk and beer to a gentle boil. Mix together cornstarch and water, then whisk into milk and beer mixture. Boil gently for 2 minutes and add water if the soup thickens too much. Add sautéed onion and bacon, sauces and cheese, stirring gently until cheese is melted. Taste and season as needed. Remove from heat, strain through fine mesh colander and serve. Garnish with fresh chopped chives and croutons, or popcorn.

Preparation: 25 minutes   Easy   Serves: 5 or 6

The Naples Pier

A landmark from the beginning when it was built as a dock for the boats that brought construction material and workers to develop the early town, the pier still plays a major role in the sophisticated city that Naples has become. If it could only talk, what fascinating tales it could tell. From the very first vacationing residents and guests it has been the place to watch the beautiful sunsets, to meet friends,to catch a fish for dinner, and to share with friends new to the area.

However, it has also seen hard times over the years.

The first Naples Municipal Pier was built in 1888; a 600–foot–long wharf that extended into the gulf to a water depth of 18 feet. The necessary pilings and timber were brought in by boat, off–loaded into the water, towed ashore, dragged from the surf by horses and left on the beach to dry. Construction workers, who also arrived by boat, were housed in nearby tents and fed in "the largest outdoor dining room in Florida" – the beach.

Continued on next page

Cream of Broccoli Swiss Cheese Soup
Moorings Park

¼ pound butter
1½ cups finely chopped onion
3 stalks celery, finely chopped
1½ pounds fresh or frozen broccoli, chopped
¾ cup flour
1 quart chicken stock
2 bay leaves
1 teaspoon thyme
½ teaspoon white pepper
1 teaspoon seasoning salt
2 teaspoons Worcestershire sauce
¾ pound Swiss cheese, grated
2 cups milk
2 cups half–and–half

In a large sauce pot sauté the onion and celery in butter, about 10 minutes. Cook the broccoli in a separate pan in 3 cups of water. Drain, reserving the liquid, and purée ¼ of the broccoli in blender or food processor. Set aside. Add flour to sautéed onion and celery, stirring about 3 minutes. Do not brown, just cook the flour to make a roux. Add chicken stock and reserved broccoli water; stir until smooth. Add bay leaves, thyme, white pepper, seasoning salt, and Worcestershire sauce; simmer 10 minutes. Remove bay leaves. Add Swiss cheese and stir until melted. Add broccoli and puréed broccoli; stir well. Add milk and half–and–half; stir well and bring to simmer. Serve hot.

NOTE: If preparing ahead: save the cheese and add just before serving.

Preparation: 40 minutes   Easy   Serves: 12
Cooking: 30 minutes   Do not freeze

Classic Onion Soup
Marie–Michelle's on the Bay

¼ cup olive oil
3 large sweet onions, julienne sliced
1½ Tablespoons fresh thyme leaves
fresh ground black pepper
¾ cup sherry wine
1 quart beef stock (low sodium canned or bouillon if
  needed)
French bread
6 slices Swiss cheese
grated Parmesan cheese

Heat the oil in a large stock pot over high heat, add the onions, thyme, and black pepper. Stir frequently until the onions are soft and some of them have started to brown. Add the sherry and stir well for 3 minutes. Add the beef stock and boil for 10 minutes. Reduce to a simmer for 45 minutes more. Check flavor; add water if too salty. To prepare the servings, cut the French bread into rounds and toast in oven until hard and dry. Ladle soup into crocks, put 1 toast round on top, covered with 1 slice Swiss cheese, sprinkled finally with Parmesan cheese. Bake crocks in 450°F. oven 3–5 minutes, until the cheese bubbles. Brown under the broiler, if needed, for appearance.

Preparation: 15 minutes　　　Easy　　　Serves: 8
Cooking: 1 hour　　　Can do ahead
Baking: 5 minutes
Cooking: 30 minutes

A hurricane in 1910 almost destroyed the pier, causing the hotel to remain closed that year. When it was repaired, a post office was added to it. In 1922 a carelessly dropped cigarette started a fire that burned the post office and required replacement of about 20 feet of boardwalk. In 1960 Hurricane Donna completely destroyed it and local residents, Lester and Dellora Norris donated the full cost of $104,000 to rebuild it of greenheart wood from South America. Eleven years later they contributed another $25,000 to shore up the far end, which now stretched 1,000 feet into the gulf. About that same time a hue and cry erupted when the city council announced it was considering an admission charge. In a public letter, Norris stated that he had been verbally promised in 1960 that no charge would ever be levied for the pier's use and the idea was abandoned. This past year the beloved pier has undergone another "rejuvenation" and is once again a favored gathering place for residents and visitors alike.

Cream of Chicken Soup
The Palm Restaurant

1 whole chicken (3–5 pounds)
1 carrot, cut into 1–inch pieces
1 onion, chopped
1 stalk celery, cut into 1–inch pieces
2 Tablespoons chicken bouillon or stock base
4 Tablespoons butter
4 Tablespoons flour
1½ cups heavy cream or milk
¼ cup shredded carrot
2 teaspoons chopped parsley
pinch garlic powder
salt and pepper to taste

Wash and clean chicken thoroughly inside and out. Place in a pot and cover with water; add the cut–up carrot, onion, and celery; bring to a boil then lower temperature and simmer for 45–60 minutes or until chicken begins to fall off the bones. Remove vegetables, chicken, bones and skin from stock. Strain the stock to remove any small pieces of bone. Add chicken boullion or stock base. Return stock to pot to simmer. When chicken is cool enough to handle, remove all bones and skin and chop the meat. Melt butter and add flour to make a roux. Slowly add roux to stock a little at a time until the soup has thickened somewhat. (It may not be necessary to use all of the roux). Add cream or milk to stock, stirring constantly. Adjust heat to low and add 2 cups chopped chicken, carrot, parsley, garlic powder and salt and pepper to taste. Continue to simmer for 15 minutes until the carrots are cooked.

NOTE: Chicken bouillon or stock base comes in many forms—cubes, dry powdered, semi-soft condensed stock base. Use whichever you prefer to enhance the flavor of the chicken stock.

Preparation: 20 minutes   Moderately easy   Yield: 2½ quarts
Cooking: 1½ to 2 hours

Cream of Tomato and Sausage Soup

Vito's Ristorante

1 large onion, diced
3 stalks celery, diced
2 cloves of garlic, diced
6 Tablespoons of butter
1 teaspoon thyme
2 bay leaves
2½ quarts rich chicken stock
1 large can (28–ounce) crushed tomatoes
1 pound Italian sausage links, cooked and diced
1 quart cream
1 bunch fresh basil, chopped
salt and pepper to taste

Roux

½ cup butter
½ cup flour

In a large saucepan melt butter and sauté onions, celery, and garlic about 5 minutes. Add bay leaves and thyme. Add chicken stock, crushed tomatoes and Italian sausage. Bring to a boil and then allow to simmer 3–5 minutes. Add cream and fresh basil; return to boil. Whisk in roux, a little at a time, thickening to desired consistency. Salt and pepper to taste.

Preparation: ½ hour   Moderately Easy   Yield: 5 quarts
Cooking: 1 hour

How-To: Prepare a Roux—Stir butter and flour together in a saucepan over medium–low heat for 10–12 minutes until roux is bubbly and swollen, being careful not to burn it.

Wild Mushroom Bisque

Truffles

½ cup butter
1 medium onion, thinly sliced
1 pound assorted wild mushrooms (shiitake,
  portobello, crimini), sliced
2 Tablespoons chopped fresh thyme
salt to taste
¼ cup flour
1 quart chicken stock
2 cups heavy cream
soy sauce
fresh ground pepper to taste

Sauté onion in butter until translucent. Add mushrooms and thyme. Sauté them until they "let out their own water," about 5 minutes (a touch of salt will help this along). Stir in the flour and lower heat to simmer. Continue stirring 2–3 minutes and then add the chicken stock. Increase heat to let the flour taste cook out. Taste to test readiness. Add heavy cream and continue cooking uncovered; the liquid should thicken a little. Stir in 1 Tablespoon soy sauce, then taste to see if more is needed. Purée the soup (in batches) in a food processor or blender and strain into another container to ensure there are no large pieces. Season with plenty of fresh ground pepper, and salt if needed.

Preparation: 10 minutes   Easy   Yield: 2 quarts
Cooking: 20 –30 minutes

Lentil Soup
Graf Rudi Restaurant

½ pound lentils
6 cups water
¼ cup butter
3 Tablespoons flour
1 cup grated vegetables - onion, carrot, parsnip,
 celery root
salt to taste
1 clove garlic minced
½ cup milk
croutons

In a large covered pot bring the lentils and water to a boil; lower the temperature and simmer slowly until tender (about ½ hour). Make a roux with the flour and butter; stir into soup bit by bit until desired consistency. Stir in grated vegetables and simmer 10 to 20 minutes more. Stir in garlic, milk, and salt to taste. Serve hot with croutons on top.

Preparation: 30 minutes	Easy	Serves: 4
Cooking: 1 hours	Can do ahead	
	Serve warm	

Split Pea Soup
Hole–in–the–Wall Golf Club Inc.

2 cups dry split peas
3 quarts water or chicken stock
1 large onion, diced
2 stalks celery, diced
2 carrots, diced
1 ham hock, smoked
2 teaspoons chopped garlic
1 teaspoon thyme leaves
1 teaspoon white pepper
1 bay leaf

Combine all ingredients in a large pot and bring to a boil. Reduce heat, cover and simmer for two hours. Remove bay leaf and ham hock, dice meat and return to soup. Serve with garlic croutons.

Preparation: 15 minutes	Easy	Serves: 6–8
Cooking: 2¼ hours		

Indian Shell Seekers—

The next time you do some beach shelling, give thought to the early Florida Calusa Indians as shell seekers.

Highly sought was the large lightning whelk which, once the interior whorls were removed, made a nifty and practical dipper which could hold up to 10 ounces of water.

Placed on the coals of a fire, it could produce boiling water in about 8 minutes.

Tomatoes

The origin of the tomato is a little fuzzy but its international reputation as a favorite "vegetable" is very clear. If you have ever eaten a "fresh" tomato purchased in the winter at a store up north, you will understand why the huge crops grown in Immokalee, Everglades City, Naples and Marco Island have earned Collier County the distinction of being known as the market basket of the East Coast. They are easily digested, low in calories and their bright color helps stimulate the appetite. What more can you ask of a "love apple?"

Tomatoes, Tomatoes, Tomatoes

In 1993–94, Collier County marketed 1.3 million tomatoes: enough to completely cover Marco Island! If the trucks were placed bumper-to-bumper on I–75, they would stretch from Naples to Tampa.

Tomato Bisque with Fresh Basil
Collier Athletic Club

2 Tablespoons olive oil
2 Tablespoons Prosciutto, finely diced
3 shallots, finely diced
4 cloves garlic, finely diced
1 14–ounce can tomatoes, diced with juice
1 Tablespoon butter
1 Tablespoon flour
2 cups (1 pint) heavy cream
2 Tablespoons grated Romano cheese
3 Tablespoons fresh basil, julienne
seasoned croutons for garnish

Heat olive oil in a 2–quart pot over medium heat. Sauté ham, shallots, and garlic until fragrant, about 3–5 minutes. Add tomatoes with juice; simmer until liquid is almost gone. Be careful not to burn nor cook the ham too long as it will get tough; set aside and keep warm. Melt the butter in a separate 2–quart pot over low heat. Add flour and cook 3–5 minutes, stirring occasionally until the roux has changed to a golden color. Do not burn! Stir in the cream, bring to a boil and simmer 10 minutes over low heat. Combine tomato mixture with the cream over low heat. Add the cheese and basil. The cheese will thicken the soup. Serve hot, garnished with seasoned croutons and a sprig of basil.

Preparation: 10 minutes
Cooking: 30 minutes
Moderately Easy
Serve immediately
Serves: 4

Tomato Consommé
Vanderbilt Inn on the Gulf

2 pounds tomatoes, quartered
2 cups tomato juice
1 stalk celery with leaves, chopped
1 cup fresh basil
5 egg whites, (and the shells)
salt and pepper to taste

In the bowl of a food processor combine tomatoes and juice; process until smooth. Pour tomato mixture into a pot and add celery, basil and egg shells; bring to a boil, reduce heat and simmer 10 minutes. Lightly whip egg whites just until frothy. Remove pan from heat and slowly add egg whites, whisking slightly. Return to medium–low heat and simmer 10 minutes. Strain well, season to taste, and serve hot. Delicious with Green Pea Pancakes and Mushroom and Tomato Duxelle. See page 187.

Preparation: 10 minutes
Cooking: 20 minutes
Moderately Easy
Serves: 4

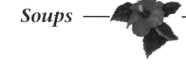

Pappa Al Pomodoro (Tomato and Bread Soup)
Asti Ristorante

6 Tablespoons extra virgin olive oil
4 cloves garlic, chopped
2 bunches fresh basil, chopped (about ¾ cup)
3 pounds ripe tomatoes, peeled, seeded, cut into large
    pieces
2 loaves cubed day–old Italian bread (with crust)
2 cups beef or chicken broth
salt and pepper to taste

In a large saucepan over low heat, combine 4 Tablespoons olive oil, 3 cloves of garlic and half of the chopped basil. Do not brown the garlic. Add the tomatoes and cook for 20 minutes; set aside. In a baking pan, mix 1 Tablespoon of olive oil and the rest of the garlic with the cubed bread. Salt and pepper to taste and bake at 350°F. until golden brown. Add the broth and bread crumbs to the cooked tomatoes and cook for 10 minutes. To serve: sprinkle each portion with fresh basil and a drizzle of extra virgin olive oil.

Preparation: 15 minutes   Easy   Yield: 1½ quarts
Cooking: 35 minutes   Can Do Ahead

Potage Four Seasons
☞ *Naples Bath & Tennis Club*

2 cups peeled, diced potato
1 cup diced carrot
½ cup diced onion
2 cups diced leek
½ cup diced celery
8 cups chicken broth

Combine all ingredients in a large stock pot. Bring to a boil; reduce heat and simmer for 20 minutes, or until vegetables are tender. Purée all in batches in a blender. Return purée to the pot to keep warm and season with salt and pepper to taste. If potage is too thick, thin with additional chicken stock. Serve hot.

Preparation: 20 minutes   Easy   Yield: 3 quarts
Cooking: 20 minutes

Pin-Hookers

Locally the gleaners who go into the fields to pick after the harvest are called "pin-hookers". The derivation of this term is unknown but several of the farmers think it is a corruption of the Spanish word "pintura" (to paint) and "hooker" for the hooking motion their hands make as they harvest only the red and pink tomatoes, the green tomatoes having already been harvested for shipping to market.

Tomato Consommé

Tomatoes are used often in the cuisine of Madrid. So the name consommé à la Madrilène is used for this consommé which uses tomatoes—in the manner of Madrid.

Jellied Consommé à La Madrilène

The Naples Yacht Club

10 ounces lean ground beef
¾ cup coarsely chopped onion
½ cup coarsely chopped celery
½ cup coarsely chopped carrots
4 large egg whites
pinch of ground thyme
1 teaspoon pickling spice
1 pound canned whole tomatoes
3 quarts chicken or beef stock
1 drop red food coloring
4 envelopes clear gelatin hydrated in 6 ounces cold
   water

Mix ground beef, onion, celery, carrots, egg whites, thyme, pickling spice and tomatoes in a large bowl. In a large pot bring the stock to a boil and add meat mixture, stirring until well blended. Simmer until foam forms and is established; continue simmering covered for 1½ hours. Strain all ingredients through fine cheesecloth. Add 1 drop red food coloring to enhance color. Stir in gelatin and dissolve. Pour into flat pan and refrigerate until jelled.

Preparation: 30 minutes   Moderately easy   Serves: 10
Cooking: 1½ hours
Chilling: 4 hours or more

Madrissoise à La Naples Yacht Club

To serve as Madrissoise: add cubes of jellied Madrilène to bowls or cups of chilled Vichyssoise. Garnish with chopped chives.

Amish Vegetable Soup

Royal Poinciana Golf Club Inc.

1 Tablespoon clarified butter
¼ cup diced leek
¼ cup diced onion
¼ cup diced carrot
¼ cup diced celery
¼ cup peeled, seeded, and diced butternut squash
¼ cup peeled, seeded, and diced acorn squash
fresh chopped thyme to taste
2 quarts chicken stock reduced to half
⅓ cup cooked brown rice (cooked in the chicken
    stock)
⅓ cup corn kernels toasted
2 Tablespoons green beans, cut into 1–inch pieces
2 Tablespoons yellow beans, cut into 1–inch pieces
salt and pepper to taste

In a large pot cook the leek, onion, carrot, celery, butternut
and acorn squash in the clarified butter until the vegetables
"sweat" (i.e. bead with water and begin to soften). Stir in
the thyme and mix well. Add the hot chicken broth that
has been brought to a boil. Add rice, corn, green and yellow beans; heat to boiling. Season to taste.

Preparation: 30 minutes   Easy   Serves: 6
Cooking: 30 minutes

*HOW-TO: Toast Corn—place corn
kernels on a cookie sheet on the top
shelf of the oven at 400°F. for about
5–10 minutes.*

Vegetarian Noodle Fagioli Soup

Noodles Cafe Inc.

2 large carrots, peeled and chopped
1 large white onion, chopped
2 stalks celery, chopped
¼ cup olive oil
1 Tablespoon chopped fresh garlic
1 Tablespoon Italian seasoning
1 teaspoon chili powder
2 bay leaves
3 cups canned cannellini beans, with liquid
4 cups crushed plum tomatoes, with liquid
½ pound pasta of choice
1½ cups grated Parmesan cheese

Sauté onion, celery, and carrots in olive oil in a large sauce pot over medium heat. Stir often until onions are translucent and soft. Add seasonings and stir about 1 minute. Add beans, tomatoes, and let simmer about 30 minutes on very low heat. Add pasta to soup and cook until pasta is tender. Serve hot and sprinkle each serving with cheese. (If too thick, add tomato juice or chicken stock).

Preparation: 40 minutes
Cooking: 40 minutes

Moderately Easy
Can do ahead
Serve warm

Serves: 8

Acorn Squash Soup with Toasted Hazelnuts
Alexander's

2 whole acorn squash
1 whole onion, chopped
1 large carrot, peeled and chopped
1 to 2 Tablespoons butter
2 quarts chicken stock
1 bay leaf
dash thyme
dash nutmeg
salt and pepper to taste
1 cup half–and–half
brown sugar (optional)
Garnish:
¾ cup chopped toasted hazelnuts or pecans

Roast the squash on a sheet pan in a 350°F. oven. After 10 minutes pierce the squash with a fork to let the steam out. Roast until soft, about 30 minutes. Cool. Sauté carrots and onions in butter for 5 minutes. Cut the squash in half, remove the seeds, scrape out the pulp and add it to the carrots and onions. Place vegetables in a 6–quart pot and cover with chicken stock and seasonings. Simmer uncovered for 1 hour. Remove bay leaf. Add half–and–half and purée in blender. Taste for seasonings and add as needed. A pinch of brown sugar may be to your taste. Strain the soup and garnish with chopped toasted hazelnuts or pecans.

Preparation: 35 minutes   Easy   Yield: 2 quarts
Cooking: 1 hour   Serve warm

The Naples Hotel

Without refrigeration or grocery stores, the hotel menus consisted of staple foods enhanced by fish or game brought in daily, but they had a fine reputation for good meals well served. Indeed, Thomas Edison and his family frequently drove down from Fort Myers for Sunday dinners and occasionally, he and Harvey Firestone would stop in for lunch.

The old hotel register lists several famous guests: Rose Cleveland (sister of the President), actress Gertrude Lawrence, novelist Daphne du Maurier, Richard Nixon (who popped in for lunch in 1956). But even more exciting, in 1951 the entire cast and crew filming *Distant Drums* stayed there, including its star, Gary Cooper, and romantic interests, Mari Aldon and Linda Darnell.

Other pleasures: Cocktails preceding the sunset were the social highlight of each day and continued to be throughout the Prohibition era. The solarium, furnished in white wicker, was a favorite place to while away a lazy afternoon, with the long porch and its rocking chairs a close second. The porch was also the site for a meeting of 13 young businessmen in 1951, which resulted in the founding of *Naples Federal Savings & Loan Association*, now known as *First Union*.

Corn

There seems to be little doubt that corn, or maize, originated in the "New World" and was introduced into Europe after Christopher Columbus discovered America. Crops have greatly increased as new uses for the product have been found. Aside from the many varieties of sweet corn as a vegetable, every movie house seems to sell tons of the ubiquitous popcorn you smell before you see it dancing in the huge popping machine. But these are only two of the uses. Corn provides the flour used for polenta in its various forms, tortillas and for bread–making. It's also valuable for its oil content, which is found in many brands of oil and margarine in today's market–place. Even the stalks and leaves are used for fodder and silage for farm animals! And finally, it's even used to make the new gasoline additive ethanol. Maize is amazing!

Roasted Onion, Corn, and Squash Soup
Bonita Bay Club

½ cup diced onions
½ cup fresh corn kernels
1 teaspoon butter
1 teaspoon minced garlic
2 Tablespoons diced celery
2 Tablespoons diced carrot
½ pound zucchini, diced
½ pound yellow squash, diced
2 cups chicken stock
¼ cup heavy cream
1 teaspoon chopped chives
salt & pepper to taste

Lightly grease two baking pans; spread the diced onions in one and the fresh corn kernels in the other. Roast these vegetables in a 450°F. oven 10–15 minutes until they are golden brown. Melt the butter in a saucepan with the garlic, celery and carrot. When they begin to "sweat" (give off their juices) add the onions, blending well. Add the zucchini, yellow squash and chicken stock. Simmer until the vegetables are tender. Purée the soup in a blender, adding more stock if necessary. Add the heavy cream and season to taste. Serve hot, garnished with chopped chives and roasted corn kernels.

Preparation: 15–20 minutes   Easy   Serves: 4
Cooking: 10–15 minutes

Roasted Corn and Crab Chowder

The Club Pelican Bay

6 ears fresh corn
1 small green pepper, diced
1 small red pepper, diced
1 small white onion, diced
¼ cup butter
½ pound crab meat
1 teaspoon Cajun spice
¼ cup dry Vermouth
1 quart heavy cream
2 medium potatoes, diced and boiled
salt and pepper to taste

Roast corn in 350°F. oven until golden brown. Cut corn from cob (reserve cobs). Sauté peppers and onion in butter. Add roasted corn, crab, Cajun spice, and Vermouth. In a large pot cover corn cobs with heavy cream. Add pepper and corn mixture. Simmer and reduce until soup thickens (about 20–30 minutes). Remove cobs, add cooked potatoes and adjust seasoning with salt and pepper.

Preparation: 1 hour   Moderately Easy   Serves: 8
Cooking: 20–30 minutes

Smoked Corn and Crab Chowder
Bay Colony Club

1 cup hickory or mesquite wood chips
12 ears fresh yellow corn
6 small white onions, diced
12 frozen or fresh soft shell crabs, diced
¼ pound smoked bacon, diced
¼ pound butter
1 quart heavy cream
1 cup diced potatoes
1 Tablespoon chopped fresh basil
1 Tablespoon chopped fresh oregano
salt and pepper to taste
¼ pound fresh crab meat
2 Tablespoons fresh basil chiffonade (cut into thin
   strips)

Soak the wood chips in water for 30 minutes. Strain and place wet chips on a sheet of aluminum foil, then place this foil with wet chips on a preheated grill. Remove the husks from the corn and place the husks on the wood chips. Cut the corn from the cobs, placing the cobs on top of the husks. Close the lid on the grill and let them smoke for 20 minutes. While the cobs are smoking, dice the onion, bacon and crabs. Heat the butter in a sauce pot and add the bacon and onions. Cover and cook until the onions are tender. Add the crabs and cut corn; cover and cook slowly for 10 minutes. Stir in the heavy cream and smoked corn husks; simmer for 30 minutes. Remove the corn husks; purée the chowder. Strain well and season. To serve, divide the fresh crab meat in the bottom of six cups and ladle the chowder over. Garnish with basil on top.

Preparation: 45 minutes   Difficult   Serves: 6
Soaking: 30 minutes
Grilling: 30 minutes
Cooking: 45 minutes

Blue Crab Soup
Michael's Cafe

1 Tablespoon butter
1 cup diced onion
1 cup diced celery
1 teaspoon thyme
2 Tablespoons lobster or fish broth
1 cup heavy cream
3 cups half–and–half
½ pound blue crab claw meat
⅓ cup sherry
salt and pepper to taste

Melt butter in a soup pot and sauté onions and celery until translucent. Add thyme, lobster broth, cream and half–and–half. Bring to a boil and simmer 10 minutes. Add sherry and crabmeat; bring to a simmer and serve hot.

Preparation: 20 minutes   Easy   Serves: 4–6
Cooking: 20 minutes

Crab

Solid lumps of sweet white meat (the most expensive in the marketplace) come from the body of the crab; flake meat also comes from the body but not in pieces large enough to qualify as lumps. Claw meat has a tan color and therefore is generally used in recipes where appearance is not vital.

Easy Bouillabaisse
Marie–Michelle's on the Bay

2 Tablespoons butter
6 3–ounce portions grouper
1 cup diced tomatoes
2 Tablespoons chopped basil
2 teaspoons chopped garlic, or more to taste
large pinch saffron
3 8–ounce lobster tails —split lengthwise and shell removed
12 sea scallops (10 count)
12 jumbo shrimp (10 count) peeled and deveined
¼ cup Pernod or Anisette
1 23–ounce can V–8 juice
5 ounces white wine
5 ounces water

Rub bottom of stock pot with butter. Place grouper on the bottom of the pot. Cover with tomato, basil, garlic and saffron. Place shellfish on top. [At this point the pot can be covered and refrigerated until ready to cook, just before serving.] Place pot on high heat, when food begins to sauté (sizzle and brown), pour in Pernod and shake (it may or may not flame). Add liquids and bring to a boil. Simmer 6 minutes covered. Serve in bowls with French bread rounds (toasted slices of French bread that may be seasoned to taste).

Preparation: 20 minutes   Easy   Serves: 6
Cooking: 15 minutes

Chowder

It is said by some of the oldsters in the area that most of the kids way back when took an old shortening can to school for a lunch pail. A piece of cornbread was put in the bottom and bacon grease was poured over it. If they were lucky, a little piece of fat back was included. The kids on Marco Island were luckier. Each child, it is said , had a tin cup on a nail at the clam factory. At noon they ran over to the factory and filled their cups with fresh clam chowder!

Bermuda Rum Chowder

Cafe de Marco

⅓ cup finely chopped celery
1 cup finely chopped carrots
½ red bell pepper, finely chopped
½ red onion, finely chopped
1 Tablespoon olive oil
3 cups clam juice
1½ cups chopped clams
¼ pound cooked shrimp, broken pieces
¼ cup marinara sauce
¼ cup rum, spiced with cinnamon and cloves
1 teaspoon garlic powder
¼ teaspoon thyme
½ bay leaf
a few grains of saffron
Maggi seasoning to taste
1 Tablespoon gravy enhancer
few drops of Tabasco
¼ teaspoon shrimp base
1 can of diced tomatoes (14½–ounce size)
Roux (optional): mix together
1 Tablespoon cornstarch
2 Tablespoons water

Sauté celery, carrots, peppers and onion in olive oil until onions are translucent. In a large pot combine clam juice, chopped clams, broken shrimp pieces, marinara sauce, spiced rum, and bring to a boil. Add vegetables and rest of ingredients. If necessary thicken with roux. Serve hot.

Preparation: 30 minutes   Moderately Easy   Serves: 4–6
Cooking: 30 minutes

Florida Shellfish Soup

The Ritz–Carlton Naples

3 carrots, peeled and finely diced or shredded
5 stalks celery, finely diced
2 fennel, finely diced
4 leeks, thinly sliced (white part only)
2 cloves garlic, minced
½ cup butter (divided)
8 cups fish stock
¼ cup flour
¼ cup Pernod or Anisette
¾ teaspoon fennel seed
½ teaspoon celery seed
pinch cayenne pepper
pinch anise seed
salt and pepper to taste
pinch saffron
2 Tablespoons tomato sauce

Garnish

cooked scallops, shrimp and stone crab claw meat
croutons spread with Gruyère, Parmesan or Boursin
    cheese

In a large soup pot sweat together over medium heat: the carrots, celery, fennel, leeks and garlic in ¼ cup butter. In a large pot bring the fish stock to a boil. Meanwhile, prepare the roux. In a small saucepan combine the remaining ¼ cup butter and flour and cook over medium heat until the roux bubbles and swells. Whisk the roux into the fish stock to a medium consistency. Add the Pernod to the vegetables and reduce until dry. Add seasonings, saffron and tomato paste. Add thickened fish stock and bring all to a boil. Check seasonings and consistency and remove from heat. Garnish with cooked scallops, shrimp, stone crab meat—and croutons spread with Gruyère, Parmesan or Boursin cheese.

Preparation: 30 minutes   Moderately easy   Serves: 8
Cooking: 30–45 minutes

Chilies

Today there are probably 200 different types of chilies grown in all parts of the tropics; red, orange, yellow and purple or green when unripe. Fresh chilies should be crisp and unwrinkled; ripe chilies are available dried, crushed, flaked and ground. If the chili you eat is too hot for you, don't try to ease it by drinking water, a piece of plain bread will do a better job!

Chili

Hole–in–the–Wall Golf Club Inc.

1½ pounds lean ground beef
1 large Spanish onion, diced
1 medium green pepper, diced
1 medium red pepper, diced
1 teaspoon salt
¼ cup chili powder
1 bay leaf
1 teaspoon garlic powder
½ teaspoon white pepper
½ teaspoon black pepper
½ teaspoon cayenne pepper
1 can (28–ounce size) whole tomatoes, diced with juice
2 cans (16–ounce size) chili beans, with liquid
1 can (8–ounce size) tomato sauce
2 Tablespoons tomato paste

In a 6–quart heavy saucepan brown meat; add onions and peppers, cooking until vegetables are tender. Stir in spices, seasonings, and remaining ingredients. Cover and simmer 1 hour. Remove bay leaf before serving.

Preparation: 30 minutes   Easy   Serves: 6
Cooking: 1¼ hours   Serve immediately

Cheeseburger Soup

The Moorings Country Club

Hamburgers

½ pound ground beef
1 large egg
¼ cup onion, minced
¼ cup green pepper, minced
¼ cup fine bread crumbs

Soup

1 Tablespoon butter
¼ cup onion, finely diced
¼ cup leeks, finely diced
1½ cups chicken stock
3 cups milk

Roux

8 Tablespoons butter
¾ cup flour

Cheese

½ pound cheddar cheese, grated

Combine all hamburger ingredients. Use a large melon ball scoop or teaspoon to form small meatballs. Place on a sheet pan. Cover with parchment or waxed paper and flatten with another pan to ¼" to ½" thickness as desired. Bake at 350°F. for 10 minutes. For soup, melt butter in stock pot; sauté onions and leeks until tender; add chicken stock and milk. Make a roux by melting butter over low heat and blending in flour. Stir to distribute evenly and cook out the raw taste of the flour without browning it. Cook 5–10 minutes. Set aside. (Extra roux may be refrigerated or frozen for future use.) When stock is almost at a boil, gradually stir in roux with whisk to desired thickness of creamed soup. Sprinkle in grated cheese, blending thoroughly with whisk to prevent lumps of cheese. Add mini hamburgers and season to taste.

Preparation: 25 minutes   Moderately easy   Serves: 8–12
Cooking: 30 minutes

Mulligan Stew

The Ridgeport Pub

1 cup medium-diced Spanish onions
5 stalks celery, French cut (medium diagonally sliced)
2 cups diced carrots
¼ cup olive oil
4 cups diced baked or cooked potatoes
½ pound corned beef, cooked, sliced thin, diced (½–inch)
2 cups chicken stock
1½ Tablespoons horseradish
½ cup unsalted butter, softened
1 quart heavy cream
2½ pounds sour cream
white pepper and salt to taste

In a large stockpot, combine onions, celery, and carrots with the olive oil. Sauté vegetables until tender. Add diced baked potatoes and corned beef and cook 5–7 minutes. Add chicken stock and boil until reduced by half. Add horseradish and butter; cook on medium heat. Add heavy cream and heat through but do not boil. Combine salt and pepper with sour cream and add to soup all at once. Continue heating over medium heat, stirring constantly until sour cream is well blended and heated through. Serve hot.

NOTE: *Butter may be reduced or eliminated. Half–and–half may be substituted for heavy cream. Low–fat sour cream may be substituted for sour cream.*

Preparation: 1 hour   Moderately Easy   Serves: 8
Cooking: 30 minutes

Stone Soup
The Ridgeport Pub

¾ cup olive oil
1 pound hot Italian sausage, bulk
1 cup chopped scallions
1 cup diced onions
2 Tablespoons crushed red pepper
2 Tablespoons granulated garlic
5 carrots, diced
5 stalks celery, medium dice
3 turnips, peeled and diced
2 cups chicken stock
½ cup unsalted butter
½ head cabbage, cored and roughly chopped
3 cups water
¾ cup uncooked pasta (macaroni, bow tie or shell)
grated Parmesan cheese for garnish
chopped parsley for garnish

In a large saucepan, heat ½ cup olive oil and brown sausage, breaking into medium–sized pieces. Drain cooked sausage and pour off all but about ¼ cup fat from the saucepan. Sauté onions and scallions in saucepan until tender, adding crushed red pepper and garlic halfway through. Add sautéed onion mixture to reserved sausage. Add remaining ¼ cup olive oil to pan and sauté carrots, celery, and turnips, until tender, about 8 minutes. Add butter and chicken stock, bring to a boil. Add chopped cabbage and reserved sausage–onion mixture. Continue cooking until cabbage is tender. Add water and the pasta; cook until pasta is tender. Serve hot, garnished with Parmesan cheese and chopped parsley.

Preparation: 1 hour
Cooking: 45 minutes

Moderately easy
Can do ahead

Serves: 6

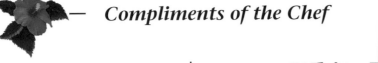

White Bean Soup with Escarole and Ham Shank

Bayside

2 cups dried cannellini beans
3 Tablespoons olive oil
2 medium red onions, diced
1 bulb garlic, minced (10–12 cloves)
2 cups canned Italian plum tomatoes
1 smoked ham shank
3 quarts strong chicken stock
1 teaspoon chopped fresh thyme
½ teaspoon chopped fresh oregano
1 head escarole, washed and chopped in 1–inch squares
salt and freshly ground pepper to taste

Pick through cannellini beans then cover with cold water and let stand overnight. In heavy 6–quart kettle, sauté onion in olive oil until soft. Add garlic and stir for 15 seconds. Add drained beans, tomato, ham shank, stock, and herbs. Cover and simmer for 2 hours or until beans are soft. Remove ham shank and add escarole. When shank is cool enough to handle, take meat off bone, dice and return to soup. Taste, and add salt and pepper as needed. Serve with crusty Italian bread.

Soaking: overnight
Preparation: 30 minutes   Easy   Yield: 3 quarts
Cooking: 2½ hours

Baked Black Bean Soup with Havarti Jalapeño Cheese

Olde Marco Inn

1 pound black beans, cleaned
2½ quarts chicken stock
2 strips bacon, chopped fine
1 cup diced onion
1 cup diced ham
2 teaspoons chopped garlic
½ cup diced green pepper
2 medium tomatoes, chopped
¼ cup raw rice
2 teaspoons chopped parsley
½ teaspoon oregano
pinch of thyme
pinch of cayenne pepper
½ teaspoon ground black pepper
¼ cup sherry (optional)
½ pound Havarti jalapeño cheese at room
    temperature

Soak the beans overnight in a generous quantity of water. Drain the beans and put into a large saucepan with chicken stock. Bring beans to a boil. Let simmer for 45 minutes. In 5 or 6–quart pan, brown bacon to a crisp. Add onion and cook till transparent, about 5 minutes. Add ham and the rest of the ingredients, except sherry and cheese. Simmer 30 minutes. Add sherry and stir in. To serve, fill bowls with about 5 ounces of soup and top each serving with 2 teaspoons of cheese. Place in a hot oven 400–450°F. until cheese is melted. Serve immediately.

Soaking: overnight	Easy	Serves: 10
Preparation: 15 minutes	Can do ahead	
Cooking: 2 hours	Can freeze	

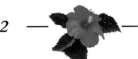

A Christmas Menu at Old Naples Hotel

Refinement, style and excellent meals were always the hallmark of the Old Naples Hotel – starting with Annie McLaughlin of Lexington, Kentucky, who literally ran the whole place for the Haldeman family. As the town became a growing city, a series of chefs with new dishes and different menus followed – until Chef William Schultz arrived to take over the considerably modernized kitchen in 1947. With a background that included a stint at Barron Collier's Useppa Island Inn in 1928, followed by several up-scale hotels, Sunday night buffets soon became a tradition for town residents and hotel guests.

Starting in 1948 the hotel was open year 'round, giving Schultz and his staff an opportunity to dazzle everyone with Thanksgiving and Christmas feasts. On Christmas afternoon an Open House was held for the entire community; carol singing and a party for the staff held sway in The Seminole Room.

Continued on next page

Tortilla Soup with Chicken, Avocado and Tortilla Strips
LA PLAYA Beach Resort

6 fresh corn tortillas, cut into 1–inch strips
¼ cup olive oil
½ yellow onion, diced
2–3 cloves garlic, chopped
1 jalapeño, seeded and diced
1 Serrano pepper, seeded and diced
½ Anaheim pepper, seeded and diced
2 tomatoes, seeded and diced
¼ cup tomato paste
¼ teaspoon cumin
¼ teaspoon cayenne
1 gallon chicken stock

Garnish

1½ grilled chicken breasts, julienne cut
1 avocado, diced

In a large pot sauté fresh corn tortilla strips in olive oil until crispy. Reserve one–third for garnish. Stir in onions and garlic; cook until golden brown. Stir in jalapeño, Serrano and Anaheim peppers, and tomatoes; cook until tender. Stir in tomato paste, cumin, cayenne and chicken stock; simmer for 30 minutes, stirring occasionally. Purée in batches. Taste and adjust seasoning to taste. To serve, ladle into cups or bowls, topping each with chicken breast, avocado and reserved tortilla crisps for garnish.

Preparation: 20 minutes   Easy   Yield: 2–3 quarts
Cooking: 40 minutes

Three Bean Soup

O——🔑 *Imperial Golf Club*

¼ cup dried black beans
¼ cup navy beans
¼ cup pinto beans
1 quart chicken stock
2 slices bacon, diced fine
¼ small onion, minced
½ clove garlic, minced
⅛ teaspoon dried chopped rosemary
½ teaspoon seeded, chopped jalapeño
½ teaspoon dried oregano
¼ teaspoon salt
¼ cup dry white wine
¼ teaspoon pepper

Soak beans overnight in water to cover, each in a separate dish. Sauté bacon, onion, garlic, rosemary, jalapeño, and oregano together, and add to chicken stock; season with salt and pepper. Divide into three pots, one for cooking each type of bean. Drain the beans, add to chicken stock and cook until tender. When beans are tender, drain stock off and set aside. Purée each type of bean separately, adding stock as needed for consistency desired. To serve, first place ¼ cup black bean soup into cup. Ladle ¼ cup white beans into center of black. Using a toothpick, make swirls on the outside edge of the black beans. Ladle ¼ cup pinto beans into center of white beans and swirl the new edge with a toothpick. Serve hot.

Soaking: Overnight
Preparation: 45 minutes   Moderately Easy   Serves: 4
Cooking: 1½ to 2 hours

In the late 40's and 50's, a full-course dinner cost $3.50, (children under 12 were served at half price). A typical menu is as follows:

– Choice of shrimp cocktail, fruit cup or a caviar canapé

– Choice of three soups

– Fish course (usually pompano)

– Main course: choice of filet mignon, baked ham, roast prime rib of beef, turkey, or roast goose

– Fresh vegetables: silver onions in cream, almond sweet potatoes, hubbard squash, and buttered cauliflower

– Chef Schultz' famous southern spoon bread

– Dessert: wide assortment of ice cream, pies, puddings, bowls of fresh fruits, and a variety of cheese

– Dishes of Christmas candies and after–dinner mints.

From an article by:
Doris Reynolds, Naples, FL

The Key Marco Cat

What's so special about a cat? Well, this one is thousands of years old and was "rescued" from its Marco Island shell–mound grave in an 1896 dig organized by ethnologist Frank Hamilton Cushing of the University of Pennsylvania Museum. While digging muck to use as fertilizer, Marco's Capt. W. D. Collier found several carved and painted objects in good condition and sent some of them to Cushing for evaluation. His examination of the objects led to the uncovering of one of the richest collections of carved and painted ceremonial and utilitarian objects ever found in the State of Florida.

The beautifully hand–carved wooden "cat," valued at 2.5 million dollars, is actually a half–cat, half–human figure just six inches tall.

Escarole and Bean Soup

Vineyards Country Club

2 Tablespoons olive oil
1 onion, chopped
2 shallots, diced
2 cloves garlic, diced
8 sun–dried tomatoes, chopped
1 head escarole, washed well, roughly chopped
1 Tablespoon tomato paste
2 cubes vegetable bouillon
2 cans cannellini beans, drained
4 cups water
1½ teaspoons fresh basil, chopped
1½ teaspoons fresh oregano, chopped
1 Tablespoon fresh marjoram, chopped

Garnish

grated fresh Romano cheese

Heat olive oil in a large pot. Add onions and cook 2 minutes. Add shallots and garlic and sauté 2 minutes. Add sun–dried tomatoes and escarole, stirring until wilted. Add tomato paste and vegetable bouillon cubes; cook 2 minutes, stirring frequently. Add drained beans, water and seasonings. Heat to simmer and simmer 25 minutes. Serve hot, garnished with grated Romano cheese.

Preparation: 20 minutes   Easy   Yield: 2½ quarts
Cooking: 30 minutes   Can do ahead

Borscht

Hilde's Tea Room

1 16–ounce can beets
1 16–ounce can beef broth
1 cup sour cream
sugar vinegar
lemon pepper

Pour beets with juice and beef broth into a blender. Blend on high speed until well blended. Pour over sour cream. Mix well. Season to taste with sugar, vinegar, and lemon pepper. Chill and serve.

Preparation: 7 minutes   Easy   Serves: 6
Chilling: 1–2 hours

Cold Cucumber Soup
Countryside Country Club

2 cups chicken broth
2 cups sour cream
4 cucumbers, peeled and seeded
salt and white pepper to taste
dash of Tabasco sauce

Garnish

chopped fresh dill or chives (optional)

Purée 3 of the cucumbers in food processor or blender. Finely dice the other cucumber. Mix all ingredients well, seasoning to taste. Serve well chilled, garnished with dill or chives.

Preparation: 15 minutes   Easy   Serves: 6
Chilling: 4 hours   Can do ahead

Gazpacho
Bayside

2 medium onions, chopped
2 cucumbers, peeled and chopped
1 red bell pepper, seeded and chopped
1 green pepper, seeded and chopped
4 cloves garlic, chopped
1 can (28–ounce) Italian plum tomatoes
1 Tablespoon chopped parsley
1 Tablespoon chopped mint
¼ cup almonds
¼ cup red wine vinegar
2 cups water
1 can (28–ounce) V–8 juice
3 Tablespoons extra virgin oil

Garnishes

1 Spanish onion, chopped
1 cucumber peeled, seeded and chopped
½ cup black olives, chopped
½ green bell pepper, seeded and chopped
½ red bell pepper, seeded and chopped
salt and ground white pepper to taste

Mix first nine ingredients and process in food processor. Pour into large glass, plastic or stainless steel bowl. Add vinegar, water, and V–8. Whisk in olive oil and add garnishes. Taste and add salt and ground white pepper as needed. Chill and serve.

Preparation: 20 minutes   Easy   Serves: 12
Chilling: 2 hours

Chilled Gazpacho

Hole–in–the–Wall Golf Club Inc.

1½ cups tomato juice
1½ cups V–8 juice
¼ cup water
¼ cup tarragon vinegar
1 small onion, peeled and finely chopped
1 medium tomato, peeled and finely diced
1 medium green pepper, seeded and finely chopped
1 medium cucumber, peeled, seeded, diced
¼ cup olive oil
1 teaspoon minced fresh garlic
1 teaspoon white pepper
1 teaspoon salt
few drops Worcestershire sauce
few drops Tabasco
cucumber slices for garnish

Mix all ingredients and chill for 2 hours. Serve cold with a slice of cucumber for garnish.

Preparation: 20 minutes   Easy   Serves: 6
Chilling: 2 hours

Sinbad's Chilled Gazpacho

Glenview at Pelican Bay

1 medium red pepper
1 medium yellow pepper
1 medium green pepper
1 jalapeño pepper
1 Tablespoon chopped cilantro
1 Tablespoon chopped mint
3 very ripe tomatoes, peeled and seeded
1 Tablespoon minced garlic
½ cup diced red onion
1 cup diced zucchini (green part only)
2 Tablespoons lime juice
¼ cup chopped green onions
2 cups low–fat yogurt
salt to taste

Roast whole peppers under broiler or over charcoal fire until they are charred on all sides. Cover with a towel for a few minutes to cool slightly so you can handle them enough to peel and seed. Dice the peeled, seeded red, yellow and green peppers but not the jalapeño. Using a food processor blend the peeled, seeded jalapeño, herbs, garlic, lime juice, yogurt, and salt (optional). Gently fold in the diced vegetables. Ladle into chilled soup plates and garnish with diced peppers, onions and mint leaves.

Preparation: 30 minutes   Moderately easy   Serves: 6
Roasting: 10–15 minutes

Peach Soup

The Naples Beach Hotel and Golf Club

1 10–ounce can of peaches, drained
1 pint plain low–fat yogurt
2 cups heavy whipping cream
⅓ cup half–and–half
1 Tablespoon vanilla
1¼ cup sugar

Blend all ingredients thoroughly in a blender; taste to see that the sugar is dissolved. Chill before serving.

NOTE: This soup can also be frozen in individual portions as a dessert or a frozen soup.

Preparation: 10 minutes	Easy	Serves: 4–5
Chilling: 4 hours		

Watercress Soup

Voilà! Wine Bar & Brasserie

1 bunch watercress
1 onion, peeled
2 large potatoes, peeled and quartered
1 cup cream
2 cups chicken stock
1 cup milk
salt and pepper to taste

In a large pot blanch the watercress, onion, and potatoes in boiling, salted water. Do not cool. Place all blanched vegetables into a pot with the cream, chicken stock and milk. Season to taste and cook 10 minutes or until potatoes are well done. Purée in blender or food processor until smooth. Serve hot or cold.

Preparation: 10 minutes	Easy	Yield: 6 cups
Cooking: 15 minutes		

Vichyssoise

The Naples Yacht Club

1¼ pounds potatoes, peeled and thinly sliced
½ pound onions, thinly sliced
2 leeks, white part only, washed and thinly sliced
1 bay leaf
3 cups chicken stock, fat skimmed off
salt to taste
3 cups half–and–half
chopped fresh chives for garnish

Combine potato, onion, leek, and bay leaf with chicken stock in a pot with a heavy bottom; simmer until the vegetables are soft. Remove bay leaf and put the contents of the pot through fine food mill, or purée in food processor or blender. Cool, season to taste and chill. At time of serving: combine chilled soup with half–and– half and garnish with chopped chives.

Preparation: 20 minutes	Easy	Serves: 8–10
Cooking: 20 minutes	Must chill thoroughly	

© Paula A. Malone

Salads

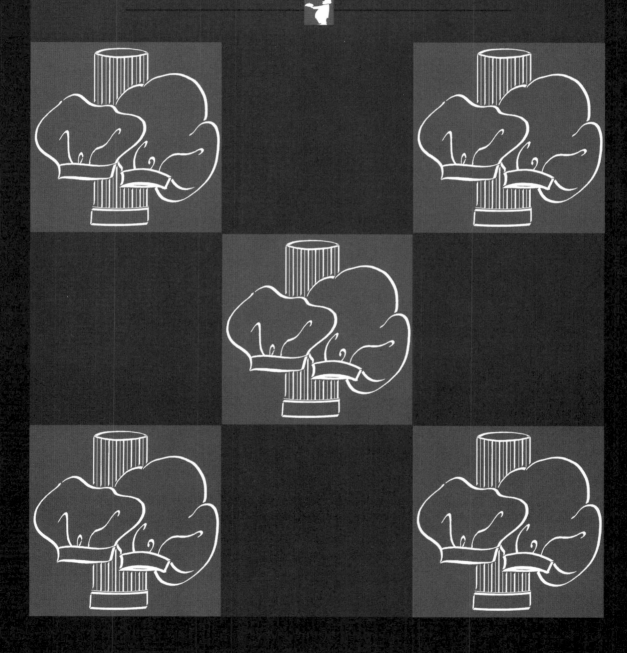

Salads and Salad Dressings

Avocado with Jalapeño Dressing
Moorings Park

3 large navel oranges, peeled and sectioned
2 large ripe avocados, peeled and sliced
1 small cucumber, thinly sliced
red leaf lettuce

On one large platter or 4 individual plates arrange the lettuce, top with orange, avocado and cucumber slices on top. Cover with jalapeño dressing.

Preparation: 10–15 minutes   Easy   Serves: 4

Jalapeño Dressing

½ cup plain low–fat yogurt
½ teaspoon cumin
½ teaspoon garlic
2 Tablespoons minced Jalapeño peppers
fresh orange juice to desired consistency
2 Tablespoons cilantro
salt to taste

In a small bowl stir all ingredients together and season to taste.

Preparation: 10 minutes   Easy   Yield: 1 cup

Fruity Tuna Salad
First Watch Restaurant

2 6–ounce cans tuna, drained
2 Tablespoons diced water chestnuts
¼ cup diced celery
¼ cup mayonnaise, or more as desired
fresh fruit, such as melon, oranges, apples, diced or
    sliced
1 thick slice tomato
4–6 leaves of lettuce or spinach

Mix tuna, water chestnuts, celery and mayonnaise together. Prepare whatever fresh fruits you have to accompany tuna. To serve, line a plate with lettuce or spinach. Place a slice of tomato on a leaf of lettuce or spinach and top with a scoop of tuna salad. Arrange diced or sliced fresh fruit around the tuna.

Preparation: 15 minutes   Easy   Serves: 4

Avocado

The avocado tree, a.k.a. as an "alligator pear," is native to tropical America and appeared in an Aztec writing about 291 B.C. describing their location. It is an evergreen tree that can grow to be as tall as 80 feet and may live for as long as a hundred years. Most bear fruit for about 25 of those years, beginning sometime between four and eight years. The pear– shaped or round fruit contains one very large seed and can weigh up to four pounds.

Bananas

The flowers on a banana tree develop into a "bunch" of bananas. Each row of fruit is a "hand"; each fruit is a "finger". And you thought the humor of bananas related to noses!

Fruit Salad Grand Marnier
⚷ *Lakewood Country Club*

1 cup cantaloupe
1 cup honeydew
¾ cup watermelon
¼ cup seedless red grapes
¼ cup seedless green grapes
½ cup apple, Red Delicious preferred
1 cup bananas
1 cup strawberries

Dice fruit into bite–sized pieces: Set aside.

Preparation: 15 minutes   Easy   Serves: 6–8

Grand Marnier Dressing

2 cups whipping cream
4 teaspoons powdered sugar
¼ cup orange juice
¼ cup pineapple juice
4 teaspoons Grand Marnier liqueur

Whip cream while gradually adding sugar until the mixture begins to hold its shape. Slowly add the liquids. Pour over fruit and mix thoroughly. Chill before serving.

Preparation: 10 minutes   Easy   Yield: 3+ cups

Citrus and Cheddar Salad
Wyndemere Country Club

1 Boston lettuce, rinsed and dried
2 ruby red grapefruit, sectioned
3 oranges, sectioned
4 ounces sharp cheddar cheese, grated
6 fresh strawberries with stem, fan cut

Arrange Boston lettuce on 6 plates. Place grapefruit and orange sections on top, sprinkled with grated cheddar cheese, and garnished with a strawberry pressed lightly to fan it.

Preparation: 15 minutes   Easy   Serves: 6

Citrus Dressing

½ cup lemon juice, reduced to half on low heat
¼ cup white wine
1 Tablespoon Dijon mustard
1½ cups salad oil
½ cup orange juice
1 Tablespoon honey
1 Tablespoon sugar
1 teaspoon poppy seeds
1 pinch salt

Prepare dressing in a quart bowl by whisking the reduced lemon juice, white wine and mustard. Continue whisking while adding salad oil in a fine stream. As dressing thickens, thin down with orange juice, a little at a time. Stir in honey, sugar, poppy seeds and salt. Dressing should be smooth. Drizzle over salad; refrigerate any leftover dressing.

Preparation: 15 minutes   Easy   Yield: 2½ cups

Citrus

In 1993–94, Collier County marketed 1.4 billion oranges, grapefruit and other citrus. If these fruits were placed side–by–side in a straight line, they would circle the globe nearly three times!

Imperial Salad

Imperial Golf Club

Raspberry Vinaigrette Dressing

6 ounces frozen raspberries (¾ cup thawed)
3 Tablespoons salad oil
3 Tablespoons vinegar
¼ cup chopped onion
2 Tablespoons chopped chives
2 Tablespoons sugar
salt and pepper to taste

Mix all ingredients in blender or food processor. Season to taste.

Preparation: 10 minutes   Easy   Yield: 2 cups

Salad

1 carrot peeled and sliced on the bias
1 tomato peeled and seeded, cut into quarters
1 sheet puff pastry (defrosted from frozen)
1 head radicchio, rinsed and chilled
1 head green leaf lettuce, rinsed and chilled
4 ounces cream cheese

Marinate the carrot and tomato slices in the Raspberry Vinaigrette dressing overnight. Cut pastry ½ inch wide and 4 inches long. Twist several times and pull ends together and pinch to make a circle. Arrange on a baking sheet and bake at 350°F. until golden brown; let cool. To serve, place puff pastry in center of plate. Place green lettuce on top of puff pastry and then radicchio on top of them. Arrange carrot and tomato slices around the side, resting on the pastry. Make a 1–oz. ball of cream cheese and place one on each salad. Top with Raspberry Vinaigrette Dressing.

Marinate: overnight   Moderately difficult   Serves: 4
Preparation: 30 minutes
Baking: 15 minutes

Seared Tuna Carpaccio

Vito's Ristorante

Marinade

½ **cup olive oil**
½ **bunch fresh basil, chopped**
½ **stalk fresh rosemary, chopped**
2 **cloves garlic, chopped**
salt and pepper to taste

Combine the marinade ingredients. Rub the tuna steak with marinade and refrigerate at least 4 hours. Remove tuna from marinade. Sear tuna in a very hot sauté pan, 15 to 20 seconds per side. Slice tuna very thin.

Dressing

½ **ripe tomato, chopped**
½ **stalk celery, chopped**
¼ **medium onion, chopped**
½ **small carrot, chopped**
1 **clove garlic, chopped**
¼ **bunch fresh basil**
2 **Tablespoons balsamic vinegar**
¼ **cup olive oil**
juice of ½ lemon
salt and pepper to taste

Purée the dressing ingredients in a blender until smooth.

Salad and garnish

arugula or baby greens
capers
fresh shredded Parmesan
fresh ground pepper
marinated roasted red pepper strips

To serve, center salad greens on four plates. Arrange tuna slices around greens. Pour ¼ cup dressing over tuna and greens. Garnish with capers, fresh shredded Parmesan, fresh ground pepper and marinated roasted red pepper strips.

Preparation: 45 minutes   Moderately easy   Serves: 4
Chilling: 4 hours
Cooking: 5 minutes

The First Golf Course

Frequently, Collier County is called "The Golf Capitol of the World," but its first golf course certainly didn't offer a glimpse of the future. The nine–hole course ran north on Third Street South and then turned east on Fifth Avenue South, about as far as Cambier Park.

It has been said that the greens weren't too bad, but you had to watch carefully where your ball landed because it could be buried in the sand by the time you reached it. In a marshy area near the center of the course, the greens–keeper, Robert Fohl, tended a very productive vegetable garden!

Shrimp and Apple Almond Salad
Bonita Bay Club

1 pound medium shrimp, steamed, cleaned, and
  chilled
2 heads romaine lettuce, torn bite–size
½ pound almond slices, oven toasted golden brown
1 red apple, cored and diced

Toss all ingredients together and divide into servings. Top with Poppy Seed Dressing.

Preparation: 20 minutes   Easy   Serves: 4–5
Steaming: 10 minutes
Oven toasting: 10–15 minutes

Poppy Seed Dressing

1 egg yolk or 2 Tablespoons egg beaters
⅓ cup honey
1 shallot, chopped
1 Tablespoon Dijon mustard
⅓ cup sesame seed oil
1½ cups canola oil
½ cup vinegar
1 Tablespoon poppy seeds
salt and pepper to taste

Place egg yolk, honey, shallot and mustard in blender and blend. With blender running, slowly drizzle oils into mixture. As mixture thickens, slowly drizzle vinegar, alternating between oil and vinegar. The dressing should be of a creamy consistency. When finished blending, stir in poppy seeds and season to taste.

Preparation: 10 minutes   Easy   Yield: 2 cups

5th Avenue Salmon Salad

Calella's Bistro Inc.

½ pound fresh Atlantic pink salmon, skinless, boneless
2 tomatoes cut into wedges
1 pound mixed salad greens
1 can hearts of palm, drained, sliced into 1–inch rounds
1 can artichoke hearts, quartered
2 teaspoons caviar

Poaching mixture

1 cup water
¼ cup white wine
2 Tablespoons fresh lemon juice
2 bay leaves
8–10 whole peppercorns

Poach salmon in a covered pan in the poaching mixture for 4 to 10 minutes, depending on the thickness of salmon; keep covered. Remove from heat. Drain and cover salmon with ice for 15 to 20 minutes. Remove salmon, place in a covered dish, and refrigerate for 2 hours. To serve, arrange mixed greens on chilled platter. Garnish with tomatoes, artichoke and hearts of palm. Top with flaked salmon. Drape with caviar and your favorite salad dressing.

Preparation: 20 minutes   Easy   Serves: 4
Cooking: 10 minutes   Cooling: 20 minutes
Chilling: 2 hours

Grilled Salmon and Spinach Salad
Bear's Paw Country Club

¾ pound salmon fillet cut into 4 pieces
salt & pepper to taste
4 slices thick–cut double–smoked bacon
2 Tablespoons olive oil
1 shallot, minced
4 ounces white mushrooms, sliced
½ cup balsamic vinegar
4 Tablespoons cold unsalted butter
1 bag (10–ounce) fresh spinach, washed and
    stemmed

Heat a Hibachi or charcoal grill for the salmon. Trim, portion and season the salmon with a little salt and pepper. Cut the bacon into large squares, the width of the strips and cook in a skillet until browned and crispy; drain and set aside. Grill the salmon to the desired doneness and keep warm. Heat the olive oil in a skillet and sauté the shallots and mushrooms until softened. Add the balsamic vinegar and boil down until syrupy. Swirl in the butter and remove the pan from the heat. Divide the clean spinach among four plates and top each salad with a piece of grilled salmon. Spoon the mushroom sauce over each salad and garnish each with crisp bacon pieces.

Preparation: 15 minutes   Easy   Serves: 3–4
Cooking: 15 minutes

Tabbouleh
Naples Beach Hotel and Golf Club

½ cup bulghur wheat*
1½ cups flat or Italian parsley, finely chopped
3 medium tomatoes, cubed
1 Tablespoon fresh mint, finely chopped
1 medium onion, finely chopped
½ teaspoon ground white pepper
¾ teaspoon salt
½ cup lemon juice
¼ cup olive oil
1 teaspoon finely chopped garlic

Pour HOT water over the cracked wheat covering the wheat by more than an inch. Soak the wheat for 15 to 30 minutes. Drain and rinse well. Spread it out on paper towels to dry further while you prepare the rest of the salad. Combine the cracked wheat, parsley, tomatoes, mint and onions. In a small bowl combine the salt, pepper, lemon juice, olive oil, and garlic; mix well. Mix this dressing with the wheat mixture, blending well; chill. Serve cold as a salad or luncheon dish.

Bulghur wheat is readily available in Natural food stores.

Preparation: 30 minutes   Moderately easy   Serves: 4–5
Soaking: 30 minutes
Chilling: 2–4 hours

Marco Island

W. T. Collier from Tennessee (not related to Barron Collier) is considered to be the founder of the Marco Island town site. Having survived a bad storm, he arrived from Clearwater in 1870 with his wife and eight children in tow. After buying the claims of four black squatters who were farming there, he paid their transportation back to Fort Myers and settled in to build a home from lumber he brought with him. The family had lived in the house just three months when it was destroyed by fire, but spent several years in the palmetto shack which replaced it. Fortunately, they fared much better with their farming operation. Their very first crop of cabbages brought a good price in Key West, and one old–timer recalled buying a single head of cabbage from him that weighed in at 14 1/2 lbs.

In later years the Collier children (increased to 11) greatly expanded the family enterprises, and one son, "Captain Bill" Collier, emerged as a guiding force in the community.

Baba Ghanoush or Mediterranean Eggplant Salad
Naples Beach Hotel and Golf Club

3 pounds eggplant
1 tomato, diced
1 small onion, chopped
1 Tablespoon chopped fresh mint
1 Tablespoon chopped fresh garlic
¼ cup chopped walnuts
salt and freshly ground pepper to taste
¼ cup lemon juice
¼ cup olive oil
pita bread
lemon twists

Bake eggplants, unpeeled, in 350°F. oven for about 35 minutes. Cool, then peel, remove seeds and cube cooked eggplant. Place in a large bowl. Add tomatoes, onion, mint, garlic and walnuts to the cubed eggplant, mixing lightly. Blend together lemon juice olive oil, salt and pepper; pour over vegetables and toss to mix well. Garnish with lemon twists and serve with pita bread.

Preparation: 30 minutes   Moderately easy   Serves: 8
Baking: 35 minutes

Grilled Portobello Mushroom Salad with Walnut Dressing
Voilà! Wine Bar & Brasserie

1 large portobello mushroom, peeled
2 Tablespoons olive oil, heated
1 head Boston lettuce
1 Tablespoon red wine vinegar
2 Tablespoons walnut oil
salt and freshly ground pepper

Soak the portobello mushroom in the heated olive oil for 2–3 minutes. Prepare a small salad with the Boston lettuce and arrange on plate. Sprinkle with red wine vinegar and walnut oil, seasoning with salt and pepper to taste. Broil the mushroom with a touch of salt until soft, slice and serve hot on the salad.

Preparation: 10 minutes   Easy   Serves: 1
Broiling: 3–5 minutes

Wild Portobello Mushroom, Roasted Garlic Herb Oil on a bed of Field Greens garnished with Goat Cheese
Noodles Cafe Inc.

4 portobello mushrooms, 4–inch diameter, dirty part of the stem removed
1 cup fresh garlic cloves, roasted
2½ cups extra virgin olive oil
12 ounces quality mixed greens, prepacked or your choice
4 plum tomatoes, each cut into 4 rounds
4 ounces goat cheese
2 teaspoons fresh dill, chopped
2 teaspoons fresh rosemary, chopped

Place mushrooms, top side down, with garlic cloves in a shallow ovenproof saucepan. Drizzle ½ cup oil on each mushroom's underside. Roast at 400°F. until mushrooms are almost soft and garlic is golden brown (if garlic browns too fast, remove from oven and let stand in remaining olive oil). To serve, fill a 10–inch plate with salad greens, place a mushroom in middle with top side up; place tomato round and goat cheese evenly around mushroom. Add dill and rosemary to ½ cup oil with roasted garlic. Drizzle over mushroom and serve immediately.

NOTE: save any extra oil for the next mushroom salad. Oil will pick up flavor of garlic and herbs for next party.

Preparation: 15 minutes   Easy   Serves: 4
Baking: 10–20 minutes

Lamb Medallion and Warm Goat's Cheese Salad

Collier's Reserve Country Club

6 ounces mixed salad greens
4 oven–dried Roma tomatoes
10 to 12–ounce boneless lamb loin, cut into
   medallions (½ inch thick)
6 ounces goat cheese (cheverole, montrachette,
   Boucheron)

Portion the lettuces and arrange the oven–dried tomatoes as a garnish. Grill the lamb medallions and place on the salads. Spray a baking pan and place the goat cheese on it to heat under the broiler until slightly brown and bubbly. Top lamb with the goat cheese. To serve, drizzle with Warm Pink Peppercorn Vinaigrette.

Warm Pink Peppercorn Vinaigrette

⅓ cup olive oil
2 Tablespoons minced shallots
3 Tablespoons pink peppercorns
¼ cup Armagnac or other Cognac
½ cup port wine
½ cup balsamic vinegar
1 Tablespoon cornstarch
2 Tablespoons water
salt
sugar

In a skillet sauté shallots in 2 teaspoons olive oil until about half cooked. Add the pink peppercorns, Armagnac, wine, and vinegar. Boil and reduce by one–third. Thicken with a little cornstarch and water mixture. Whisk in oil and season to taste with salt and sugar.

Preparation: 20 minutes   Moderately easy   Serves: 4
Cooking: 20 minutes   Can prepare part ahead

Caribbean Black Bean Salad

O══▶ *Country Club of Naples*

1 pound dried black beans
2 celery stalks
1 whole carrot cut lengthwise
1 Tablespoon salt

In a large bowl cover black beans with 2 inches of water and refrigerate overnight. Drain beans and transfer to pot with celery, carrot stalks, and Tablespoon of salt. Add water to cover beans 2 inches. Bring to a boil and simmer until beans are tender (1½ to 2 hours). Remove celery and carrot and strain. Cool beans.

Preparation: 5 minutes   Easy   Serves: 8
Soaking: overnight
Cooking: 1½–2 hours
Cooling: 1 hour

Salad

2 tomatoes, large dice
2 green peppers, finely diced
2 red peppers, finely diced
1 bunch green onions, finely diced
1 Tablespoon chopped garlic
1 Tablespoon chopped cilantro
1 teaspoon black pepper
2 teaspoons salt
¼ cup olive or vegetable oil
¼ cup red wine vinegar

Mix beans with remaining ingredients in a large bowl. Toss well and refrigerate for 1 to 2 hours. Retoss before serving.

Preparation: 25 minutes   Easy   Serves: 8

Citrus

Orange trees first appeared in St. Augustine, Florida in 1565, believed to have been grown from seeds brought here by Ponce de Leon. The grapefruit is a relative newcomer, having been introduced into Florida in 1823 from the Bahamas.

The true lime is native to Malaysia and was introduced into Florida in 1838, variously known as the Key, Mexican or West Indian Lime.

Arugula, Radicchio, Pear and Walnut Salad with Sun–Dried Tomato Citrus Vinaigrette
Vito's Ristorante

Sun-Dried Tomato Citrus Vinaigrette

½ cup fresh orange juice
½ cup olive oil
¼ cup balsamic vinegar
2 cloves garlic, chopped
2 Tablespoons chopped sun–dried tomatoes, softened in
1 Tablespoon warm water
1 Tablespoon sugar
salt & pepper to taste

Combine all ingredients and let stand 15 minutes. Purée mixture in blender.

Salad

½ pound arugula, washed and dried
¼ pound radicchio, bite size
¼ cup (heaping) walnut pieces
2 ripe pears

Combine arugula, radicchio and walnuts in a large salad bowl. Peel and dice pears, then toss them with the salad.

Garnish

orange segments
fresh Parmesan cheese

To serve: arrange salad on four salad plates, garnish with orange segments and top with fresh shredded Parmesan cheese. Dress with vinaigrette.

Preparation: 15–20 minutes   Easy   Serves: 4
Must make vinaigrette first.

Tossed Baby Greens with Raspberry Vinaigrette
℗━━ *Collier Athletic Club*

Raspberry Vinaigrette

¼ cup raspberry vinegar
2 teaspoons Dijon mustard
¼ cup chopped red onion
¼ teaspoon ground black pepper
1 teaspoon sugar
¾ cup salad oil
salt to taste
4–6 cups assorted Baby Greens, washed and dried

Garnish

1 cup fresh strawberries and raspberries

Combine the vinegar, mustard, chopped onion, pepper, and sugar in a bowl. Whisk in the oil and salt to taste. To serve, toss with washed and dried baby greens and garnish servings with fresh strawberries and raspberries.

Preparation: 10 minutes   Easy   Serves: 4

Baby Lettuces with Grilled Vegetables and Balsamic Dressing
Trio's

Balsamic Dressing

1 Tablespoon sugar
½ cup balsamic vinegar
1 medium shallot, finely diced
⅛ teaspoon salt
ground pepper to taste
½ teaspoon dried basil
½ teaspoon dried oregano
1 cup olive oil and 1 cup vegetable oil mixed
   together

In food processor place sugar, ¼ cup vinegar, shallot, salt, pepper and herbs. Process on high, adding 1 cup of the oil mix in a steady thin stream. Add remaining vinegar, then remaining oil, processing on high all the while. Chill 1 hour or more.

Preparation: 5 minutes   Easy   Yield: 2½–3 cups
Chilling: 1 hour

Salad

1 pound mixed baby lettuces
1 medium zucchini
1 medium yellow squash
1 medium eggplant
1 red onion
olive oil
salt and pepper to taste

Wash, drain and tear lettuce, refrigerate. Cut vegetables crosswise into circles ⅛ inch thick. Lay on a cookie sheet. Brush lightly with olive oil, sprinkle with salt and pepper. Grill or broil until tender.

Preparation: 20 minutes   Easy   Serves: 6
Cooking time: 5–10 minutes

To serve, toss lettuces with ½ of the dressing. Divide up on chilled plates. Arrange grilled vegetables around lettuce. Drizzle with dressing as desired.

Southwestern Chicken Salad on a Sweet Potato Biscuit
Collier's Reserve Country Club

14 ounces boneless, skinless chicken breast
2 red bell peppers
2 green onions
1 small bunch cilantro
2 cloves garlic
½ teaspoon cumin
2 Tablespoons heavy mayonnaise
2 Tablespoons sour cream
dash cayenne pepper
salt and pepper to taste

Grill the chicken breast over mesquite; set aside to cool. Roast the red peppers over mesquite, turning frequently to insure even roasting. Scrape the black off the peppers when they are finished roasting. Slit and remove the seeds and stem. Cut into small dice and place on towel to drain. Chop the green onions and cilantro; mince the garlic; cut cooled chicken into small dice. Place all ingredients in a mixing bowl, mix together, and season to taste. To serve, split fresh biscuits and fill with the salad. Garnish with cilantro.

Preparation: 10 minutes   Easy   Serves: 4
Cooking: 35 minutes

Sweet Potato Biscuits

¾ cup mashed sweet potato
¼ cup melted butter
1¼ cups flour
4 teaspoons baking powder
1 Tablespoon sugar
1 teaspoon salt

Beat together the mashed sweet potato and melted butter. Sift together the dry ingredients and gently fold into the sweet potato mixture. Take care not to mix too much as this will produce a tough biscuit. Drop biscuits on ungreased baking pan. Bake at 400°F. 12–18 minutes.

Preparation: 10 minutes   Easy   Serves: 4
Baking: 12–18 minutes

Walnut and Wild Rice Chicken Salad

Countryside Country Club

1 cup white & wild rice blend, cooked and cooled
½ cup sliced green onion
¼ teaspoon grated lemon peel
1½ Tablespoons lemon juice
⅔ cup plain yogurt
3 Tablespoons olive oil
salt & pepper to taste
2 cups finely diced cooked chicken
1 cup chopped walnuts

Mix first seven ingredients together and blend well. Add the chicken and walnuts, mix well. Refrigerate until serving.

Preparation: 15 minutes   Easy   Serves: 4
Cooking: 30 minutes to pre–cook rice and chicken
Chilling: 1 hour

Madras Curry Chicken Salad

Countryside Country Club

2 pounds chicken, cooked and diced (about 2½ to 3 cups)
4 stalks celery, diced fine
1 teaspoon curry powder
¼ teaspoon white pepper
1 teaspoon garlic powder
1 teaspoon Old Bay seasoning
1 cup walnut halves and pieces
1 cup canned pineapple chunks, drained
1 cup mayonnaise or more as desired

Combine all ingredients together until well mixed. Chill at least one hour before serving.

Preparation: 30 minutes   Easy   Serves: 6
Cooking: 20–30 minutes to pre–cook the chicken
Chilling: 3–4 hours

Salad Annette with Citrus Dressing

Island Club of Naples Inc.

1 chicken breast, poached and cubed
1 small onion, sliced
1 carrot, cut into chunks
1 stalk celery, cut into chunks
1 teaspoon sesame seeds
½ cup toasted rice noodles
½ cup toasted almonds
1 head lettuce
1 romaine lettuce

Poach chicken breast with sliced onion, carrot, and celery in water to cover for 20 minutes. Remove chicken from poaching liquid, save chicken; discard vegetables and liquid. Cool chicken slightly then cut into cubes. Toast almonds and sesame seeds in 350°F. oven for 10–15 minutes. Tear lettuces into desired size. Toss all ingredients together with Citrus Dressing to taste.

Preparation: 10 minutes   Easy   Serves: 2–3
Cooking: 20 minutes

Citrus Dressing

½ cup salad oil of your choice
¼ cup vinegar of your choice
2 teaspoons sugar
¼ cup chopped fresh parsley
juice of 1 orange

Garnish

1 orange cut into wedges

Whisk ingredients together and pour over Salad Annette, toss lightly. Serve on chilled salad plates. Garnish with orange wedges.

Preparation: 5 minutes   Easy   Yield: 1 cup

Everglades/Rod and Gun Club

Generally recognized as the founder of Everglade, George W. Storter Jr. arrived in 1882 to help harvest William Allen's crop; five years later he built his first home and in 1889 he purchased the Allen property – the entire Everglade town–site for $800 – and moved into the Allen house. The trading post he established downriver in 1892 became a gathering place for both Indians and whites and was enlarged over the years, thanks to the growth of seasonal hunters, fishermen and yachting parties. Known for the lavish and delicious meals served, it was the foundation for today's Rod and Gun Club, famous for its cuisine.

In 1923 Everglade changed to the plural Everglades and became the county seat of the new Collier County, the main location of Barron Collier's Florida holdings. It was a transportation and communications center and the site of two great engineering projects: building a town, directing the construction work on the Tamiami Trail and a north/south highway from Everglades to the Trail then up to Immokalee.

First Watch Salad
First Watch Restaurant

1 teaspoon celery seed
1 teaspoon dry mustard
1 teaspoon salt
3⁄8 cup sugar
½ cup vinegar
1 cup salad oil
1 cup finely diced onion
1½ cups diced tomatoes
1½ cups diced celery
1½ cups diced zucchini

Mix dry ingredients together in medium bowl. Whisk in vinegar, oil and onion. Mix well and let stand for 1 hour. Stir in tomatoes, celery and zucchini. Refrigerate at least 2 hours. Serve as a salad dressing for lettuce, tossing just before serving. OR, marinate cooked pasta in dressing for a delicious pasta salad.

Preparation: 15 minutes   Easy   Yield: 1 quart +
Standing time: 1 hour   Chilling time: 2 hours

Cauliflower

Cauliflower is nothing more but cabbage with a college education.
Mark Twain (1835–1910)

Country Cauliflower Salad
Country Club of Naples

1 head cauliflower
¼ cup spinach, chopped
¼ cup bacon, cooked and crumbled
3 Tablespoons grated Parmesan cheese
2 Tablespoons finely diced onion
½ cup mayonnaise
½ teaspoon salt
½ teaspoon pepper

Cut cauliflower into small florets. In a large mixing bowl toss together all ingredients until completely coated with mayonnaise. Chill and serve.

Preparation: 35 minutes   Easy   Serves: 4–5
Must do ahead   Must chill

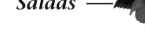

Sweet Cole Slaw

The Moorings Country Club

8 cups shredded cabbage
2 cups kale, shredded
2 cups mayonnaise
¾ cup sugar
Garnish:
lettuce leaf
mandarin orange sections or peach slices

Toss cabbage and kale together in a large bowl. In a small bowl blend sugar into mayonnaise. Pour mayonnaise mixture over cabbage mixture and toss well to combine thoroughly. Serve chilled on a piece of lettuce leaf and garnish with mandarin orange sections or peach slices.

Preparation: 15 minutes	Easy	Serves: 10–12
Chilling: 1 hour or more	Must do ahead	

Cabbage

A familiar kitchen–garden vegetable about as large and wise as a man's head.

Ambrose Bierce
The Devil's Dictionary (1906)

Bayside Spinach Salad with Port Vinaigrette

Bayside

Salad

fresh spinach leaves
grilled red onion
diced Gorgonzola cheese
dried currants
walnut pieces

Tomato Concassé

Fresh tomato, peeled, seeded, evenly diced

Toss salad ingredients together and top each portion with 2 Tablespoons Port Vinaigrette. Garnish with Tomato Concassé.

Port Vinaigrette

2 shallots, diced
1 teaspoon oil
1 Tablespoon sugar
1 cup Ruby Port
¼ cup raspberry vinegar
¾ cup extra virgin olive oil
¾ cup canola oil
salt and white pepper to taste

In stainless (non–corrosive) sauce pot, sauté shallots in oil until soft. Add sugar and stir with a wooden spoon until sugar begins to caramelize. Carefully add Port and reduce to about 6 Tablespoons (3 ounces) of syrup. Remove from heat. Add raspberry vinegar and whisk in olive and canola oils. Season to taste with salt and white pepper.

Preparation: 30 minutes   Moderately difficult   Yield: 2 cups
Cooking: 30 minutes

Spinach Gelatin Mold
The Moorings Country Club

½ cup cold water
3 envelopes unflavored gelatin
2 cups beef broth
10 ounces fresh spinach, washed, stemmed, chopped
  fine
½ cup finely chopped onion
6 large eggs, hard cooked, chopped
¾ pound bacon, crispy cooked, crumbled
½ cup mayonnaise
3 Tablespoons lemon juice
black pepper to taste

Sprinkle gelatin into cold water, stir, let stand 10 minutes. Heat beef broth to almost boiling, remove from heat. Dissolve gelatin in hot beef broth. Combine remaining ingredients in a large bowl. Add beef broth to spinach mixture and mix well. Pour into oiled 1½ quart ring mold and chill 4–6 hours or overnight to set. Unmold gelatin by holding mold in hot water for a few seconds till loosened. Cover with plate and turn over carefully. Serve wedges of molded salad on a bed of red–leaf lettuce, if available. Serve with your choice of dressing.

Preparation: 30–40 minutes   Easy   Serves: 6–8
Chilling: 4–6 hours

Blue Heron House Dressing
Blue Heron Inn

1 Tablespoon Dijon mustard
1 Tablespoon chopped mixed fresh herbs (basil, dill, oregano, thyme)
2 Tablespoons white wine vinegar
2 Tablespoons balsamic vinegar
1¼ cups salad oil
½ cup beef broth (reduced for beefy taste)
salt and pepper to taste

Mix mustard, herbs and vinegars together. While whisking, slowly add salad oil. Finish by adding beef broth. Salt and pepper to taste. To serve, toss with mixed baby lettuces, homemade croutons. Delicious topped with crumbled Gorgonzola, freshly grated Parmesan.

Preparation: 15 minutes   Easy   Yield: 4 cups
Cooking: 5–10 minutes to reduce beef broth

Cucumber and Shrimp Dressing
Blue Heron Inn

1 cup mayonnaise
¼ cup tomato ketchup
¼ cup brandy
¼ cup lemon juice
1 splash Worcestershire sauce
1 splash Tabasco sauce
salt and pepper to taste
½ cup baby shrimp, cooked
½ cup finely diced, peeled and seeded cucumber

Mix first 7 ingredients in a mixing bowl. Add shrimp and cucumber; mix. Refrigerate 1 hour. Serve over mixed baby lettuces.

Preparation: 10 minutes   Easy   Yield: 3 cups

Entrees

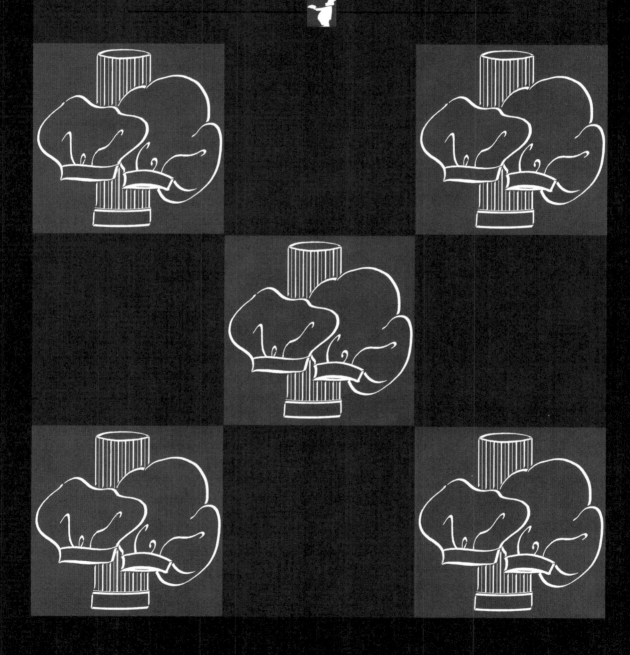

Entrees

Potato Crusted Salmon with Chives and Lump Crab Vinaigrette
Bistro 821

2 Tablespoons sweet butter
3 Tablespoons lemon juice
6 6–ounce salmon fillets
salt and pepper to taste
½ pound medium red Bliss potatoes
2 Tablespoons olive oil
⅓ cup chopped chives for garnish

Melt butter and add the lemon juice, whisking well. Brush the tops of the salmon fillets with lemon butter (reserve about one–third of this mixture). Season the tops of the fillets with salt and pepper. Peel the potatoes and slice into rounds as thinly as possible. Arrange them on the fillets to look like scales, overlapping them from one side to the other. Heat a non–stick pan. Add 1 Tablespoon olive oil and reserved lemon butter to pan and carefully sauté fillets (potato side–down) until nicely browned. When brown, carefully turn over and place on an oiled baking sheet to finish cooking in the oven at 400°F. about 10 minutes. Serve with fresh green salad with lump crab vinaigrette. Sprinkle with chives for color.

Preparation: 45 minutes   Moderately Easy   Serves: 6
Cooking: 10 minutes

Lump Crab Vinaigrette

¼ cup rice wine vinegar
¾ cup olive oil
1 red bell pepper, finely chopped
1 yellow bell pepper, finely chopped
2 Tablespoons chopped fresh herbs, of your choice
salt and pepper to taste
½ pound lump crab (picked over to remove bits of shell, etc)

Whisk together the vinegar, oil, peppers, and herbs. Add the crab and season to taste. Serve over fresh greens.

Preparation: 15 minutes   Easy   Serves: 6

Salmon Au Poivre with Green Peppercorn Sauce

Naples Sailing & Yacht Club

2 pounds salmon
1 leek
2 Tablespoons black peppercorns (coarsely cracked)
2–4 Tablespoons oil or butter for sautéing
½ shallot, finely chopped
2 Tablespoons green peppercorns
½ cup brandy
½ cup fish stock
¼ cup heavy cream
2 Tablespoons butter for sauce
pinch of salt

Garnish

4 sprigs fresh dill
4 Tablespoons tomato concassé (finely diced tomato)

Cut salmon into 1–inch strips across the length of the fillet. Turn the pieces onto their sides and form two pieces into a circle. Cut the leeks lengthwise into ¼ inch strips, and very lightly blanch them. Use the leek strips to tie the salmon, to hold it together securely during cooking. (A square knot works well.) Coat both sides of the fish with the cracked black pepper, pressing down firmly to ensure that it stays on. Preheat a holding oven to 300°F. then preheat a sauté pan large enough for the four portions of fish. Sauté the salmon with butter or oil for 3–5 minutes per side. Remove the fish from the pan and place on an oven-proof dish, in preheated oven while you make the sauce. In the same sauté pan you cooked the fish; add the shallots and green peppercorns, sauté slightly, making sure not to burn them. With the pan away from the burner add the brandy. It will flame, so be careful! After the flame goes out, add the fish stock and reduce by half. Add the heavy cream and continue to reduce until it is of a sauce consistency. Remove from heat and add the butter, swirl it until all the butter is melted and incorporated. Add pinch of salt, if desired. Take the fish from the oven and place on serving plate. Spoon the peppercorn sauce over the top and garnish with fresh dill sprigs and tomato concassé.

Preparation: 30 minutes   Moderately Easy   Serves: 4
Cooking: 15–20 minutes

Pan–Fried Salmon Cakes with Sour Cream Sauce, Baby Lettuces and Ginger Lime Vinaigrette

The Chef's Garden

Salmon Cakes

1 pound fresh fillet of Norwegian salmon
¼ cup water
¼ cup sliced green onions
½ cup mayonnaise
¼ cup Kikoman soy sauce
3 large or 2 extra large eggs
2 Tablespoons minced ginger or pickled ginger
1 Tablespoon chili paste with garlic
¾ cup bread crumbs
½ cup vegetable oil

Place salmon fillet in baking pan; add ¼ cup water and bake at 350°F. for 10–15 minutes or until done. Remove salmon from pan and refrigerate until cool enough to handle. While salmon is cooling, lightly mix the next six ingredients together in a mixing bowl. Crumble cooled salmon into mixture and stir until well incorporated. Refrigerate 10–15 minutes (or more if you want to prepare ahead of serving). Shape salmon mixture into ¼ cup balls. Dredge in bread crumbs and flatten to ½" thick discs. Pan fry in hot vegetable oil until honey–browned. Serve with Sour Cream Chive Sauce and baby lettuces with Ginger–Lime Vinaigrette.

Sour Cream Chive Sauce

1 cup sour cream
2 Tablespoons finely chopped chives
salt and freshly ground pepper to taste

Place sour cream in mixing bowl. Add chives and mix well. Season to taste.

Ginger–Lime Vinaigrette

2 Tablespoons freshly squeezed lime juice
1 teaspoon peeled, minced, fresh ginger
2 Tablespoons vegetable oil

Whisk the lime juice and minced ginger together. Slowly add the vegetable oil, whisking constantly until oil and juice are blended. Serve with baby lettuces.

Preparation: 45 minutes   Moderately Easy   Serves: 6–8
Cooking: 15 minutes   Can do ahead

"Mayor" Speed S. Menafee

Although the 1923 state legislature authorized the incorporation, it was not completed until 1925. For several years council meetings were held in the Naples Improvement Company offices, where rooms five and six were designated as the Town Hall.

Officially, the first mayor is listed as Speed S. Menafee, who had come to Naples 20 years earlier and, at some point, had worked for "The Company." But he was only mayor for as long as it took him to walk up to the podium and resign, at which time he was "succeeded" by Judge E. G. Wilkerson, who held the office for many years.

In today's world, Menafee would probably be known as a free spirit. A soldier of fortune who had traveled the world over while gathering a liberal education, he was a man of many talents and owner of a wonderful sense of humor. Funny stories about him abound, but he seems to be known best as a man who could spin the most unlikely tales with an absolutely straight face. He also had a guitar, could sing a few old songs, roamed all over the area – and was always warmly welcomed.

Alaska Salmon Cakes with Red Pepper Coulis

Merriman's Wharf

Salmon Cakes

1 egg
2 Tablespoons mayonnaise
1 Tablespoon Dijon mustard
2 teaspoons dry mustard
2 Tablespoons chopped cilantro
2 Tablespoons chopped scallions
juice of 1 lemon
2 pounds poached salmon, flaked
1 cup white breadcrumbs
salt and pepper to taste
clarified butter

In a large bowl combine the egg, mayonnaise, Dijon mustard, dry mustard, cilantro and scallions. Blend thoroughly and add lemon juice. Add the salmon and bread crumbs, being careful not to overmix. Add salt and pepper; form into 8 patties. Heat a large sauté pan to medium heat and sauté the patties in clarified butter 2 to 3 minutes on each side until golden brown. Drain on paper towels. Center Red Pepper Coulis on each plate, top with salmon cake and drizzle with coulis.

Preparation: 45 minutes Moderately Easy Serves: 6–8
Cooking: 15 minutes Can poach salmon ahead

Red Pepper Coulis

1 large red pepper
½ teaspoon rice vinegar
¼ teaspoon poppy seeds
¼ teaspoon salt

Roast the pepper over an open flame or under the broiler until soft and charred all over. Place in a paper bag and let steam for 10 minutes. Scrape the skin off and remove the core, seeds and ribs. Cut into small pieces and place in a blender or food processor and purée until smooth. Add vinegar, poppy seeds and salt; pulse until blended.

Preparation: 10 minutes Easy Yield: ½ cup
Roasting: 10 minutes Can do ahead

Salmon Teriyaki & Mango with Mixed Vegetables
Vanderbilt Inn on the Gulf

Mixed vegetables

2 cups mixed vegetables, coarsely chopped (carrots,
    zucchini, celery, onion, or any that you like)
½ bunch parsley
½ bunch basil
1 sprig fresh thyme
1 teaspoon salt
½ teaspoon white pepper
2 Tablespoons olive oil

Place vegetables, herbs and seasonings in a medium pot
and cover with cold water. Boil or steam, if you prefer, over
medium– high heat for 5 minutes, or until tender. Strain
and toss with olive oil. Serve hot.

Salmon

2 7–ounce fillets of salmon, skin removed
¼ cup flour
3 Tablespoons olive oil
¼ cup teriyaki sauce
1 mango, peeled, seeded and puréed

Lightly dust salmon with flour. Place in heated sauté pan
with olive oil. Cook 1 minute on each side over medium–
high heat. Remove and place in a baking dish with teriyaki
sauce. Cover and bake at 300°F. about 10–15 minutes or
until done. To serve, lift salmon out of the pan and place
in center of plate. Cover ⅔ of salmon with the mango purée.
Place hot vegetables around salmon.

Preparation: 30 minutes   Easy   Serves: 2–3
Cooking: 5 minutes   Serve immediately
Baking: 10–15 minutes

Crusted Cappellini Salmon Sun–Dried Tomato Beurre Blanc Sauce

Noodles Cafe Inc.

Pesto

4 cups fresh basil
½ cup walnuts
10 large cloves garlic
1 cup olive oil
½ cup grated Pecorino Romano cheese

Fill a blender with all of the basil. Add garlic, walnuts, ½ cup oil and cheese; blend together. Add the rest of the oil a little at a time until all is used. *Add more cheese if the mixture is too oily.*

Cappellini Crust

8 ounces pasta
¾ cup dry bread crumbs
2 egg yolks
1 cup pesto
2 Tablespoons grated citrus zest (lemon, orange or lime)

Cook pasta in a large pot of boiling, salted water 10 minutes, until well done. In a large bowl, mix together the cooked pasta, bread crumbs, egg yolks, pesto and citrus zest. Continue mixing together until the mixture is of a soft sticky consistency.

Sun–Dried Tomato Beurre Blanc Sauce

4 ounces sun–dried tomatoes (about 20 tomato halves)
1 pound unsalted butter
1 cup white wine
1 Teaspoon diced shallots

In a saucepan combine sun–dried tomatoes, white wine, and shallots; let it reduce by half. Over LOW HEAT, add the butter, a little at a time, until all butter is incorporated into the wine mixture. Set aside and keep warm.

Continued on next page

Crusted Cappellini Salmon
Sun–Dried Tomato Beurre Blanc Sauce (continued)

Salmon

3 Tablespoons oil
1½ pounds fresh salmon fillets (cut into 4 6–ounce
  portions)

Heat oil in a large sauté pan over medium heat. Pack the Cappellini Crust mixture on top of salmon fillets, turn salmon over (crust side down) and cook in heated oil until brown (about 2 minutes). Turn over, (crust should be facing up) cover and cook another 2 minutes. Remove from sauté pan and place in an ovenproof dish and finish cooking in a 450°F. oven for 2 minutes or until salmon is pink inside when flaked with a fork. Serve on a bed of julienned vegetables of your choice, which have been steamed *al dente.* Top with Sun–Dried Tomato Beurre Blanc Sauce

Preparation: 30 minutes   Moderately easy   Serves: 4
Cooking: 30 minutes
Baking: 5 minutes

Sweet Potato Crusted Salmon

Apollo's Oceanview Restaurant

2 large sweet potatoes
8 6–ounce fillets of salmon, no skin or bone
¼ cup Dijon mustard
½ Tablespoon fresh dill, chopped
¼ cup butter, melted
¼ cup white wine

Peel and shred sweet potatoes into ⅛ inch strips. Blanch in boiling water about 5 minutes. Remove from water and chill. Place salmon fillets on a greased or sprayed shallow baking pan. Spread ½ Tablespoon of Dijon mustard on each fillet. Sprinkle chopped dill on each fillet. Mix sweet potatoes and melted butter until all potatoes are coated with butter. Place potatoes on top of each fillet to get an even coat. Add wine to baking pan. Cover and bake for 15 minutes at 375°F. Uncover and cook for 5 minutes at 450°F. to brown potatoes.

Preparation: 25 minutes   Easy   Serves: 8
Cooking: 20 minutes

Sweet Potato

The Sweet Potato is a root member of the morning glory family. It is totally unrelated to the yam, and produces more calories, minerals and vitamin A than the white potato.

Columbus brought the sweet potato to Europe after his first voyage to the New World. Today it is now cultivated in the sub–tropical parts of the world.

Peppers

Peppers, which originated in South America and were cultivated in America for years before being introduced into Europe, are generally classified as sweet (for eating) or hot (for seasoning). Forget about eating them for a moment and picture them placed in a wide low bowl: smooth firm "fruit" in a myriad of shapes and shiny jewel colors of red, dark green and shades of yellow... Instant decoration for your kitchen – – until you can no longer resist adding them to a salad, stuffing and baking them for dinner, mixing them with such other vegetables as eggplant and tomatoes or whipping up a batch of chili.

Sauté Florida Snapper, Risotto and Yellow Pepper Fennel Sauce
The Ritz–Carlton Naples

Risotto

2 Tablespoons olive oil
½ cup yellow onion, diced
½ cup celery, diced
1 cup Arborio rice
1¼ cups tomato juice
1 cup fish stock
¼ cup zucchini, diced
¼ cup yellow squash, diced
¼ cup eggplant, diced

In a medium–size sauce pot sweat the onions and celery in olive oil over medium heat. Add rice and mix well. Add half the tomato juice and fish stock. When the liquid has been absorbed, add the rest. Then add the diced vegetables and cook over slow heat until the rice has reached a creamy consistency.

Preparation: 20 minutes   Easy   Serves: 4
Cooking: 20–30 minutes

Yellow Pepper Fennel Sauce

3 Tablespoons olive oil
3 yellow peppers, cored, seeded and coarsely chopped
2 bulbs fennel, chopped
2 shallots, chopped
pinch of saffron
1¼ cups fish stock
¼ cup Pernod or anise flavored liqueur
pinch chopped Italian parsley
pinch chopped thyme
salt and white pepper to taste
1 Tablespoon butter, softened

Heat the olive oil in a medium sauce pot; sweat together the peppers, fennel and shallots. Add saffron and Pernod, reducing mixture until dry. Add fish stock and bring to a boil. Reduce to a simmer over medium heat for 15 minutes. Add herbs and seasonings and purée. While the ingredients are in the blender add soft butter. Remove and serve.

Preparation: 15 minutes   Easy   Yield: 2 cups
Cooking: 30 minutes

Continued on next page

Sauté Florida Snapper, Risotto and Yellow Pepper Fennel Sauce (continued)

Snapper

4 snapper fillets (6 to 8 ounces each)
3 Tablespoons olive oil
salt and pepper to taste

Heat olive oil over high heat in sauté pan. When oil begins to smoke, season fillet with salt and pepper on both sides. Remove pan from heat and place snapper in pan. Return to medium heat and cook snapper for approximately 3 minutes. Turn fillet over and cook for another 3 – 4 minutes. Remove snapper from pan. To serve: Place Risotto in center of plate and lay snapper on top. Top with sauce. Serve immediately.

Preparation: 5 minutes   Easy   Serves: 4
Cooking: 10 minutes

Hazelnut Crusted Snapper
Michael's Cafe

2 6–ounce fresh snapper fillets
1 egg
2 Tablespoons milk
2 Tablespoons flour
3 Tablespoons hazelnuts, chopped fine
1 Tablespoon oil or butter
salt and pepper to taste

Rinse the snapper and pat dry with a paper towel. Make egg wash by beating the egg and milk together. Mix flour and hazelnuts together. Dip the snapper in the egg wash to cover, and then into the flour/hazelnut mixture, pressing lightly to cover. Heat oil in a sauté pan and sauté the coated snapper until brown on both sides. To serve, place Mango Coulis on plate with the fish on top. Garnish with diced mango.

Preparation: 15 minutes   Easy   Serves; 2
Cooking: 5–10 minutes

Mango Coulis

2 mangoes, peeled, seeded and diced
¼ cup white wine

Save ¼ cup of the diced mango in the refrigerator for garnish. Simmer mango and wine in a saucepan for 10 minutes. Purée in blender or food processor. Spoon on plate with fish on top. Refrigerate unused portion of coulis.

Preparation: 10 minutes   Easy   Yield: 2 cups
Cooking: 10 minutes

Snapper

Of the roughly 250 species of snapper, about 15 of them are available in Gulf waters.

The Red Snapper and the Yellowtail Snapper are abundant in Florida. Found in depths of 60–200 feet, they grow to 35 pounds – although they are usually sold in the marketplace from four to six pounds in size. Snapper may be cooked by any method, especially baked and stuffed or poached and glazed like salmon.

Yellowtail Snapper with Pesto and Pine Nuts

Blue Heron Inn

Pesto

2 cups fresh basil
½ cup Parmesan cheese
½ cup pine nuts
¼ cup chopped garlic
1 cup olive oil

Purée all ingredients in a food processor or blender. Set aside.

Preparation: 10 minutes   Yield: 2 cups

Lemon Butter Sauce

½ cup white wine
2 teaspoons lemon juice
1 cup chopped cold butter
a little demi–glace (optional)

In a small saucepan bring the wine and lemon juice to a boil; whisk in butter a little at a time until well blended and smooth.

Preparation: 5 minutes   Easy   Yield: 1½ cups
Cooking: 10 minutes

Fish

4 8–ounce snapper fillets, skinned
½ cup flour
¼ cup olive oil

Egg Wash

2 eggs
¾ cup milk
1 Tablespoon Pesto Sauce

Garnish

2 Tablespoons toasted pine nuts

Dip snapper in flour and shake off excess. Heat olive oil in a large fry pan. Beat egg wash ingredients together in a bowl. Dip floured fish fillet in egg wash and sauté in hot olive oil. When lightly browned (about 3 minutes), turn fillet over and finish cooking. To serve, transfer to plate and drizzle with Lemon butter sauce. Garnish with toasted pine nuts and fresh pesto sauce.

Preparation: 15 minutes   Easy   Serves: 4
Cooking: 15 minutes

Nut–Crusted Red Snapper
Bentley Village

1 Tablespoon unsalted butter
¼ cup finely ground pistachio nuts
¼ cup finely ground almonds
4 red snapper fillets (6 to 8 ounces each) about
  1–inch thick
1 Tablespoon olive oil
¼ teaspoon ground white pepper

One hour before you begin cooking, bring butter to room temperature. Pulverize the nuts in a food processor until they are very finely ground (similar to granulated sugar). Do not overprocess or they will turn to butter. Dust the fish fillets with this ground nut flour. In a sauté pan, heat the oil and 1 Tablespoon of butter. Sauté the fish over very low heat for about 3 minutes on each side or until done. Sprinkle with white pepper and remove fish to a warm platter.

Mustard and Ginger Sauce

1 large shallot, peeled and finely minced
½ teaspoon finely minced fresh ginger
¼ cup Champagne or dry white wine
½ cup heavy whipping cream
1 Teaspoon Dijon mustard
3 Tablespoons butter
salt and freshly ground white pepper to taste

In the sauté pan used to cook the fish, add the minced shallot and sauté for 1 minute. Add the ginger and Champagne. Bring the mixture to a boil, and lower the heat to medium. Add the cream and let it reduce for 2 minutes. Lower the heat to the lowest temperature and add the remaining butter (1 Tablespoon at a time) and the mustard, stirring continuously. Add salt and pepper to taste. To serve, spoon 3 Tablespoons sauce onto the bottom of each plate, place fillet on top of sauce.

Preparation: 20 minutes   Easy   Serves: 4
Cooking: 20 minutes

Macadamia Nut Crusted Snapper with Tropical Fruit Beurre Blanc

Marco Island Hilton Beach Resort

Sweet Potato Purée

2 medium–size sweet potatoes
2 Tablespoons heavy cream
⅛ teaspoon cinnamon
⅛ teaspoon nutmeg
1 teaspoon honey

Peel and steam sweet potato until soft. Purée in food processor; blend in cream, cinnamon, nutmeg and honey. Reserve.

Tropical Fruit Brunoise

1 Kiwi fruit, peeled, chopped, finely diced
½ cup papaya, finely diced
½ cup fresh pineapple, finely diced
½ cup fresh mango, finely diced

Mix all fruits together and reserve.

The Snapper:

4 yellow–tail snapper fillets, about 6 ounces each
½ cup flour, seasoned with salt and pepper
½ pound unsalted butter, softened
½ cup macadamia nuts, pulverized
2 teaspoons finely chopped shallots
1 teaspoon finely chopped garlic
salt and white pepper to taste

Dredge snapper fillets in seasoned flour. Melt 4–ounces of butter in a large sauté pan. Sauté snapper fillets quickly, about 2 minutes, to sear them. Mix the pulverized nuts with the remaining 4 ounces of butter, shallots, garlic, salt and white pepper. In an uncovered glass baking dish large enough to hold the fish fillets in one layer, cover the fillets with the nut mixture and bake at 400°F. for 10 minutes. While the fish is baking make the following Beurre Blanc.

Beurre Blanc

1 cup dry white wine
1 teaspoon finely chopped shallots
juice of half a lemon
4 ounces unsalted butter, cut into 8–10 chunks

In a small saucepan, blend the wine and shallots and reduce over medium–high heat to about 2 Tablespoons. Off

Continued on next page

Macadamia Nut Crusted Snapper with Tropical Fruit Beurre Blanc (continued)

heat, whisk in the butter chunks, one at a time until all are blended in. Add the lemon juice.

Garnish

asparagus spears
chopped fresh chervil
lemon wedges

To serve: spoon Fruit Brunoise and Beurre Blanc onto four plates. Place fish fillet on top. Garnish with Sweet Potato Purée, chervil, asparagus spears and a lemon wedge.

Preparation: 30 minutes Moderately difficult Serves 4
Cooking: 10 minutes
Baking: 10 minutes

Wyndemere's Yellowtail Snapper
Wyndemere Country Club

4 Yellowtail snapper fillets, skin off
1 large baking potato, finely grated
1 lemon zest and juice
1 lime zest and juice
salt and pepper to taste
¼ cup oil
½ cup unsalted butter
1 teaspoon fresh chopped dill weed

Pat Yellowtail fillets dry with paper toweling. Grate potato as fine as possible and mix in the zests, salt and pepper. Carefully press the potato mixture on top of each fish fillet. Heat oil in sauté pan and carefully place fish in hot oil, potato side down. While fish is cooking, prepare sauce in a small pan by reducing the lemon and lime juices by half. Reduce heat and stir in butter and add dill. Turn fish over and brown on other side, about 4 minutes. Remove fish from pan and place potato side up on serving platter. Pour hot sauce over fillets and serve immediately.

Preparation: 30 minutes Moderately Easy Serves: 4
Cooking: 15 minutes Serve immediately

Almond Encrusted Snapper
The Fifth Season Restaurant

Sauce

1 teaspoon finely chopped shallots
1 teaspoon finely chopped ginger
2 Tablespoons white wine
½ cup orange juice concentrate
2 Tablespoons Grand Marnier
1 Tablespoon finely chopped mint
¼ cup butter, softened
clarified butter
1 orange, sliced for garnish
parsley for garnish

Place shallots and ginger in saucepan with white wine and reduce by half. Add orange juice concentrate, Grand Marnier and mint. Bring to a boil and reduce heat. Gradually add butter and stir with a wooden spoon until all butter is thoroughly mixed. Remove from heat and keep warm.

2 pounds red snapper fillets, skinless and boneless
¼ cup flour
2 eggs, lightly beaten
¼ cup blanched, sliced almonds

Dredge snapper in flour, dip into egg wash, then dip into almonds (both sides). Sauté snapper at a moderate heat in clarified butter until golden brown on both sides. For thin fillets, no additional cooking is required. For thick fillets, complete cooking fish in 350°F. oven until flaky, about 10 minutes.

To serve, set fillet on plate, ladle hot sauce on top and garnish with parsley and 2 slices of orange.

Preparation: 30 minutes
Cooking: 15 minutes

Moderately easy
Serve immediately

Serves: 4–6

Baked Snapper Casino
Olde Marco Inn

6 snapper fillets, boned, about 6 ounces each
¼ pound butter
1 medium red pepper, diced fine
1 medium green pepper, diced fine
1½ teaspoons chopped garlic
1 bunch green onions
1 heaping Tablespoon chopped parsley
⅓ cup lemon juice
1 cup clam juice
¼ teaspoon black pepper
1 cup dry seasoned bread crumbs
3 pieces bacon, finely diced and cooked until crisp

Lay snapper fillets on well–buttered (or sprayed) baking tray, skin side down. In a saucepan, melt butter; add all the peppers, parsley, green onions and garlic. Cook another 3–4 minutes. Stir in the lemon juice, clam juice and black pepper. Add bread crumbs; stir and remove from heat. Spread the bread crumb mixture evenly over the fillets. Spread the bacon pieces evenly over the bread crumbs. Bake in a 450°F. oven until done, about 10–15 minutes. Serve immediately with lots of lemon wedges and parsley.

Preparation: 30 minutes   Easy   Serves: 6
Cooking: 15 minutes   Can prepare ahead and bake when needed

E. W. (Ed) Crayton

In 1914, E. W. Crayton, a successful real estate executive in Ohio and St. Petersburg, Florida, purchased The Naples Company from Walter Haldeman's two sons, who owned the business after their father's death in 1902, and gave it the new name of Naples Improvement Company. He intended to operate the Naples Hotel as a business and eventually develop the land. In 1916 he built the southern wing of the hotel and aggressively began to attract wealthy, northern visitors to the area.

As owner of the company and guiding force of the town for close to 25 years, Ed Crayton is the focus of many stories of his time and was variously described as single–minded, hard, honorable, humorless, and tightfisted; but in his book *Early Naples and Collier County*, Dr. Earl Baum pictures him as a very astute businessman who tried to hide his softer nature.

However he was perceived, there is no question that it was his vision, his planning, his guidance and his achievements that led the way to the present–day Naples.

Red Snapper Paloma
Konrad's Seafood & Grille Room

2 Tablespoons flour
1 teaspoon cayenne pepper
1 teaspoon dry oregano
1 6 to 8–ounce red snapper fillet
3 Tablespoons olive oil
½ lime

Combine flour, cayenne and oregano. Dredge fillet in this mixture. Heat olive oil in skillet, and place snapper in pan, skin side UP. When golden brown, turn snapper over and add juice of half lime to pan. Cover and cook until tender. Serve with salsa and rice or pasta.

Preparation: 5 minutes   Easy   Serves: 1
Cooking: 5–10 minutes   Serve immediately

Salsa

1 large tomato, chopped
2 sprigs cilantro
1 Tablespoon ketchup
3 Tablespoons red wine vinegar
½ teaspoon chopped garlic
½ lemon
1 jalapeño, chopped
2 sprigs parsley, chopped

Combine all ingredients and marinate overnight. To serve, spoon generously over snapper fillet.

Preparation: 10 minutes   Easy   Yield: 1+ cup
Marinate: overnight

Grouper de Marco
Cafe de Marco

4 6–ounce portions grouper fillet, skinless and
  boneless
salt and pepper to taste
2 shallots, freshly diced
2 cups sliced fresh mushrooms
¼ cup finely ground bread crumbs
3 Tablespoons garlic butter, melted
2 Tablespoons white wine
2 Tablespoons water

Garnish

2 lemons, cut in half with a zig–zag cut to form a
  crown
fresh parsley sprigs

Lay grouper fillets in baking pan and lightly season with
salt and pepper. Rub the top with the freshly diced shallots. Cover the fillets generously with the mushrooms and
sprinkle bread crumbs over the top. Drizzle the garlic butter over the bread crumbs for flavor and to prevent burning the crumbs. Mix the water and wine and pour around
the fillets to keep them moist during baking. Bake at 450°F.
for 8–10 minutes, or until fish is cooked through. Serve
hot, garnished with a lemon crown and fresh parsley sprig.

Preparation: 15 minutes   Easy   Serves: 4
Baking: 8–10 minutes

Kitchen Mounds

*Some homes in Marco are
sitting on other people's kitchen
refuse. Once Caxambas was a
major Calusa settlement as the
great temple mounds and small
"kitchen middens" still testify
today. Built from discarded oyster
shells and other debris, the mounds
served as foundations for the home
of a chief, as observation posts, as
temple sites or for burial – all great
ways of using land fill.*

Deep–Fried Macadamia Crusted Grouper with Cold Rémoulade Sauce
Wilderness Country Club

Rémoulade Sauce

1 shallot minced
3 Tablespoons chopped chives
3 Tablespoons chopped tarragon
2 Tablespoons capers
1 quart mayonnaise
2 ounces cornichons (tiny pickles), chopped
salt and pepper to taste
Tabasco sauce to taste
1 teaspoon anchovy paste
1 Tablespoon Dijon mustard

Combine all ingredients and serve. Store leftovers in refrigerator.

Preparation: 10 minutes   Easy   Yield: 4½ cups

Fish

2 pounds grouper fillets
salt and pepper to taste
2 Tablespoons water
2 eggs
½ cup flour
2 cups bread crumbs
1 cup crushed macadamia nuts

Cut fish into portion sizes and season with salt and pepper. Mix water and eggs in a bowl. Dredge fish in flour; dip in egg wash. Mix bread crumbs and macadamia nuts. Roll and dredge fish in bread crumb mixture. Deep fry at 350°–375°F. on a frying thermometer for 2 or 3 minutes, or until golden brown and the fish flakes easily when tested with a fork. Drain on absorbent paper. Serve with Rémoulade Sauce.

Preparation: 20 minutes   Moderately Easy   Serves: 6
Deep Frying: 15 minutes

Roasted Fillet of Grouper Stuffed with Stone Crab Meat and Shiitake Mushrooms
Edgewater Beach Hotel

4 6–ounce fillets of grouper
¼ cup olive oil
1 teaspoon chopped fresh rosemary
salt and pepper to taste
1 rib celery, diced
½ green pepper, diced
½ red pepper, diced
2 small shallots, diced
8 ounces shiitake mushrooms, diced
2 cloves garlic, chopped
8 ounces stone crab meat, diced
4 ounces butter
½ cup Japanese bread crumbs
4 strips smoked bacon or Italian pancetta

Marinate grouper with 1 Tablespoon olive oil, rosemary, salt and pepper. Set aside. Sauté celery, green pepper, red pepper and shallots in 3 Tablespoons olive oil. Add garlic and shiitake mushrooms. Simmer 10 minutes. Add stone crab, butter and bread crumbs. Cook 4 more minutes. Remove from heat and cool to room temperature. Slice a pocket in the grouper fillet and fill with one–quarter of the stuffing mixture. Wrap one slice of bacon around each grouper fillet, securing with a toothpick. Roast in a 350°F. oven for 10–15 minutes.

Preparation: 20 minutes   Moderately Easy   Serves: 4
Cooking: 20 minutes
Baking: 10–15 minutes

Grouper

A member of the sea bass family, grouper is very popular in Southwest Florida. It appears in some form on almost every restaurant's seafood menu, is usually available at the marketplace and is the source of great pride on the dinner table of the fisherman who caught it.

The grouper's white–fleshed meat is generally sweet and lean but its skin is tough and strong–tasting; not recommended for cooking whole.

Grouper Luigi
Calella's Bistro Inc.

¼ cup olive oil
6 cloves garlic, peeled and finely chopped
½ cup white wine
juice of 1 lemon
salt and pepper to taste
4 6–ounce boneless, skinless grouper fillets
¼ cup chopped fresh parsley
½ pound linguini
½ cup butter

In a 14–inch skillet on medium high heat add olive oil. Sauté garlic until golden brown. Add wine, lemon juice, salt and pepper to taste. Add fish, cover, and simmer for 6 to 10 minutes (thicker cuts may take a little longer). Fish is done when a fork inserted causes the fish to flake. Boil linguini so it is ready when the fish is done. To serve, toss the linguini with the fish sauce and place the fish on the side.

Preparation: 15 minutes   Easy   Serves: 4
Cooking: 15 minutes   Serve immediately

Grilled Grouper with
Sweet and Sour Mango Mustard
Bonita Bay Club

4 grouper fillets, 6 to 8–ounce portions, skinless and boneless
salt and pepper to taste
olive oil
2 cups Sweet and Sour Mango Mustard

Season fillets with salt and pepper, brush with olive oil and grill on both sides until flesh is firm, about 5 minutes on each side. Serve on plate with mango mustard around fish, exposing nice grill marks. Serve with your choice of pasta or rice. Garnish with fresh cilantro sprigs.

Preparation: 5 minutes   Easy   Serves: 4
Grilling: 10 minutes

Sweet and Sour Mango Mustard

2 Tablespoons canola oil
1 red onion, diced
4 mangoes, skinned, pitted, and diced
½ cup brown sugar
½ cup cider vinegar
2 Chipotle peppers, chopped
⅓ cup Dijon mustard
salt and pepper to taste

In a saucepan, sauté onions in oil until golden brown. Add mangoes, sugar, vinegar and peppers. Bring to a boil and then reduce heat to low and simmer for about 1 hour. Stir frequently to avoid burning. Purée mixture and cool; season with salt, pepper and mustard. Serve warm with fish.

Preparation: 30 minutes   Easy   Serves: 4
Cooking: 1 hour   Can do ahead

Rooting For A Meal?

Look for a fern with a root the size of a turnip. It is the coontie plant also known as Florida arrowroot, or more scientifically Zamia Floridiana. The root provided the equivalent of flour for the Calusa Indians as far back as a couple of millenniums and for the Seminoles for the last couple of centuries. The Indian recipe calls for the root to be cut up in pieces and then pounded to pulp in wooden bowls. Mix in water and stir. After allowing all sediment to settle to the bottom, drain off the water and you are left with the flour. Mix the flour with cornmeal and fry in fresh bear fat to make your coontie burger, or add honey and warm water to the flour and allow to cool into a jelly.

Nut Crusted Grouper with Ginger Citrus Sauce

Maxwell's on the Bay

8 grouper fillets, (about 7 ounces each) rinsed and patted dry
½ cup buttermilk
1 pound unsalted nuts, finely chopped

Dip grouper in buttermilk, then dredge in chopped nuts. Place on baking pan and bake at 400°F. until done (about 10–12 minutes). Serve with ¼ cup sauce on plate and poured over fish.

Preparation: 15 minutes   Easy   Serves: 8
Baking: 10–12 minutes

Ginger Citrus Sauce

1 Tablespoon chopped garlic
½ cup peeled, chopped fresh ginger
1 cup sugar
3 lemons, zest and juice
3 limes, zest and juice
3 oranges, zest and juice
1 quart orange juice
2 teaspoons chopped cilantro
2 teaspoons raspberry vinegar
2 cups water
½ cup arrowroot

In a stock pot combine the chopped garlic, ginger, zests and sugar; cook, stirring over medium heat for 5 minutes. Deglaze by adding the citrus juices. Add cilantro, vinegar, and bring to a boil; lower to simmer. Blend arrowroot and water until smooth; stir into sauce and return to simmer and cook to medium thick consistency, about 2 minutes. Serve with Nut Crusted Grouper.

Preparation: 20 minutes   Easy   Yield: 1 quart
Cooking: 30 minutes

Blackened Grouper with Mango Sauce
The Little Bar

2 pounds grouper fillets, cut into portions
½ cup Cajun seasoning
3 Tablespoons butter

Heat a cast iron skillet until very hot. Sprinkle Cajun seasoning on one side of grouper. Add butter to skillet; lay fish Cajun side down in skillet. Cook until almost done (about 3 minutes). Flip to other side and finish cooking. To serve, spoon ¼ cup Mango sauce onto plate. Put grouper on sauce blackened side up. Drizzle ½ line of sauce over grouper. Garnish with edible flowers and/or parsley.

Preparation: 5 minutes   Easy   Serves: 4–6
Cooking: 7 minutes

Mango Sauce

6 mangoes, peeled and seeded, cut into 2–inch pieces
2½ cups orange juice, divided
1½ teaspoon ginger
½ teaspoon cinnamon
1 dash Worcestershire sauce
1 dash Tabasco sauce
1 Tablespoon sherry
3 Tablespoons cornstarch

In a saucepan bring to a boil the mangoes, 2 cups orange juice, seasonings and sherry. Whisk together ½ cup orange juice and cornstarch, and whisking briskly, add the cornstarch mixture to the boiling mango mixture. Stir until desired thickness is reached or when mixture will coat a spoon.

Preparation: 10 minutes   Easy   Serves: 8–10
Cooking: 10 minutes

A Canal for Fish

Early settlers in Naples tell stories of a canal that ran from the Gulf to the Bay, roughly where 12th Street South is today. This shallow, ancient waterway was a legacy of the Calusa Indians and has long since disappeared. It probably was never built for navigation but for fishing, as the tides funneled the fish into easy entrapment.

The snook is referred to as the Rolls Royce of the local game fish. Anyway you cook them, they are a taste treat.

Crispy Fish with Pineapple Chutney

Truffles

Marinade

½ cup Sherry
2½ cups soy sauce
2 Tablespoons fresh ginger, grated
¼ cup brown sugar
juice of 1 lemon
juice of 1 lime
3 eggs

Whisk all ingredients together.

Fish

6 8-ounce portions of Grouper
1 cup cornstarch
½ pound snow peas, julienned
1 carrot, julienned
1 bell pepper, julienned

With a sharp knife, score the fish portions making ⅛" or 1/16" cuts across the fish. Place the fish in the marinade and refrigerate for 1 hour. Remove the fish from the marinade and place in a colander to hold. Lightly coat each portion of fish in cornstarch and deep fry at 375°F. until cooked through (about 2–3 minutes depending on the thickness). Blanch the vegetables quickly in boiling water and strain.

Preparation: 20 minutes   Moderately Easy   Serves: 6
Cooling: 1 hour
Cooking: 15 minutes

Brown Rice

2 cups uncooked Brown Rice

Cook Brown Rice and keep warm until ready to use when serving the fish.

Cooking: 40 minutes

Continued on next page

Crispy Fish with Pineapple Chutney (continued)

Pineapple Chutney

¼ cup butter
1 shallot, minced
1 cup sugar
1 cup rice vinegar
¼ teaspoon crushed, dried red pepper
1 pineapple, diced small
2 Tablespoons fresh ginger, peeled and grated
2 limes, zest and juice
1 Tablespoon cornstarch mixed with 2 Tablespoons
    water
¼ cup each red, yellow and green peppers, diced
    very small
8 basil leaves, julienned

Sauté the shallot in butter until softened. Add the sugar, rice vinegar and crushed red pepper. Boil the mixture until it becomes syrupy. Add the diced pineapple and cook about 5 minutes. Add the grated ginger, lime, and cornstarch mixture, stirring well. Simmer 2 minutes and remove from the stove to cool. Add the diced peppers and basil.

Preparation: 30 minutes   Moderately Easy   Yield: 2½–3 cups
Cooking: 15 minutes

Serve the Crispy Fish on Brown Rice with the vegetables mounded on top, spooning the Pineapple Chutney around the fish.

Pineapple

Early New England sea captains brought home pineapples from their sea voyages to South America and the Caribbean. A pineapple would be placed on the door step to announce the safe arrival of the seaman and to invite visitors. Soon the pineapple became a symbol of hospitality and was often carved in wood and placed over the door in the broken pediment of the door frame.

Pan Seared Tuna with Fresh Tomato and Kalamata Salsina

Collier Athletic Club

Fresh Tomato and Kalamata Salsina
½ pound tomatoes, seeded and finely diced
2 Tablespoons shallots, finely diced
1 Tablespoon crushed garlic
1 Tablespoon lime juice
¼ cup fresh basil, roughly chopped
2 Tablespoons Kalamata olives, seeded and diced
2 teaspoons Kosher salt

Combine all ingredients; let stand at room temperature 30 minutes. Store left–overs in refrigerator.

Preparation: 10 minutes   Easy   Yield: 3 cups
Marinating: 30 minutes

Fish

2 8–ounce tuna steaks
1 Tablespoon olive oil
1 teaspoon salt
1 teaspoon black pepper
1 teaspoon diced fresh garlic

Garnish

sprigs fresh rosemary

Rub tuna with oil and spices. Grill to medium or medium rare, about 5 minutes per side. Serve with risotto and Tomato and Kalamata Salsina. Garnish with sprigs of rosemary.

Preparation: 5 minutes   Easy   Serves: 2
Grilling: 10 minutes

Mediterranean Orzo–Crusted Tuna Steaks

Collier Athletic Club

2 cups cooked orzo pasta, *al dente*
¼ cup finely chopped fresh basil
2 Tablespoons finely chopped fresh thyme
¼ cup finely chopped fresh oregano
1 Tablespoon finely chopped rosemary
½ cup finely chopped kalamata olives
6 6–ounce portions Yellowfin tuna fillets
1 cup flour, seasoned with salt and pepper
2 eggs, beaten with ¼ cup water
½ cup olive oil
salt and pepper to taste
½ cup balsamic vinegar
2 cups white wine
6 Tablespoons butter, softened

Mix orzo, basil, thyme, oregano, rosemary and olives. Lightly flour tuna fillets and dip in egg wash. Press orzo mixture around tuna and sear in olive oil; season with salt and pepper and cook to rare with crisp crust, turning once. Remove fillets to hot platter to keep warm. Deglaze pan with vinegar and white wine, reducing it slightly. Remove from heat and stir in softened butter. Mix well and strain through fine strainer, sieve or cheese cloth. To serve, place fillet on plate and pour small amount of sauce on top.

Preparation: 20 minutes   Moderately easy   Serves: 6
Cooking: 15–20 minutes-

Red Pepper Crusted Tuna Steak with Mango Salsa

Merriman's Wharf

2 dried red cayenne peppers
1 Tablespoon black peppercorns
6 6–ounce tuna steaks
½ cup olive oil
salt to taste

Coarsely grind the peppers and peppercorns together. Dredge the tuna steaks in the pepper mixture on one side only. Heat the olive oil in a large pan over medium–high heat until it begins to smoke. Add the tuna pepper side down and cook for 1 minute or until crust forms. Lower the heat to medium, turn the steaks and cook for 3 minutes more. The fish should be rare. Season to taste with salt. To serve, place steak on plate pepper side up, with Spicy Mango Salsa to taste. Serve immediately.

Preparation: 10 minutes   Easy   Serves: 6
Cooking: 10 minutes

Mango Salsa

½ cup coarsely chopped mango
2 Tablespoons finely diced red onion
1 teaspoon finely diced jalapeño pepper
2 Tablespoons coarsely chopped cilantro
3 Tablespoons fresh lime juice
salt and freshly ground pepper

Combine the mango, onion, jalapeño, cilantro and lime juice. Season to taste with salt and pepper. Cover and set aside or refrigerate, if prepared a day ahead. Bring to room temperature before serving. Serve with fish.

Preparation: 20 minutes   Easy   Yield: 1 cup
Chilling: 1 hour (if desired)   May be prepared day ahead

Triangle of Tuna with Basil and Roasted Garlic

L'Auberge on Fifth Restaurant Français

¾ pound tuna steak (about 2 inches thick)
2 Tablespoons coarse ground or cracked black
  pepper
1 sprig fresh basil
1 Tablespoon olive oil
24 garlic cloves, peeled
1 teaspoon brandy
1 teaspoon white wine

Cut tuna steak in the middle to form two triangles. Dip each small edge in pepper. Chop basil and set aside. Slowly sauté the garlic cloves in olive oil until they are light brown and very soft, about 5 minutes. Flambé with brandy and white wine. Reduce. Grill or sauté the tuna on both sides until the steak is medium rare, about 3 minutes a side. Remove steaks to platter. Garnish with basil and cloves of garlic.

Preparation: 10 minutes   Easy   Serves: 2
Cooking: 15 minutes

Fresh Yellowfin Tuna Roulades

THE DOCK at Crayton Cove

1½ teaspoons olive oil
1 teaspoon chopped fresh garlic
2 teaspoons finely diced onion
2 Tablespoons finely diced red bell pepper
1 Tablespoon chopped fresh basil
salt and pepper to taste
4 ounces goat cheese or farmers cheese
2 6–ounce tuna steaks
juice of 1 lemon

Heat olive oil in sauté pan; add garlic, onion, red pepper and basil. Season with salt and pepper, cooking lightly without browning. Remove from heat. Place cheese in a small mixing bowl, adding sautéed mixture; stir and set aside. Pound tuna steaks between two sheets of plastic wrap or wax paper. Remove top paper and drizzle lemon juice over each fish steak. Place half of the sautéed mixture on each steak and roll firmly. Place seam side down on buttered baking dish. Bake at 450°F. uncovered for 12 minutes, be careful not to let the fish dry out. Let rest 5 minutes, then slice to expose colorful stuffing and arrange on plates.

Preparation: 20 minutes   Easy   Serves: 2
Baking: 12 minutes

Fish

"Fruit from the sea," although not as bountiful in our area as it was a hundred years ago, is a gift from God – nourishing food that needs no digging, planting, cultivating, weeding or picking. It offers an extremely wide choice, a variety of ways to prepare it, it's delicious and it's good for you. To men of the sea it provides a living; to the sports fishermen on the pier, the shore, in the Gulf, bay, lake, pond or stream, there is nothing as exciting as pulling in "the big one."

The Advent of Railroads

The need for rail transportation had been obvious for a long time, but Naples really hit the jackpot when TWO separate railroads arrived within 10 days of each other near the end of 1926.

First to arrive was the Atlantic Coast Line on December 27th, which pulled into its sturdy, practical station well out of town at what is now the intersection of Airport and Radio Roads. The records are not clear on the subject, but apparently the ACL was primarily a freight line for shipping fresh fruits and vegetables to the northern markets and only occasionally carried passengers. This service continued until May, 1971, although for the final two decades they ran only one train a day.

The Seaboard Air Line pulled into its Spanish–style stucco depot on Tenth Street South, the heart of Naples, on January 27, 1927. The layout of their tracks indicated that

Continued on next page

Paupiettes of Sole
Collier's Reserve Country Club

Oven–Dried Tomatoes

6 large plum tomatoes
2 teaspoons chopped fresh thyme
salt and pepper to taste
2 teaspoons sugar

Core tomatoes and cut them in half lengthwise. Arrange on a baking sheet and season with a bit of fresh thyme, salt, pepper, and a touch of sugar. Bake at 200–225°F. about 3 hours to dry them until moist but not too juicy.

Preparation: 5 minutes   Easy   Yield: 12 halves

Fish

4 6–ounce fillets of sole
4 ounces fresh spinach
6 large plum tomatoes, oven–dried

Place sole fillets between 2 sheets of waxed paper or heavy plastic and carefully pound them to an even thickness. Blanch the spinach and ice it to chill quickly and halt the cooking process. Lay the spinach over ⅔ of each sole fillet, leaving one end uncovered. Cover this end with the oven dried tomatoes, about 2 or 3 pieces per fillet. Roll the fillets starting with the tomato end, arriving at a pinwheel design, with the tomato in the center. Place on an oiled baking dish and either refrigerate until later or bake immediately, about 15 minutes in 375°F. oven. To serve, remove from baking dish and cut in half. Stand each half on the cut end in a Tablespoon or more of fresh Herb Beurre Blanc Sauce, and top with a Tablespoon of Hollandaise Sauce.

Preparation: 20 minutes   Moderately easy   Serves: 4
Cooking: 5 minutes
Baking: 15 minutes

Fresh Herb Beurre Blanc Sauce

3 Tablespoons white wine vinegar
3 Tablespoons dry white wine
2 minced shallots
1 Tablespoon heavy cream
1 cup very cold butter in small cubes
1½ teaspoons chopped fresh tarragon
1½ teaspoons chopped fresh basil
1½ teaspoons chopped fresh chives
1½ teaspoons chopped fresh thyme
1½ teaspoons chopped fresh parsley
salt and white pepper to taste

In a small saucepan boil the vinegar, wine and shallots to a

Continued on next page

Paupiettes of Sole (continued)

glaze. Add the cream and reduce again to a glaze. Whisk in the butter cubes and season with the fresh herbs, salt, and white pepper to taste.

Preparation: 15 minutes   Easy   Yield: 1 cup
Cooking: 15 minutes

Hollandaise Sauce

¾ **cup butter**
3 Tablespoons water
3 egg yolks
salt and white pepper to taste
1 teaspoon lemon juice

Melt butter and remove the froth from the top. Allow to cool to tepid. In a stainless steel bowl whisk the water and egg yolks about 30 seconds to mix well. Set the bowl in a pan of *simmering* water and whisk until the mixture begins to thicken. You will have a thin light custard that should form a ribbon trail from a spoon for about 5 seconds. Whisk in melted butter, a little at a time, and season with salt, white pepper and lemon juice to taste.

Preparation: 5 minutes   Moderately easy   Yield: 1 cup
Cooking: 5–8 minutes

they expected to bring in building materials as well as passengers, but freight was certainly secondary to the townspeople. The first train arrived with great fanfare, and almost immediately the depot became "the place to be" when the 6 p. m. train arrived. Aside from its novelty there was always the possibility of the unannounced arival of celebrities during the season.

Just before World War II started, financial difficulties forced the end of this service. During the early part of the war, a portion of the depot was used as a USO club for the Air Corps personnel stationed at the airport. A local resident provided a jukebox and the women used their ingenuity to decorate the barren area and maintain a supply of refreshments.

Today the restored depot is a cherished landmark used for various purposes – from art classes to wedding receptions.

Top Choice

The snook is referred to as the Rolls Royce of the local game fish. Any way you cook them, they are a taste treat.

Snook

If you tell a Florida fisherman the snook are running, get out of his way because he'll be heading for the reported location in nothing flat.

Common along the Florida coast, snook is a good food fish averaging about 3–5 pounds. They can be caught from bridges, a boat in the inlet, or close to shore and can be found in brackish and fresh waters. Use shrimp (dead or alive) and strip–cut mullet for bait.

Marco Island Snook Cakes
Kretch's Garden Restaurant

2½ pounds snook
3 egg yolks
1½ teaspoons chopped garlic
4 green onions, finely chopped
1 Tablespoon Old Bay Seasoning
1 Tablespoon Dijon mustard
2 Tablespoons diced pimento
2 Tablespoons fresh lemon juice
¼ cup mayonnaise
2 or more cups Ritz cracker crumbs, as needed
¼ cup melted butter

Simmer snook in boiling water until cooked throughout. Refrigerate until well–cooled. Flake the meat, discarding any bones, skin and dark pieces of meat. Place flaked snook in a large bowl and add the next eight ingredients. Mix all together and add enough crumbled Ritz crackers so you can form the mixture into cakes. Coat with additional Ritz cracker crumbs. Place on a well–buttered baking sheet. Drizzle melted butter over the cakes and bake at 375°F. until golden brown. Serve with your favorite seafood sauce.

Preparation: 20 minutes — Moderately easy — Serves: 8
Chilling: 2 hours
Cooking: 15 minutes
Baking: 15 –20 minutes

Broiled Mahi Mahi with Fruit Salsa

Maxwell's on the Bay

8 mahi mahi fillets (about 7 ounces each)

Broil or grill mahi mahi fillets until desired doneness. Serve, topped with ¼ cup Fruit Salsa.

Preparation: 5 minutes   Easy   Serves: 8
Broiling or grilling: 10 minutes   Serve immediately

Fruit Salsa

1 mango, diced into ¼–inch cubes
1 papaya, diced into ¼–inch cubes
½ cup finely chopped red onion
2½ cucumbers, peeled, seeded and diced (¼–inch cubes)
1 Tablespoon chopped cilantro
1½ teaspoons salt
¼ teaspoon ground white pepper
1 seeded, chopped jalapeño pepper
½ cup orange juice
¼ teaspoon cayenne pepper
¾ to 1 cup canola oil

Place all ingredients in a stainless steel or glass bowl; mix together well. Taste for seasonings and adjust as needed.

Preparation: 30 minutes   Easy   Yield: 6 cups

Pepper Seared Fillet of Black Bass on Baby Lettuces with Tomato and Fried Onion–Mango Relish
Bay Colony Club

Fried Onion–Mango Relish

2 Tablespoons extra virgin olive oil
2 white onions, peeled and thinly sliced
2 Tablespoons minced garlic
1 Tablespoon minced ginger
1 teaspoon star anise
1 Tablespoon curry powder
1/8 teaspoon cinnamon
2 Tablespoons molasses
2 Tablespoons orange juice
2 Tablespoons white vinegar
salt and pepper to taste
1 ripe mango, diced

Using the Relish ingredients listed, heat the olive oil in sauté pan; add the onions and cook until nicely browned. Add the rest of the ingredients except the mango. Cook them for 5 minutes. Remove from heat and fold in the diced mango. Let cool at room temperature. (Tightly covered Relish will keep one week in refrigerator.)

Preparation: 20 minutes   Easy   Yield: 2 cups

Baby Lettuces with Tomato

1 small head each of these lettuces (or any combination)
radicchio, arugula, baby red leaf, Iola Rosa, frisee, mâche, watercress
2 ripe tomatoes, peeled, seeded and julienned
1 pound asparagus, peeled and blanched
1 can artichoke bottoms
3 white mushrooms thinly sliced
1 carrot peeled, julienned and blanched
1/3 cup extra virgin olive oil
2 Tablespoons white wine vinegar
1 tablespoon each chopped chives, basil, tarragon
salt and pepper to taste

Clean the lettuces and dry them well. Toss with the rest of the the ingredients. Place lettuce on 6 chilled plates.

Preparation: 30 minutes   Easy   Serves: 6

Continued on next page

Pepper Seared Fillet of Black Bass on Baby Lettuces with Tomato and Fried Onion–Mango Relish (continued)

Fish

6 6–ounce black bass fillets, skin on (grouper or
    snapper substitute well)
3 Tablespoons course cracked black pepper
3 Tablespoons extra virgin olive oil

Score the skin side of the fish with a sharp knife in a diagonal fashion. Heat a sauté pan; add the olive oil. Lightly coat the flesh side of the fish with black pepper and place into hot pan, skin side down to begin. Once the skin had crisped, turn over and cook 3 to 5 minutes depending on the degree of doneness you like. Remove from pan and place on top of the salad. To garnish, add a dollop of Fried Onion–Mango Relish on top of the fish.

NOTE: Star anise may be purchased at a specialty store or oriental grocery.

Preparation: 30 minutes   Easy   Serves: 6

Orange Crusted Swordfish with Lemon Beurre Blanc
The REGISTRY Resort

1 cup bread crumbs
1 teaspoon horseradish
¼ teaspoon ground orange zest
2 teaspoons chopped parsley
2 teaspoons chopped basil
2 teaspoons chopped cilantro
salt and pepper to taste
4 8–ounce swordfish steaks
olive oil to brush on fish
2 teaspoons olive oil for sauté

Combine the bread crumbs, orange zest, and chopped herbs in a food processor. Process for 30 seconds. Season swordfish with salt and pepper; brush with olive oil and lightly press crumb mixture on both sides of fish. Heat olive oil in a medium Teflon sauté pan and cook 10 to 12 minutes over medium heat. Serve with Lemon Beurre Blanc.

Preparation: 10 minutes   Easy   Serves: 4
Cooking: 10–12 minutes

Lemon Beurre Blanc

½ cup minced shallots
½ cup white wine
2 Tablespoons lemon juice
2 Tablespoons vinegar
1 cup heavy cream
1½ cups unsalted butter
salt and pepper to taste

In sauté pan cook shallots, wine, lemon juice and vinegar until reduced by half. Add heavy cream and reduce slightly. Gradually blend in butter until all incorporated. Adjust seasoning with salt and pepper. Serve with fish.

Preparation: 10 minutes   Moderately easy   Yield: 2 cups
Cooking: 15 minutes

Swordfish with Mediterranean Salsa

The Fifth Season Restaurant

Mediterranean Salsa

3 medium tomatoes, peeled, seeded and diced small
½ medium red onion, chopped fine
½ red bell pepper, diced small
½ green bell pepper, diced small
4 cloves garlic, chopped fine
½ cup basil leaves, chopped fine
2 Tablespoons oregano leaves, chopped fine
¼ cup Italian parsley, chopped fine
16 pitted black olives, quartered (your choice of
   type)
3 Tablespoons drained capers
3 Tablespoons extra virgin olive oil
2 teaspoons balsamic vinegar
juice of 1 lemon
½ teaspoon ground black pepper
½ teaspoon salt

Mix all salsa ingredients in a non–corrosive bowl; taste for seasoning and let sit for 1 hour at room temperature.

Fish

2 pounds swordfish, sliced 1" thick, cut into serving
   portions
olive oil
fresh parsley

Baste swordfish with olive oil; grill or broil on both sides until brown (about 6 minutes on each side). To serve, place swordfish on plate and top with salsa; garnish with a sprig of parsley.

Preparation: 45 minutes   Easy   Serves: 4 to 6
Chilling: 1 hour
Cooking: 12 – 15 minutes

Lemon Pepper Penne with Shrimp
Pazzo!

2 Tablespoons olive oil
5 large cloves garlic, sliced
1 Tablespoon diced red onion
3 pieces oven–dried tomato
1 medium tomato, coarsely chopped
¼ cup white wine
2 Tablespoons orange juice
2 Tablespoons lemon juice
2 Tablespoons clam juice
6 shrimp, peeled and deveined
salt and black pepper to taste
1 teaspoon basil
5 leaves arugula WELL WASHED
cooked penne pasta for one

In a large sauté pan heat the olive oil and sauté the garlic and onions until fragrant; add oven–dried tomato and chopped tomato. Continue to simmer for 3–5 minutes. Add wine, orange, lemon and clam juices; stir well. Add shrimp; season with salt and pepper; simmer until the shrimp turn pink. Add basil and 4 leaves of arugula. To serve: spoon penne pasta into bowl, pour sauce over top and garnish with 1 arugula leaf.

Preparation: 20 minutes   Easy   Serves: 1
Cooking: 15 minutes

Shrimp Feta with Pernod
Olde Marco Inn

1 strip bacon, chopped fine or 1 Tablespoon olive oil
½ cup diced onion
1 10–ounce bag fresh spinach, cleaned and roughly chopped
½ to ¾ cup heavy cream
salt and pepper to taste
dash of Tabasco
2 teaspoons Pernod
1½ pounds raw shrimp, cleaned, tails removed
8 ounces Feta cheese

Sauté bacon until crisp (or heat oil), add onion and cook until transparent. Add spinach and cook 5 minutes. Add cream, salt, pepper, Tabasco and Pernod and cook another few minutes. Remove from heat. Place shrimp in 6 individual casseroles or in 1 large one. Cover shrimp with spinach mixture and top with Feta cheese. Bake at 350°F. until hot and bubbly, 10 to 15 minutes.

Preparation: 20 minutes   Easy   Serves: 6
Cooking: 20 minutes
Baking: 10–15 minutes

Shrimp Veneto
Frascati's Italian Restaurant

Polenta

½ cup cream
¾ cup water
½ cup cornmeal

Pour cream and water into a large pot and bring to a boil. Slowly add the cornmeal, stirring to keep it from getting lumpy. Continue cooking and stirring, about 8 minutes until thick. Set aside and keep warm until sauce and shrimp are ready.

Sauce and Shrimp

2½ Tablespoons butter
2½ Tablespoons shallots, chopped
2½ Tablespoons garlic
⅓ cup lemon juice
5 cups cream
20 medium shrimp, peeled and deveined
salt and pepper to taste

Garnish

8 sprigs fresh parsley

Heat the butter in a large sauté pan and sauté the shallots and garlic until light brown, stirring frequently. Add the lemon juice and 5 cups cream. Bring to a boil and then turn heat down and let the mixture simmer until it thickens. Add the shrimp and continue cooking about 2–4 minutes, until the shrimp are a bright pink. Season with salt and pepper to taste. To serve: portion out the polenta into 4–ounce dishes, invert the polenta onto the serving plate, arrange 4 shrimp near the polenta and ladle sauce over the polenta. Garnish with the parsley sprigs.

Preparation: 20 minutes   Moderately easy   Serves: 4–5
Cooking: 20–30 minutes

Cajun Shrimp with Linguini
Apollo's Oceanview Restaurant

2 pounds raw unpeeled jumbo shrimp
½ cup butter
2 cloves garlic, chopped
1 large onion, chopped
1 Tablespoon crushed red pepper
2 Tablespoons flour
½ cup white wine
1 quart heavy cream (can substitute half–and–half
  but then reduce amount of chicken stock)
1 quart chicken stock
3 Tablespoons Cajun spices
fresh parsley, chopped
1 pound linguini, cooked

Clean shrimp and remove tails. Sauté garlic and onion in butter in a large sauté pan over medium heat for about 6 minutes, stirring constantly. Add crushed red pepper, shrimp and flour. Add white wine to deglaze pan. Add heavy cream, chicken stock, and Cajun spices. Bring to a boil, about 5 minutes or until the sauce thickens. Serve over freshly cooked linguini. Top with fresh chopped parsley.

Preparation: 30 minutes   **Moderately easy**   **Serves: 8**
Cooking time: 20 minutes

Barron G. Collier/ Tamiami Trail

Barron Collier was a brilliant entrepreneur who, after earning a fortune in the streetcar advertising business, acquired more than 900,000 acres of land in what became Collier County; then he pushed through the necessary legislation and completed the construction of the Tamiami Trail, thus connecting the east and west coasts of Florida. Collier placed in charge of the entire operation, D. Graham Copeland, a graduate of the Naval Academy who had retired after World War I to apply his engineering expertise in the private sector. Headquartered in Everglades City with telephone lines direct to "the front," the enormous project, a model of efficiency, was underway by October, 1923.

With the Florida land boom at its peak, finding and keeping laborers was almost impossible. When asked how many shifts they ran, Collier only half–jokingly replied: "Three. One on the way down from Tampa, one on the job, and one on the way back to Tampa." That changed when the start of the 1926 depression created a large pool of good workers happy to have *any* job offering a steady income.

Continued on next page

Shrimp and Crawfish Cakes
Savannah a Fine Traditional Restaurant

2 Tablespoons olive oil or butter
½ small red bell pepper, diced
½ small green pepper, diced
½ onion, diced
½ pound small shrimp, cooked and deveined
½ pound crawfish meat, cooked
1 teaspoon ground cardamom
1½ teaspoons ground coriander
2 Tablespoons Dijon mustard
¼ cup mayonnaise
2 Tablespoons chopped parsley
3 cups bread crumbs
salt and pepper to taste
additional olive oil for frying

Sauté diced peppers and onion 2–3 minutes, and set aside to cool. Chop shrimp and crawfish; place in bowl with cardamom, coriander, mustard, mayonnaise and parsley and mix well. Mix in cooled peppers and onions. Mix in bread crumbs, a little at a time, until mixture can be formed into cakes. Season to taste with salt and pepper. Form into balls about 1½ inches in diameter, roll in bread crumbs and flatten into cakes. Sauté in olive oil until golden brown on both sides. Serve on top of Peach Citrus Butter.

Preparation: 1 hour   Difficult   Serves: 6
Cooking: 10 minutes

Peach Citrus Butter

½ cup white wine
¼ cup peach schnapps
¼ cup heavy cream
1 cup unsalted butter
Juice of 1 lime and 1 lemon
salt and white pepper to taste
½ cup fresh, canned or frozen peaches, chopped fine
1 Tablespoon chopped parsley

In a small saucepan heat white wine and peach schnapps on high until reduced by half. Add heavy cream, reduce until thick. On low heat whisk in a little of the butter at a time until all butter is used. Remove from heat. Add lime and lemon juices, salt and white pepper to taste, chopped peaches and parsley. Gently heat to serve (or sauce may separate). To serve, spoon some sauce on plate, placing crawfish cakes on top.

Preparation: 15 minutes   Difficult   Serves: 6
Cooking: 10 minutes

Interesting statistics of that time: common laborers received 20 cents; drivers were paid 25 cents; engineers received $150 per month and supervisors were paid $200. The total cost was almost $8 million, or about $25,000 per mile.

It was back–breaking work under extremely difficult and dangerous conditions; aside from necessary dynamiting, the men had to contend with the broiling sun, hordes of mosquitos, black flies and snakes, many of which were poisonous. Copeland's efficiency provided a mobile camp consisting of three mess sections and portable bunkhouses which were moved ahead about every seven days, and women who prepared meals around the clock, augmenting food from the commissary with venison and wild turkey purchased from local Indians.

Tamiami Trail was officially opened on April 26, 1928, celebrated by an exuberant crowd at a county fair held in Everglades City. Everyone was invited, with a special invitation to all the Seminoles, without whom "the crews could never have made their way though the swamps."

Scampi á la Lakewood

O━━━ *Lakewood Country Club*

White Clam Sauce

2 Tablespoons olive oil
2 cloves fresh garlic, chopped
¾ cup clam juice
¾ cup chopped clams
¼ teaspoon ground white pepper
½ teaspoon salt
½ teaspoon chopped fresh parsley

Sauté garlic in olive oil. Add clam juice and chopped clams, pepper, salt and parsley. Simmer for 5 minutes. Keep hot while preparing Scampi.

Scampi

1 pound linguini, cooked *al dente* and kept hot
½ medium onion, diced
¼ cup unsalted butter
12 large shrimp, peeled and deveined
2 cloves fresh garlic, chopped
1 teaspoon lemon juice
4 teaspoons sherry
½ teaspoon salt
¼ teaspoon ground white pepper

Sauté onion in butter until translucent; add shrimp, garlic, lemon juice, sherry, salt, pepper and cook 4-7 minutes, depending on size of shrimp. Add White Clam Sauce and blend. Serve over a bed of hot linguini.

Preparation: 30 minutes   Easy   Serves: 4
Cooking: 30 minutes

Linguini Alla Vongole — White
Frascati's Italian Restaurant

2 pounds linguini
6 Tablespoons olive oil
6 Tablespoons minced garlic
5 8–ounce cans clams
1¼ cups clam juice
6 Tablespoons butter
¾ cup parsley, chopped
fresh ground black pepper

Cook the linguini *al dente* (about 7 minutes). In a large sauté pan heat olive oil and sauté garlic until lightly browned. Add the clams and clam juice and bring to a boil. Add the butter and parsley; simmer 7 to 10 minutes. Finish with black pepper to taste. Serve over linguini, garnished with lemon and parsley.

NOTE: *This recipe is even better made with fresh clams.*

Preparation: 5 minutes   Easy   Serves: 8–10
Cooking: 10 minutes

Crab Cakes
The REGISTRY Resort

2 Tablespoons butter
2 shallots, minced
½ red bell pepper, diced
2 Tablespoons flour
2 Tablespoons Pernod or Anisette
½ cup heavy cream
salt and pepper to taste
dash of Tabasco
1 pound lump crab meat (flake and remove shell pieces)
4 eggs, beaten
1 teaspoon Old Bay Seasoning
1 cup fresh white bread crumbs
2 cups vegetable oil

Sauté shallots and pepper in butter; add flour and cook over low heat for 2 minutes. Add Pernod and cream and cook until thick. Add salt, pepper and Tabasco; remove from heat. Blend in crab meat, eggs, Old Bay Seasoning and bread crumbs. Let rest 30 minutes before next step. Form into 12 patties (or drop by large spoonsful). Pour oil into skillet to height of 1–inch and heat to 350°F. Fry patties until golden brown on each side. Do not crowd the patties in the pan while frying the cakes.

Preparation: 15 minutes   Moderately Easy   Serves: 6
Resting: 30 minutes
Cooking: 45 minutes

Clams

Back in the early days of Southwest Florida, the waters of the Ten Thousand Islands produced both clams and oysters in such great abundance that a clam cannery began operations at Caxambas in 1904 and another opened in Marco Island in 1911. Each one employed about 100 people; half for collecting the clams and the other half for the canning process. In knee–deep water, the digger would find the clams by stepping on them barefooted, then he would reach down, hold the clam in place with his thumb, slide a two–tined clam hook under it and drop the clam into the floating skiff beside him. On a single tide, the digger might collect thirty bushels, for which he was paid twenty–five cents per bushel. Later, Captain Bill Collier invented a dredge that mechanized clam digging, making it possible to work waters that were up to 12 feet deep and gather as many as 500 bushels in a 12–hour shift.

The canneries closed up shop sometime during the Great Depression, but a true clam–lover can still dig clams on his own.

Gumbo

Gumbo originated in south Louisiana kitchens. The word comes from the Congolese word for okra—"quin–gombo". The Choctaw Indians made filé from the powdered leaves of the sassafras tree.

How–To: Add Filé to a Gumbo— The okra and the gumbo filé will both thicken the soup. The okra may be added at any time but NEVER add the filé while the gumbo is cooking because cooking after the filé is added tends to make the gumbo stringy and tough.

Wyndemere's Filé Gumbo

Wyndemere Country Club

3 cups chicken stock
2 cups beef stock
1 ounce salt pork
12 ounces fresh or frozen okra
1 Tablespoon butter
1 Tablespoon flour
1 cup diced onions
6 spring onions, sliced thin
3 green bell peppers, cored, seeded, diced
1 cup lean cooked ham, diced
2 cups andouille sausage, medium dice
½ teaspoon white pepper
pinch ground red pepper
½ teaspoon fresh ground black pepper
4 cloves garlic, chopped fine
1 teaspoon chopped fresh thyme
4 tomatoes, diced
1½ teaspoons ground cumin
pinch ground cloves
pinch allspice
½ teaspoon ground coriander
6 bay leaves
1 Tablespoon filé
1 chicken breast, poached and diced
1 cup shrimp, cooked, peeled, deveined, cut into thirds
½ cup cooked rice

Pour stocks into a 6–quart pot; add salt pork and okra. Cook for 1 hour. Remove salt pork. Make a brown roux. Melt the butter in a small sauté pan; add the flour, let the roux cook over medium heat until it turns golden brown, bubbles and puffs up. Add the roux and all other ingredients except filé, chicken, shrimp and rice to the pot. Simmer 30 minutes; add filé, chicken, shrimp and rice. Check for seasoning and consistency. Adjust if necessary.

Preparation: 1¼ hours   Moderately Easy   Serves: 12
Cooking: 2 hours

Everglades Gumbo
The REGISTRY Resort

1 pound each of the following vegetables diced:
onions, celery, red bell peppers, carrots
3 Tablespoons oil or bacon drippings
3 Tablespoons flour
salt and pepper to taste
cloves to taste
1 bay leaf
Cajun spice to taste
1½ quarts fish stock
1½ quarts water
1 pound tomatoes, diced
1 pound okra, diced
1 pound baby shrimp
10 ounces white fish, diced
3–5 teaspoons gumbo filé (optional)

Simmer onions, celery, red bell peppers and carrots for 10 minutes. In a separate pan make a dark Cajun roux of the oil and flour, stirring constantly as it browns and cooks off the flour taste; it will bubble and puff up. Mix in the salt, pepper, cloves, bay leaf, and Cajun spice to taste. Add this roux gradually to the vegetables and stir to coat all the vegetables. Add fish stock, water, okra and diced tomatoes; bring to a boil then lower heat and simmer for 2 hours, stirring to keep it from sticking. Add more water if needed. Add baby shrimp and white fish and simmer for 20 minutes. Just before serving, remove the pot from the heat and add the gumbo filé; stir well and serve. Serve in a soup bowl over cooked rice.

NOTE: *Filé is available from a speciality store.*

Preparation: 20 minutes   Moderately Easy   Yield: 4 quarts
Cooking: 2½ hours

Pompano

Back in the earliest days of the old Naples Hotel, pompano was always on the menu as their most popular fish dinner and, although the supply is dwindling, it is still the standard–bearer by which other fish are judged. The average weight of a pompano is two pounds or less, but occasionally a jubilant fisherman will crow over the five pounder he reeled in.

Pompano are especially numerous from October to May in Florida and uncountable thousands are taken by amateur fishermen from piers, bridges and in the surf.

Seafood with Sauvignon Sauce

Maxwell's on the Bay

Sauvignon Sauce

4 Tablespoons clarified butter
½ cup sliced onions
½ cup sliced carrots
½ cup sliced celery
2 teaspoons chopped fresh thyme
6 cloves garlic, chopped
8 plum tomatoes, diced
2½ teaspoons oregano
2 teaspoons sage
1 Tablespoon chopped fresh basil
½ cup white wine
½ cup lemon juice
1 gallon fish stock
4 teaspoons salt
2¼ teaspoons white pepper

Heat the clarified butter in a stock pot and sauté the onions, carrot, celery, thyme and garlic until they are translucent. Add all other ingredients, bring to a boil, then lower to simmer and cook for 1½ hours.

Seafood

8 mussels
8 clams
½ cup white wine
3 Tablespoons olive oil
½ pound scallops
8 large shrimp (16–20 count)
½ pound white fish (sea bass, grouper or other firm white fish)

In a large pan poach the mussels and clams in the white wine until they open. In a sauté pan heat the olive oil and sauté the scallops, shrimp, and white fish until about half cooked. Add the mussels and clams to the seafood. Add ¾ cup of the Sauvignon broth. Heat well together about 5 minutes and serve with boiled new potatoes.

Preparation: 30 minutes   Moderately easy   Serves: 4–6
Cooking: 2 hours

Gator Changa with Plantain Sauce

LA PLAYA Beach Resort

½ pound alligator tail meat
1 tomato, peeled and seeded
½ red onion, peeled and quartered
2 Tablespoons olive or salad oil
½ bunch cilantro, finely chopped
½ teaspoon cumin
½ teaspoon paprika
½ teaspoon kosher salt or sea salt
½ teaspoon freshly ground black pepper
½ teaspoon Old Bay seasoning
4 ounces cheddar cheese, shredded
20 6–inch flour tortillas
1½ quarts oil for frying
2½ cups plantain sauce (from specialty food shop)
1 plantain, shoestring cut and deep fried crisp

Garnish

parsley, finely chopped

In a food grinder with the largest die or disk, grind the alligator meat, tomato and red onion into a bowl. Mix well. Heat 2 Tablespoons oil in a large sauté pan until hot. Sauté ground meat mixture about 6–8 minutes until fully cooked. Remove from heat and cool. Blend cilantro, cumin, paprika, salt, pepper, Old Bay and cheddar cheese into cooled meat mixture. Cut each tortilla into a square. Place 2 Tablespoons of seasoned meat mixture on each tortilla and fold ends in and then one end to and over the other to form an envelope around the meat mixture. In a deep fat fryer or large saucepan, heat 1½ quarts oil to 375°F. And fry the tortillas in batches about 3–4 minutes or until golden brown. Remove from oil with a slotted spoon and drain briefly on absorbent paper towels. Cut each tortilla in half to serve. Serve 4 halves per plate, garnished with ¼ cup plantain sauce, deep–fried shoestring plantain and chopped fresh parsley or other leafy herb.

Preparation: 30 minutes   Moderately Easy   Serves: 10
Cooking: 45 minutes

Alligator Snacks

The Spaniards called the sleepy creatures on the banks of the Caloosahatchee el lagarto, *the lizard. Alligator provides a nourishing if characterless meat, most popular as small chunks fried like chicken. For many diners the problem is catching the prey first. Indians say its easy – just rub its belly and it will fall asleep.*

Alligator Fritters with Orange Chipotle Salsa

⌐ *Bonita Bay Club*

Orange Chipotle Salsa

2 cups orange sections
1 small red onion, diced
½ cup diced red and green pepper
1 teaspoon minced garlic
1 Tablespoon cumin
3 Chipotle peppers, chopped
¼ cup chopped cilantro
¼ cup lime juice
salt and pepper to taste

Combine salsa ingredients and refrigerate.

Preparation: 20 minutes   Easy   Yield: 1½ cups

Jamaican Seasoning

2 Tablespoons cumin
2 Tablespoons chili powder
2 Tablespoons chopped chives
2 Tablespoons chopped cilantro
2 Tablespoons black pepper
2 Tablespoons salt
2 Tablespoons red pepper flakes
1 Tablespoon cinnamon
1 Tablespoon brown sugar
1 Tablespoon thyme
¼ cup allspice

Combine all ingredients. Set aside.

Preparation: 10 minutes   Easy   Yield: 1½ cups

Fritters

2 large eggs
¼ cup heavy cream
1 Tablespoon minced garlic
¼ cup chopped celery
6 ounces alligator meat, diced
1½ cups flour
1 Tablespoon Jamaican Seasoning
1 teaspoon baking powder
¼ cup diced red and yellow peppers
¼ cup chopped scallions
salt and pepper to taste
8 cups canola oil for frying

Whisk eggs and cream until frothy. Fold in remaining ingredients except canola oil. Refrigerate for 20 minutes. Heat

Continued on next page

Alligator Fritters with Orange Chipotle Salsa
(continued)

oil in deep saucepan until very hot (375°F.). Form fritters into balls and spoon into hot oil. Cook until golden brown or until the fritters float to the surface. To serve, spoon Orange Chipotle Salsa onto plate, covering the bottom. Place fritters on top and garnish with lemon wedge and chopped parsley. Sprinkle Jamaican seasoning over whole plate and serve.

Preparation: 20 minutes   Moderately Easy   Serves: 4–5
Chilling: 20 minutes
Deep Frying: 10–15 minutes

Conch Fritters

Kelly's Fish House Dining Room

½ **large onion, diced fine**
½ **green pepper, diced fine**
5 stalks celery, diced fine
1 cup flour
Tabasco to taste
salt and pepper to taste
2½ pounds chopped conch

Mix all ingredients in a bowl, shape into 1"-2" balls and deep fry in peanut oil until golden brown, 2 to 5 minutes.

Preparation: 15 minutes   Easy   Serves: 6
Deep frying: 2–5 minutes each batch

Conch

It's pronounced "Konk" and has a long history in the story of Florida. How is it served? In salads, chowder and plain fried. The edible queen or pink conch is found in the Florida Keys and has become the nickname of long–time natives of that area, first used to describe settlers to Florida from the Bahamas in the 1880's.

Keys–Style Conch Fritters
Edgewater Beach Hotel

2 ounces raw conch
½ red bell pepper
½ yellow pepper
1 ripe tomato
3 limes, segmented
2 jalapeño peppers, seeded
3 cloves garlic
3 shallots
3 whole eggs
1 cup tempura flour

Process conch in a food processor for 1–2 minutes. Add peppers, tomato, lime segments, garlic and shallots and pulse 1–2 minutes to dice further. Remove this mixture and place, covered, in refrigerator overnight. The following day add eggs and enough flour to hold the mixture together for deep frying. Heat small home fryer with vegetable oil to 350°F. Fry fritters 3–4 minutes or until golden brown. Drain on paper towel. Serve with Orange Lime Relish.

Preparation: 5 minutes
Refrigerate: overnight
Cooking: 20 minutes

Serves: 6

Orange Lime Relish

2 oranges, peeled, seeded, and segmented
2 limes, peeled, seeded, and segmented
½ red onion, diced
½ green pepper, diced
½ red pepper, diced
2 Tablespoons white vinegar
salt and pepper to taste
1 Tablespoon chopped cilantro

Mix all ingredients in small bowl. Let marinate overnight. Test for seasonings and adjust as needed. Serve cold with conch fritters.

Preparation: 10–15 minutes
Cooling: overnight

Easy

Yield: 1½ cups

Florida Queen Conch with Piccata Sauce
Edgewater Beach Hotel

6 whole conch, butterflied and trimmed of all outer
  skins
½ cup flour
6 Tablespoons butter
⅓ cup white wine
2 lemons, sliced
capers (optional)
salt and pepper to taste
fresh chopped Italian parsley (optional)

Place the conch on a cutting board, cover with plastic and
pound as thin as possible (about ¼ inch). Remove plastic
and dust conch with flour, salt and pepper on both sides.
Heat 3 Tablespoons of butter in a sauté pan. Sauté conch
3–4 minutes or until golden brown on both sides. Add white
wine to the pan and reduce by half. Add lemon slices to
taste. Place remaining 3 Tablespoons butter in pan, swirling it around until the sauce thickens. Add capers and parsley. Transfer conch and sauce to a serving plate. Garnish
with remaining lemon slices.

Preparation: 20 minutes   Easy   Serves: 6
Cooking: 20 minutes

Turtle

*The meat in a Logger Head turtle is
tender but the meat in the flippers
is tough, the nearest thing to a boot
heel you'll ever want to tackle.*

"Early Naples and Collier County"
*by Earl L. Baum, M.D.
Courtesy of Collier County
Historical Society*

Seafood Crêpes with Lobster Sauce
Marco Island Hilton Beach Resort

Crêpes

1 cup flour
3 eggs
1 egg yolk
2 cups milk
1 Tablespoon butter, melted
salt, pepper and chopped parsley to taste

In a food processor, blend together the flour, eggs, yolk and milk. Then add the hot butter. Blend another 30 seconds; add salt, pepper and chopped parsley to taste. In a 7–inch non–stick pan, fry your crêpe shells one after the other. Reserve and keep warm.

Preparation: 10 minutes   Easy   Serves: 4
Cooking: 10 minutes

Stock

1 quart fish stock
1 onion
1 carrot
1 stalk of celery
6 cloves garlic
½ cup white wine
1 bay leaf
1 teaspoon thyme
salt and pepper to taste
½ pound lobster meat (1½ pound Maine lobster)
4 ounces bay scallops
4 ounces button mushrooms
16 pearl onions

Seafood Filling

1 Tablespoon chopped shallots
1 cup cream
3 Tablespoons butter
3 Tablespoons flour
4 ounces lump crab meat, cooked
4 ounces shrimp, cooked

Sauce

½ cup Cognac
1 cup cream
1 small can tomato paste (6–ounce size)
2 Tablespoons flour
2 Tablespoons butter

Pour the fish stock into a large stock pot and add the on-

Continued on next page

Seafood Crêpes with Lobster Sauce (continued)

ion, carrot, celery, garlic, thyme, bay leaf and white wine. Bring to a boil and then lower heat and simmer for 30 minutes. Strain the juice and reserve the stock. Add salt and pepper to taste. Then, poach one after the other—the lobster (if not already cooked), scallops, mushrooms and pearl onions. If the lobster is raw, it will take 15–18 minutes to poach. The scallops, mushrooms and pearl onions will only take 5–10 minutes. So time accordingly. Remove seafood, mushrooms and pearl onions from broth and reserve them. Divide the broth in two pots. Remove meat from lobster and dice. Stuffing: Melt butter in a sauté pan and add shallots; sauté until they are fragrant. Add the flour and stir and simmer until it bubbles, puffs up and loses the flour taste. Add 1 cup of cream and the first half of broth. Simmer and stir until it thickens. Add all seafood, mushrooms and pearl onions. Reserve. Sauce: Add to the second part of broth, the Cognac, 1 cup of cream and the tomato paste. Bring to a boil and thicken with roux made of 2 Tablespoons of flour mixed with 2 Tablespoons melted butter. Set aside as sauce. To serve: Stuff two crêpes per person with seafood stuffing and arrange in the middle of a plate. Pour sauce across the top and serve.

Preparation: 45 minutes   Difficult   Serves: 4
Cooking: 1 hour 30 minutes

Bouillabaisse with Risotto

Bayside

¾ cup dry white wine
1 teaspoon saffron threads
¼ cup olive oil
2 cups chopped onion
1 cup chopped fennel bulb
2 cups chopped leeks, washed well
6 cloves garlic, minced
3 cups crushed Italian plum tomatoes
2 quarts clam juice
2 Tablespoons chopped fresh herbs (basil, thyme, chives)
½ pound grouper fillet, cut in half
½ pound monk fish, in 2 medallions
½ pound snapper fillet, cut in half
6 littleneck clams
6 large shrimp, peeled and deveined
6 large sea scallops
4 Tablespoons butter

Soak saffron in wine. Heat olive oil in a heavy non–reactive sauce pot. Add the onions and fennel and sauté until soft. Add the leeks and cook 2 minutes. Add the garlic and toss well. Deglaze the pot with the wine and saffron mixture. Stir well and add the tomatoes, clam juice and chopped herbs. Bring to a boil, then reduce to a simmer for 20 minutes. Remove from heat but keep warm. Meanwhile make the Risotto (recipe follows). Measure 1 quart of the broth and pour into a heavy saucepan; bring to a boil. Add the 3 varieties of fish and the clams, cover and boil for 4 minutes. Add the shrimp and sea scallops and cook for another 3 minutes, then remove from heat. To serve: place Risotto in the center of a soup bowl. Surround it with the seafood. Swirl the butter into the warm broth and pour over the seafood. Serve with hot, crusty baguettes of French bread.

Preparation: 30 minutes   Moderately easy   Serves: 6+
Cooking: 45 minutes   Serve immediately

Risotto

2 cups Bouillabaisse broth
1 Tablespoon olive oil
3 Tablespoons minced shallot
1 cup Arborio rice
¼ cup heavy cream
¼ cup grated Pecorino Romano cheese
salt and white pepper to taste

Keep the broth heated. In a medium saucepan heat the olive oil and sauté the shallot until it is transparent. Add the

Continued on next page

Bouillabaisse with Risotto (continued)

raw rice and stir until it is well coated with the oil. Add just enough broth to barely cover the rice. Cook, stirring continually with a wooden spoon until the broth is absorbed. Continue cooking in this manner until the rice is *al dente*. Add the heavy cream and grated cheese; season with salt and pepper to taste.

Preparation: 10 minutes   Easy   Serves: 6
Cooking: 20–30 minutes   May do ahead or serve immediately

Scallop Beggar's Purses with Leeks and Ginger

Bistro 821

1 pkg. phyllo pastry (in frozen section of grocery store)
2 large leeks, white part only, diced
6 Tablespoons unsalted butter, melted
1 Tablespoon chopped fresh ginger
salt and pepper to taste
¼ cup heavy cream
1 pound bay scallops, washed and trimmed

Thaw phyllo pastry. Sauté diced leeks in 2 Tablespoons butter over medium-low heat. Do not brown! Add ginger, salt and pepper. Cook for 5 minutes. Add cream and reduce until very thick. Cool mixture in refrigerator. Unroll phyllo pastry and cut in half to form squares. Lay one square down and brush with melted butter. Lay another square on top, rotating about 45°, brush with melted butter, and repeat until 5 sheets are used. Place a Tablespoon of leek mixture in center of stack and top with 1/6 of the scallops. Gather up the edges of the phyllo to make a "Purse". Continue to make 5 more purses. Chill until ready to bake. Bake at 400°F. about 15 minutes until well browned.

NOTE: If you have forgotten to thaw the phyllo pastry in advance, this dish can be made as a casserole. Remove the roll of phyllo from the box and very carefully cut through the roll of phyllo sheets and the separating papers about six inches from the end of the roll. Let this portion rest on a cutting board while you prepare the filling. Then carefully unroll this phyllo portion only one turn—the sheets will break off, because it is still somewhat frozen. Handle with care and separate your small sheets (about 4" x 6" in size) and cover the bottom of your casserole with a layer of them. Brush with melted butter. Then add two or three more layers of phyllo, buttering each layer. Gently mix the raw scallops with the cooked leek mixture and spoon over the phyllo base. Cover with several additional layers of the phyllo, brushing melted butter between each layer and over the top layer. Then bake the casserole for 15 minutes in a 400°F. oven.

Preparation: 1 hour   Difficult   Serves: 4–6
Cooking: 15 minutes   Serve immediately

Caribbean Fried Basmati Rice with Lobster Mango

Collier Athletic Club

1 cup basmati rice
2 cups chicken stock or cold salted water
2 Tablespoons extra virgin olive oil
¼ cup chopped garlic
¼ cup chopped ginger
2 Florida lobster tails, cut into ½ inch strips
1 red onion, finely sliced
1 finger hot pepper, seeded and diced
1 ear corn roasted (peel before) or grilled (peel after) corn
1 cup sliced mushrooms
2 cups chopped scallions, divided white and green
¼ cup Szechuan hot bean sauce
⅓ cup fish sauce
⅓ cup mushroom soy sauce (or less as desired)
2 mangoes, peeled, seeded and diced
1 teaspoon fresh ground black pepper

Mix rice and stock or water in a pot and bring to a boil. Immediately reduce heat to simmer, cover tightly for 10–15 minutes or until tender. Remove from heat and keep tightly covered 10 minutes. Heat oil in large sauté pan and sauté garlic and ginger. Add lobster and sauté 1 minute. Stir in red onion, hot pepper, corn, mushrooms, and whites of scallions. Sauté until vegetables are translucent. Add hot bean sauce, fish sauce, and mushroom soy sauce, cooked rice, scallion greens and mangoes. Season to taste with fresh ground black pepper.

Preparation: 30 minutes   Moderately easy   Serves: 4–6
Cooking: 20 minutes

Lobster

Florida–style lobster is a cousin of the more famous Maine lobster, usually only one or two pounds and without any meat in the claws. However, its popularity is well known in Naples!

Crispy Chicken
Golden China Chinese Restaurant

1 whole chicken
1 Tablespoon soy sauce
1 Tablespoon white wine
¼ teaspoon black pepper
7 ounces ground pork
2 slices fresh ginger, finely diced
4 green onions, finely chopped
2 teaspoons soy sauce
2 teaspoons white wine
1 egg white
½ cup cornstarch
8 cups oil for frying
1 tomato, cut into quarters or eighths
1 mustard green leaf, torn in half or quarters
½ red pepper, sliced

Cut legs from chicken, remove bones and chop with back of cleaver, remove meat from breast. Marinate legs and breast for 20 minutes in a marinade of soy sauce, wine and black pepper. Mix ground pork with ginger, chopped green onion, 2 teaspoons soy sauce, 2 teaspoons wine, egg white and 1 Tablespoon cornstarch. Sprinkle 2 Tablespoons cornstarch on chicken meat and rub ground pork mixture over chicken meat. Heat oil in a wok. Coat chicken with cornstarch and deep fry in hot oil over low heat for about six minutes. Remove. Place on platter and garnish with tomato, mustard green and red pepper.

Preparation: 30 minutes   Moderately easy   Serves: 2–4
Marinating: 20 minutes
Cooking: 10–15 minutes

Diced Chicken with Cashew Nuts

Shing Long Gourmet Chinese Restaurant

¾ pound breast of chicken, skinned, boned, diced

Marinade

1 Tablespoon water
1½ teaspoons soy sauce
1½ teaspoons cornstarch

Stir–fry

¼ cup oil
5 green onions, sliced white and green parts
6 slices fresh ginger
½ green pepper, cored, seeded and diced
1 Tablespoon water
1 Tablespoon soy sauce
1½ teaspoons white cooking wine
1½ teaspoons cornstarch
1 teaspoon sesame oil
⅛ teaspoon black pepper
3½ ounces cashew nuts

Mix marinade ingredients in a bowl; add chicken, toss all together and let chicken marinate for 30 minutes. Heat wok, add ¼ cup oil; heat to 350°–375°F. Stir fry chicken in hot oil and then lift it out to drain. Keep 1 Tablespoon oil in wok and drain off the rest. Stir fry green onion and ginger until fragrant; add green pepper to fry. Return chicken and rest of stir–fry ingredients except cashew nuts. Stir fry 3–5 minutes; add cashew nuts and continue stir–frying 1–2 minutes.

Preparation: 20 minutes   Easy   Serves: 2
Marinating: 30 minutes
Cooking: 15 minutes

Chicken Scarpariello
Frascati's Italian Restaurant

2½ Tablespoons olive oil
1 pound boneless, skinless chicken breast, cut into strips
1 pound Italian sausage cut into 1–inch pieces
10 black olives
10 pepperoncini
1 green pepper, seeded and chopped
1 large onion, chopped
2½ Tablespoons chopped garlic
⅔ cup Balsamic vinegar
salt and pepper to taste

In a large sauté pan cook the chicken and sausage in the olive oil for about 3–5 minutes, until slightly browned. Add the garlic, peppers and onions and cook until they are soft. Add the olives and pepperoncini. Stir to mix well and heat through. Deglaze the pan with Balsamic vinegar. Cook for 5 minutes to let the Balsamic vinegar cook down and reduce. Season with salt and pepper.

Preparation: 20 minutes   Easy   Serves: 8–10
Cooking: 20 minutes

Pollo Marsala
Busghetti Ristorante

4 chicken breasts, 6 ounces each
½ cup flour
½ cup butter
¼ cup diced shallots
24 large mushrooms, sliced
1 cup sweet Marsala wine
1 pound cooked pasta of your choice

Pound chicken breasts flat; dip in flour. Melt butter in a sauté pan; add shallots and mushrooms to quickly sauté. Add chicken and brown on both sides. Add wine and simmer until wine is reduced. Serve at once over the pasta.

Preparation: 15 minutes   Serves: 4
Cooking: 35 minutes

The First Library

Members or guests accustomed to our modern main library with its many satellites, will doubtless appreciate them much more when they read this brief description of Naples' first public library – just 64 years ago.

Originally, the only library was in the Fourth Street South school, which was open to the general public; but in 1932 the Naples Women's Club bought their first building on 11th Avenue South and started another library "of sorts." Formerly a private home donated by Mrs. Ed Crayton and Mr./Mrs. William Clarke, the most practical place for the purpose was in a powder room with a large closet – once part of a dressing room and bath combination. Stocked with donated second–hand books plus a few new ones, it operated on the honor system, with late–returners dropping the "fines" in a coin box. No one ever cheated, nor were any coins stolen.

Dill

A frequently used spice – especially for pickling – dill has an interesting history. Its name comes from an old Norse word meaning "to lull" and it was believed to soothe the digestive system and to relieve babies of hiccups and colic. It was also used as a protection against witchcraft and as a love potion.

Creamy Avocado and Dill Chicken over Boston Lettuce with Honey Pistachio Rice

Collier Athletic Club

1 quart heavy cream or half–and–half, if desired
1 cup chicken stock
1 Tablespoon oil
4 chicken breasts, diced
salt and pepper to taste
2 small avocados, peeled and diced
½ cup fresh dill, chopped fine
3 heads Boston lettuce, washed and dried

Simmer heavy cream to reduce by half. Add chicken stock and continue to simmer. Heat oil in a medium sauté pan, season chicken with salt and pepper and sauté 5 minutes over medium heat. Add avocado and sauté 5 more minutes. Add dill and cream mixture. Reduce heat and simmer 7–8 minutes. To serve, place lettuce leaves around plates and spoon creamy chicken in center on top of lettuce. Serve with Honey Pistachio Rice.

Preparation: 1 hour   Easy   Serves: 6–8
Cooking: 1 hour

Honey Pistachio Rice

¼ cup water
½ teaspoon salt
½ cup honey
¼ cup ground pistachios
3 cups cooked white rice

Combine all ingredients, heat and serve.

Preparation: 10 minutes   Easy   Serves: 6
Cooking: 10 minutes

Saffron Chicken
Imperial Golf Club

4 8–ounce boneless, skinless chicken breasts
2 cups water
½ cup white wine
3 pinches saffron
½ teaspoon salt
½ teaspoon white pepper

Combine all ingredients and marinate chicken overnight. Pour all into a large fry pan to poach chicken in marinade. Begin uncovered, over medium heat, and partially cover with paper or lid; replenish liquid if needed. Poach 12–15 minutes or until done. To serve, slice chicken on bias and serve with White Champagne Caper Sauce. [For a colorful and flavorful presentation you can arrange buttered baby carrots and steamed spinach on the plates first, then top with bias cut chicken and sauce.]

Preparation: 10 minutes   Easy   Serves: 4
Marinate overnight   Serve immediately
Cooking: 20 minutes

White Champagne Caper Sauce

2 teaspoons capers
½ teaspoon minced garlic
¼ cup Champagne
1 cup cream
salt and white pepper to taste

Combine all ingredients in a small pan; bring to boil and reduce until cream becomes thick and coats the back of a spoon. Season to taste with salt and white pepper. Serve with poached chicken or fish.

Preparation: 10 minutes   Easy   Yield: 1 cup
Cooking: 10 minutes

Chicken Scarpariello (Shoemaker's Chicken)
Asti Ristorante

2 Tablespoons olive oil
1 chicken (2½ to 3 pounds) cut into 8 pieces
½ pound sweet Italian sausage
¼ cup chopped onion
2 garlic cloves, chopped
¼ teaspoon red pepper flakes
½ pound mushrooms, sliced or quartered
½ teaspoon oregano
¾ cup chicken stock
2 Tablespoons lemon juice
¼ cup dry white wine
salt and pepper to taste
2 Tablespoons unsalted butter
2 Tablespoons chopped Italian parsley

Pour the olive oil into a large sauté pan over medium high heat and sauté the chicken skin side down until browned. Turn the chicken over and add the sausage. Cook, turning the sausage until brown all over. Add onion, garlic and red pepper and cook until onion is soft. Add mushrooms and cook for 2 minutes. Add the oregano, then chicken stock and lemon juice to deglaze pan. Cover and cook over low heat for 15 minutes. Remove cover and add the wine; cook over high heat to reduce. Turn off heat, add salt and pepper to taste and parsley. Stir while slowly melting butter into sauce. Serve with oven–roasted or garlic mashed potatoes.

Preparation: 30 minutes   Moderately Easy   Serves: 6–8
Cooking: 45 minutes   Can do ahead

Pan Steamed Chicken Breast

Bear's Paw Country Club

4 boned, skinless chicken breast halves (1½ pounds total)
salt and white pepper to taste
1 Tablespoon fresh parsley, minced
1 Tablespoon fresh basil, chopped
1 Tablespoon fresh dill, chopped
1 Tablespoon extra virgin olive oil
1 large shallot, minced
1 cup chicken stock or unsalted canned broth
1 Tablespoon cold unsalted butter

Trim each chicken breast of all fat and sinew. Pound with the side of a heavy knife and flatten to an even thickness (¼ inch or so). Season the chicken with salt and pepper and cover with the chopped herbs. Film a cold pan with the olive oil and sprinkle with the minced shallot. Place the chicken breasts in the pan, not touching each other, and add ¼ of the chicken stock. Over low to medium–low heat gently bring the stock to a simmer. Allow the chicken to "steam" for 7 to 10 minutes. Turn each piece and steam 3 to 5 minutes longer until firm and done. Remove the chicken breasts from the pan and place on a warm serving plate. Add the remaining stock to the pan and bring to a boil. Boil the stock down until it is slightly syrupy and then swirl in the cold butter. Pour over the chicken and serve at once.

Preparation: 15 minutes	Easy	Serves: 4
Cooking: 15–20 minutes	Serve immediately	

Herbs

Herbs like basil, dill, cilantro, mint, etc. are grown in South Florida for the wholesale fresh markets in New York, Boston, Philadelphia, Washington, D. C., and even Chicago. They are harvested by hand, boxed in the field and shipped the same day in refrigerated semi–trucks to market, arriving at the wholesale market in New York in 36 to 48 hours.

Naples Airdrome (WW II)

On October 14, 1941, Naples and Collier County jointly purchased from the Collier family 635 acres of ground on Airport Road for $12,466.78 (roughly $19.60 per acre), with the county paying two–thirds and Naples the remaining third. World War II was declared just six weeks later. Training centers became essential and the federal government quickly claimed the property for an airport. A company from Maine rushed its workers down to the old railroad depot on Airport Road with all the needed equipment loaded on flatcars. From the swampland of palmetto, pine and cypress trees complete with water moccasins, their instructions were to build a complete airport in 90 days. With several teams of men working together, it was completed in 102 days.

Christened "The Naples Airdrome," the Army Air Corps used it for target practice over the gulf for gunners on bomber planes that flew down from Fort Myers' Buckingham Airfield. Beginners fired their weapons into the water; advanced gunners shot bullets designed to shatter on impact at a moving, live target – a red windsock on the tail of a plane which had the cockpit sheathed in thick steel to protect the pilots. The only recorded tragedy was the death of 10 crew members when two planes collided in a dive over the gulf.

Chicken Douglas
Country Club of Naples

4 boneless, skinless chicken breasts, cubed
1 Tablespoon olive or vegetable oil
2 heads of broccoli, cut into florettes
4 cups heavy cream or half–and–half
4 egg yolks
1 cup grated Parmesan cheese
1½ cups ham, sliced into 1–inch sticks
2 teaspoons salt (if desired)
½ teaspoon white pepper
1 pound linguini or fettucini pasta

Sauté chicken cubes in a little oil until fully cooked. Set aside. In a large pot steam broccoli until just tender. Set aside. Cook pasta in a large pot of water and drain. In a small bowl mix 1 cup of cream with the egg yolks. Set aside. Heat remaining 3 cups of cream, then slowly whip in the cream and egg mixture, stirring until heated through. Stir in Parmesan cheese, ham, salt (if desired) and pepper. Let simmer for 3 to 4 minutes. Add chicken and broccoli and serve over cooked pasta.

Preparation: 15 minutes   Easy   Serves: 6
Cooking: 20 minutes

Pecan Crusted Chicken
Mangrove Cafe

2 boneless chicken breasts
½ cup flour for dredging
1 egg
2 Tablespoons half–and–half
½ cup ground pecans
2 teaspoons butter or oil
¼ cup Beurre blanc or other white wine sauce

Dredge chicken in flour. Mix egg and half–and half in a small bowl; dip one flat side of chicken into egg mixture. Cover dipped side with pecans. In a hot sauté pan melt butter and sauté chicken for a moment until lightly browned. Be careful not to burn the pecans. Turn chicken and splash with white wine sauce. Bake in 375°F. oven for 8 minutes or until chicken is cooked. Serve laced with Beurre Blanc sauce.

Preparation: 45 minutes   Moderately easy   Serves: 2
Cooking: 10 minutes
Baking: 8–10 minutes

Pollo Busghetti
Busghetti Ristorante

4 teaspoons curry powder
4 teaspoons EACH of the following fresh chopped
  herbs:
  tarragon
  thyme
  oregano
  rosemary
4 teaspoons garlic powder
4 teaspoons paprika
4 teaspoons Worcestershire sauce
salt and pepper to taste
4 chicken breasts (each 6 ounces) boneless and
  skinless
½ cup fresh crushed garlic
½ cup red wine
½ cup lemon juice
½ cup soy sauce
¼ cup olive oil

Mix together the curry powder, herbs, garlic powder, paprika, Worcestershire sauce, salt and pepper and set aside. Pound the chicken breasts flat; place in a glass or non–reactive baking dish. Mix the fresh garlic, wine, lemon juice, soy sauce and olive oil. Surround the chicken with the mixture. Cover all with the herb mixture. Bake at 350°F. for 15 minutes. Serve over the pasta of choice with the pan sauce.

Preparation: 20 minutes   Moderately Easy   Serves: 4–6
Baking: 15 minutes   Serve immediately

Chicken Breast with Roasted Garlic and Rosemary Sauce

The Club Pelican Bay

8 cloves garlic, peeled
2 Tablespoons sugar
⅓ cup butter
½ cup dry Vermouth
½ cup chicken stock
6 sprigs fresh rosemary
½ cup heavy cream
4 boneless, skinless chicken breasts

In a small saucepot place garlic, sugar, ¼ cup butter and Vermouth. Heat and reduce slowly until garlic caramelizes. Add chicken stock and 2 sprigs of rosemary. Simmer slowly until reduced by one–half. Strain and add heavy cream. Reduce until sauce thickens. Remove from heat and swirl in rest of the butter. Grill chicken breasts. To serve, spoon sauce over half of each breast and garnish with fresh rosemary sprig.

Preparation: 30 minutes   Moderately difficult   Serves: 4
Cooking: 30 minutes

Bohemian Grilled Chicken Breast

Glenview at Pelican Bay

6 semi–boneless 5–ounce chicken breasts (skin on)
1 bunch fresh rosemary
1 bunch fresh dill weed
1 bunch fresh basil
¼ cup balsamic vinegar
2 Tablespoons canola oil
1 Tablespoon stone ground mustard
1 Tablespoon honey
salt and pepper to taste

Place a sprig of rosemary, dill, and one basil leaf under the skin of each chicken breast. Chop remaining herbs and mix with vinegar and oil. Pour mixture over chicken and marinate 1 hour. Grill over heat, skin side down (or under oven broiler skin side up). Remove and finish cooking in 375°F. oven for 10–12 minutes. Mix honey and mustard and brush over breasts either before baking or after baking (or both times if preferred).

Preparation: 20–25 minutes   Easy   Serves: 6
Grilling: 10–15 minutes
Cooking: 10–12 minutes

Bow Tie Pasta with Grilled Chicken

The Club Pelican Bay

4 6–ounce boneless, skinless chicken breasts
2 Tablespoons olive oil
4 cloves garlic, crushed
¼ cup sliced shiitake mushrooms
8 sun–dried tomatoes, sliced
4 plum tomatoes, diced
12 thin asparagus stalks, peeled, cut into 1–inch
  pieces
½ cup chicken stock
1 Tablespoon chopped fresh basil
1 Tablespoon chopped fresh parsley
salt and pepper to taste
8 ounces bow tie pasta, cooked

Grill chicken breasts and dice them; set aside. In a large pan sauté garlic in olive oil. Add mushrooms, tomatoes and asparagus. Sauté quickly, then add diced chicken and stock. Add chopped basil and parsley. Salt and pepper to taste. Serve over cooked pasta. Garnish with a sprig of fresh basil.

Preparation: 10 minutes   Easy   Serves: 4
Cooking: 25 minutes   Serve immediately

Pelican

Mr. Bembery Storter was one of the pioneers in Collier County and liked to tell newcomers how to cook a pelican. "First you catch and kill the pelican, then pluck all the feathers and thoroughly dress the bird. Then you stuff him with plenty of onion, sweet potatoes and cabbage. You then plank him and tuck him in the oven until he is a deep brown. Then cover him with brown gravy and when it is all completed, you throwed it overboard! Ha Ha!"
"Early Naples and Collier County"
by Earl L. Baum, M.D.
Courtesy of Collier County Historical Society

Angel Hair Pasta with Chicken, Vegetables and Gorgonzola Cheese
Trio's

2 Tablespoons olive oil
6 chicken breasts, cut into strips
1 bunch broccoli, florets only
1 red bell pepper, sliced lengthwise
½ pound mushrooms, sliced
1 Tablespoon chopped garlic
¼ cup chopped basil, loosely packed
salt and pepper to taste
2 pounds angel hair pasta
½ pound Gorgonzola cheese

In large sauté pan over medium high heat, add a little olive oil to pan, enough to coat bottom. Sauté chicken strips just until cooked through. Remove from pan. Add balance of olive oil to pan, cooking broccoli over medium heat a few minutes. Add peppers, mushrooms and garlic. Return chicken to pan, cooking 3 to 5 minutes. Add a little more olive oil if needed. Cook pasta; strain; add to chicken and toss with half of the basil. Add salt and pepper to taste. To serve, divide up in dishes or pasta bowls. Crumble Gorgonzola on top and sprinkle with remaining basil.

Preparation: 20 minutes   Moderately Easy   Serves: 6
Cooking: 20 minutes

Turkey Helena
Naples Bath & Tennis Club

4 turkey escalopes, 4 ounces each
½ cup cooked spinach, minced
1 or 2 cloves garlic, crushed
¼ cup shelled walnuts
½ cup low–fat curd cheese
6 Tablespoons chicken stock
salt and pepper to taste

Preheat the oven to 350°F. Remove any fat from the turkey and pound the escalopes with a tenderizer mallet until they are ⅛ inch thick. Blend the spinach, garlic, cheese and walnuts together; season to taste. Lay the escalopes out flat and place one quarter of the spinach mixture in the middle of each. Close or roll the turkey around the filling to form an envelope. Place turkey rolls, seam side down, in a baking dish with the chicken stock; cover and bake (poach) 30 minutes. Can serve with a port and raspberry sauce.

Preparation: 1 hour   Easy   Serves: 4
Baking: 45 minutes   Can do ahead
Serve warm

Southern Fried Quail Stuffed with Rosemary–Garlic Mashed Potatoes and Bread Sauce

The Dock Restaurant at Crayton Cove

4 pounds red bliss potatoes
5 cloves garlic
1½ Tablespoons fresh rosemary
1 cup sour cream
salt to taste
8 quail, boned
2 cups flour
1 Tablespoon black pepper
1½ teaspoons salt
1 cup buttermilk
2 cups oil for frying

Boil red bliss potatoes, skin on, with garlic until potatoes are soft. Drain; add rosemary, sour cream and salt; mash or whip until smooth. Taste and season as needed. Spoon potato mixture into the cavity of each quail. Mix flour, salt and pepper together. Roll each stuffed quail first in flour mix, then in buttermilk, and back into the flour mix. Fry in hot oil, 4 minutes on each side.

Preparation: 40 minutes	Moderately Easy	Serves: 8
Cooking: 10–15 minutes	Serve warm	

Bread Sauce

2 shallots, finely diced
2 cups rich chicken stock
1 Tablespoon fresh thyme (or 1 teaspoon dried)
½ cup bread crumbs or diced stale bread

Place shallots in a saucepan on medium heat. Add chicken broth and thyme and bring to a boil. Add bread and boil 5 minutes. Serve hot with Southern Fried Quail.

Preparation: 10 minutes	Easy	Yield: 2 cups
Cooking: 10 minutes		

Skins and Feathers

Dealing with the Indians for skins in the Collier area brought the first trading outposts to the Everglades, such as Ted Smallwood's famous store in Chokolaskee. While the Seminole Indians hunted alligators, bears and other wild life, they had less stomach for the exotically plumed birds that flocked here in winter. That took the tougher hides of white men, hunters more concerned with profit than beauty. They slaughtered such birds of plumage as the Egrets, Roseate Spoonbills, and Herons for feathers that were sometimes worth as much as twice their weight in gold. For a time plumage was the largest income earner for the southern part of the county.

Demi-Glace

Demi–glace is a rich brown sauce which can be purchased or made at home.

It is made of a rich meat stock, a mixture of browned vegetables, a brown roux, and herbs. Sometimes it has added tomato sauce. It cooks for 4–6 hours until reduced by half and the sauce will coat the back of a spoon.

Tournedos "Norvegienne"
Moorings Park

2 beef tenderloins (4–ounces each)
1 ounce smoked salmon or Nova, divided
crushed black pepper to taste
1 Tablespoon butter
1 Tablespoon chopped shallots
1 ounce brandy
¼ cup demi–glace (or substitute)
2 Tablespoons heavy cream

Slit and stuff each tenderloin with ½ oz. smoked salmon. Coat the outside with coarse crushed black pepper. In a sauté pan melt the butter and add the meat. Cook until tenderloin is cooked to your desire and remove to a hot plate. Add shallots and brandy to the pan drippings and sauté until liquid is reduced one–third. Add demi–glace and heavy cream; cook until reduced one–third. Pour sauce through a strainer over the tournados. Serve.

NOTE: Salmon must be fresh and mild so as not to overpower the taste of the meat.

Preparation: 15 minutes   Moderately easy   Serves: 1
Cooking: 20 minutes

Beef with Green Pepper
Shing Long Gourmet Chinese Restaurant

¾ pound beef tenderloin, thinly sliced

Marinade

1 Tablespoon water
1½ teaspoons soy sauce
1½ teaspoons salad oil
1 teaspoon cornstarch
¼ teaspoon baking powder

Stir–fry

¼ cup oil
½ large green bell pepper, sliced
½ large red bell pepper, sliced
2 slices fresh ginger
1 Tablespoon sliced garlic
1 green onion sliced (both white and green)

Sauce

1 Tablespoon water
1½ teaspoons oyster sauce
1½ teaspoons cooking wine
1 teaspoon soy sauce
1 teaspoon sesame oil
1 teaspoon cornstarch
½ teaspoon sugar
¼ teaspoon pepper

Mix the marinade ingredients and toss sliced beef in the marinade. Let the beef marinate for 10 minutes. Heat a wok, add ¼ cup oil; heat to 350°–375°F. Cook the beef in hot oil until beef turns pale, lift out and drain. Cook the green pepper in the hot oil, 1 to 2 minutes, lift out and drain. Keeping 1 Tablespoon oil in the wok, pour off the rest of the oil. Stir fry red pepper, ginger, garlic and green onion until fragrant. Return the beef and green pepper to stir fry; add sauce ingredients mix well and heat through. Serve.

Preparation: 30 minutes   Moderately Easy   Serves: 2–3
Marinating: 10 minutes
Cooking: 15 minutes

Beef

Where's the beef? In Florida, that's where. Six and a half million pounds of beef were marketed from Collier County in the 1993–94 season. That's enough beef to make 25 million quarter–pound hamburgers. This would satisfy the beef needs of Naples residents for five years!

Cattle Country

Everyone seems to know about Florida's phenomenal growth but very few are aware that it is also the biggest cattle state east of the Mississippi River, involving more than a million head of cattle and 2,000 cowboys!

The largest operation is the 300,000–acre Deseret Ranch, owned by the Mormon church in Salt Lake City, spreading out over Osceola and Brevard counties; but big, privately owned ranches thrive throughout central and south Florida, where places like Kissimmee, Arcadia and Okeechobee are still known as cow towns. In all, about five million acres of the state are used for cattle raising, and there are nearly three thousand registered brands. Because the rangeland is largely grass and marshes, hammocks and brush, cowboys on horseback still do the work.

Bisteca Donizetti (Grilled Sirloin)
Frascati's Italian Restaurant

½ cup butter
¾ pound sliced button mushrooms
¾ pound prosciutto, julienned
¾ pound roasted red peppers, cut in strips
1¼ cups Marsala wine
6 10–ounce sirloin strip steaks
salt and pepper to taste

In a large pan melt the butter. Sauté mushrooms, prosciutto and roasted red peppers until soft and tender. Deglaze the pan with Marsala wine; let simmer. Season to taste with salt and pepper. Grill the steaks to desired doneness. To serve, place steak on plate and top with the sauce.

Preparation: 30 minutes   Moderately Easy   Serves: 6
Cooking: 20 – 30 minutes

Grilled Veal Chops
Royal Poinciana Golf Club Inc.

4 Tablespoons olive oil
4 pounds veal chops (8–ounce portions)
½ cup onions, chopped
¼ cup carrots, diced
¼ cup celery, diced
¼ cup green beans, cut into 1–inch pieces
¼ cup peas
5–6 cloves garlic, sliced
¼ pound mushrooms, sliced
½ cup Demi-Glace (brown sauce)

Heat olive oil in a sauté pan and sauté veal chops until browned outside but still rare inside. Place in ovenproof dish and bake in a 350°F. oven 15 minutes. Steam onions, carrots, celery, green beans and peas. Sauté the garlic and mushrooms in the sauté pan with some of the drippings from the veal chops. Heat the demi-glace. To serve: arrange 2 chops on each plate and surround them with the mushroom mixture and the vegetables. Serve with the heated demi glace.

Preparation: 30 minutes   Easy   Serves: 8–10
Cooking: 30 minutes   Serve immediately
Baking: 15 minutes

Roast Stuffed Shoulder of Veal
Vineyards Country Club

Stuffing

1 chopped onion
6 cloves garlic, diced
4 shallots, diced
1 pound crimini mushrooms, quartered
12 sun–dried tomatoes diced
1 teaspoon basil
1 teaspoon thyme
1 teaspoon oregano
2 bunches red Swiss chard, stems removed, washed, steamed
¼ pound stale country French bread, cubed
1 cup chicken stock
salt and pepper to taste

Sauté onion until translucent, add shallot and garlic, cook 2 minutes more. Add mushrooms, sun–dried tomato and herbs. Cook 2 minutes. Add Swiss chard and bread crumbs; mix well; add enough chicken stock to moisten and salt and pepper to taste. Set aside to cool.

Veal

4 pounds veal shoulder, trimmed, boned and butterflied
1 onion, small dice
2 carrots, small dice
2 stalks celery, diced
1 cup white wine
2 cups demi–glace

Lay butterflied veal shoulder flat. Place Swiss chard stuffing evenly on veal, roll up and tie. Heat oil in Dutch oven on stove. Sear veal roast on all sides. Place Dutch oven with seared veal in 350°F. oven 30 minutes uncovered. Add diced vegetables and wine, cover and finish roasting in oven 30–45 minutes. Add demi– glace. Roast 15 minutes longer. Remove any greens from top. Slice veal, lay on plates and ladle sauce on top.

Preparation: 30 minutes   Moderately easy   Serves: 8
Cooking: 30 minutes
Roasting: 2 hours

Cracker Barons

In Georgia "cracker" was the name for poor white folk earning a living from "crackin corn". In Florida a "cracker" today may refer to anyone who is native to the state, living the rural life, but Floridians believe the origin of the word is different. In what is still the second largest cattle producing state, they claim that their original "crackers" were the local cowboys, taking the name from the crack of their long leather whips.

Medallion of Veal a la Piemontese

Il Posto Restaurant

2 pounds tenderloin of veal, cut in medallions
¾ cup flour
2 to 3 Tablespoons 100% virgin olive oil
salt and pepper to taste
4 fresh or frozen porcini mushrooms, (or 3 dried
    porcini soaked 20 minutes in water)
¾ cup dry white wine
1 bunch parsley, chopped
1 cup chicken broth
2 Tablespoons white truffle oil or fresh black
    truffles, diced

Cut the loin in medallions; dust them in flour. Heat a very large fry pan, add the oil and add the veal. Season with salt and pepper to taste. Turn the veal until they are nicely cooked. Slice and add the porcini, mixing with the veal. Add the wine and stir until the alcohol is gone; add the chicken broth and stir until the sauce is nice and creamy. When ready stir in the truffles. Serve with roasted rosemary potatoes and fresh spinach sautéed with garlic and lemon.

Preparation: 30 minutes   Moderately easy   Serves: 6
Cooking: 30 minutes

Veal Scaloppine Voilà

Voilà! Wine Bar & Brasserie

2 or 3 thin–cut veal scallops
1 Tablespoon flour
1 Tablespoon olive oil
juice of 1 lemon
2–3 thin stalks asparagus, sliced into 1–inch pieces
¼ cup chopped shiitake mushrooms
1 Tablespoon butter
1 teaspoon capers
salt and pepper to taste

Lightly flour the veal scallops. Sauté the veal in a hot sauté pan with the olive oil until light brown on each side. Do not overcook. Remove veal and set aside. Drain fat from pan and deglaze pan with the lemon juice. Add sliced asparagus with chopped mushrooms. Add butter, capers, seasoning and reduce slightly, 3 or 4 minutes until sauce is thick and coats veal. Serve at once.

Preparation: 15 minutes   Easy   Serves: 1
Cooking: 10 minutes

Vitello Romano

Vito's Ristorante

1 pound veal scallops, 4–ounce size portions
4 thin slices Prosciutto ham
seasoned flour
olive oil
2 large Portabello mushrooms, sliced
6 to 8 ounces Marsala wine
1½ cups rich veal stock (can substitute beef or
    chicken)
1 pound spinach leaves, washed and stemmed
½ cup butter
2 garlic cloves, sliced
salt and pepper to taste
nutmeg to taste

Pound veal to flatten and tenderize. Press 1 piece of Prosciutto onto each scaloppine. Heat large sauté pan over medium high heat. Dredge veal in flour and sauté in olive oil, about 20 seconds per side. Remove veal and add mushrooms. Cook about 1½ minutes. Drain excess oil from pan and add Marsala wine to deglaze. Add veal stock and reduce to half. Remove from heat and add scaloppine to sauce to keep warm. In large sauté pan melt butter over medium–high heat. Season with garlic, salt, pepper, and nutmeg. Add spinach and cook until totally wilted. Pour off any excess liquid. Bring scaloppine pan to boil. To serve, arrange spinach on 4 plates. Place veal over spinach; arranging mushrooms on top of meat. Pour sauce over all.

Preparation: 10 minutes   Moderately Easy   Serves: 4
Cooking: 15 minutes   Serve immediately

Naples Airport

When the war ended, the federal government returned the Airdrome to its owners but for several years it suffered benign neglect. The buildings were rented out for storage, housing and offices – and just a few feet off the runway, a field of cucumbers, melons and corn were raised for the northern market. In 1951 the city bought the county's share for the exact amount they paid for it 10 years earlier. Roy Smith (at that time the combination tax assessor/clerk of the court/city manager/judge) recalled many years later how he "was chewed out for throwing the taxpayers' money away."

John Van Arsdale brought his Provincetown–Boston airline to Naples in 1957 and in November of that year the Naples Airport was born. With his wonderful sense of humor, Van Arsdale once described those start–up days this way: "By then 'the farm' was gone, but nobody in Naples seemed to have any money unless they first collected what someone else owed them. We used to call it Naples–on–the–Cuff."

But over the next three decades, he established regularly scheduled commuter flights, managed the airport, built its first terminal and operated a very successful business.

Cattle

The Spanish settlers introduced cattle to Florida when they brought with them a breed now known as the Florida Cracker. Scrawny, tough relatives of the Texas Longhorn, they were the only breed that could survive the heat, bugs and parasites. Almost extinct today, supporters are determined to breed them in large numbers again because they produce a lean type of beef that should prove to be profitable in our fat–conscious society. In the meantime, the Brahma, also resistant to Florida's heat and disease, has been crossed with the Angus, Charolais and Herefords, with excellent results.

Because Florida has no feed grain production, the ranchers sell and ship about three–quarters of a million calves each fall to such western states as Colorado, Texas, Oklahoma and Arizona. And because rustling continues to be a problem, the Department of Law Enforcement has assigned four undercover agents to chase down cattle thieves.

Veal Salvatore
The Fifth Season Restaurant

2 medium tomatoes, diced small
1 medium onion, diced small
½ cup basil leaves, chopped
¼ cup Italian parsley, chopped
¼ cup olive oil
½ teaspoon garlic powder
¼ teaspoon black pepper
½ teaspoon salt
2 pounds veal scaloppine, sliced thin
olive oil
seasoned bread crumbs

In a glass bowl, mix together the tomatoes, onion, basil and parsley, ¼ cup olive oil, garlic powder, pepper and salt. Cover and refrigerate for one hour. Remove tomato mixture from refrigerator to warm to room temperature while preparing the veal. Dip veal scaloppine into olive oil and then into seasoned bread crumbs, coating both sides. Fry veal in skillet in olive oil until golden brown, about one minute on each side. Remove and keep warm. Wipe pan clean before frying additional pieces so that the bread crumb mix left behind does not burn. To serve, place 2 or 3 pieces of veal on a plate and cover with room temperature tomato mixture. Garnish with fresh parsley.

Preparation: 30 minutes   Easy   Serves: 6
Cooking: 25 minutes

Viennese Veal Cutlets
Graf Rudi Restaurant

1½ pounds leg of veal, cut into 4 slices
salt to taste
3 Tablespoons flour
2 eggs beaten
1 cup bread crumbs
½ to ¾ cup oil
4 lemon wedges

Pound the veal to ⅛–inch thin. Sprinkle with salt. Dip the veal first in the flour, then in the eggs, then in the bread crumbs. Heat the oil in a large fry pan and fry veal until golden brown. Serve with lemon wedge.

Preparation: 10 minutes   Easy   Serves: 4
Cooking: 15 minutes

Piccata of Pork with Sauce Normande
Quail Creek Country Club

6 Tablespoons butter
½ cup sliced fresh mushrooms
2 apples, cored, peeled and cut into ⅜ inch wedges
1 pound lean pork tenderloin cut ¼ inch thick (veal may be substituted)
¼ cup flour
salt and pepper to taste

In a large sauté pan over high heat, quickly sauté mushrooms in butter just until softened. Remove mushrooms, and sauté wedges of apple just until tender (lower heat if necessary to prevent scorching). Remove and keep warm. Dredge pork in seasoned flour to coat lightly, and sauté in hot butter until golden, about one minute on each side. While cooking pork, prepare 4 plates, arranging apple wedges and mushroom slices pinwheel fashion around the rim. When pork is done arrange slices in the center of each plate and keep warm while making the Sauce Normande in the same pan.

| Preparation: 30 minutes | Moderately Easy | Serves: 4 |
| Cooking: 30 minutes | Serve immediately | |

Sauce Normande

2 shallots
¼ cup apple jack (or cider)
½ cup dry white wine
1 cup heavy cream

Peel and slice shallots. Sauté shallots in pan you used for cooking the pork. Deglaze the pan with the apple jack or cider and wine. Flambé for fun and flavor. Add heavy cream, stirring well. When hot and bubbling, pour over pork and serve.

| Preparation: 10 minutes | Easy | Serves: 4 |
| Cooking: 10 minutes | Serve immediately | |

Medallions of Pork with Black Peppercorn Sauce

The KeyWester Fish & Pasta House

3 pounds pork tenderloin (about 3 whole tenderloins)
½ cup cracked black peppercorns
¾ cup clarified butter
¾ cup brandy
½ cup whipping cream
½ cup basic brown sauce

Remove all excess fat and silverskin from the tenderloins, slice them (12–15 slices per tenderloin) and pound each slice to ¼" thickness. Heat clarified butter in large fry pan. Pat medallions of pork on each side with peppercorns; place in a hot pan and cook on one side for about 3 minutes; turn over and remove pan from heat. Add brandy and return to heat to flame off alcohol. Add heavy cream and brown sauce. Bring to a boil and simmer about 2 minutes.

Preparation: 20 minutes   Moderately Easy   Serves: 8–10
Cooking: 10–15 minutes

Roasted Pork

Fernandez de Bull

5–pound pork loin roast
salt and pepper to taste
2 teaspoons cumin
2 crumbled bay leaves
2–3 teaspoons oregano
3 cloves minced garlic or ½ teaspoon garlic powder
juice of 2 lemons

Puncture the meat a few times all around. Mix the seasonings with the lemon juice. Rub this mixture well into the meat. Place the seasoned meat in a large plastic bag and refrigerate for 3–4 hours to soak in the flavors. Remove roast from the plastic bag and place the pork in a roasting pan, fat side up. Pour any juice and seasonings that may have settled over it. Roast at 350°F. for at least 2 hours, then check for doneness (170°F. on a meat thermometer when tested).

Preparation: 10 minutes   Easy   Serves: 6–8
Chilling: 3–4 hours
Roasting: 2–2½ hours

The Cultural Life

The Naples Community Concerts Association was started in 1951 by a group of residents who hungered for fine artists and good music in a sparsely developed area. It was made feasible through the efforts of several groups working through a national organization, and the use of Gulfview Middle School auditorium for performances, limited to subscription members.

The Naples Players began in 1953, performing in storefronts, warehouses, school auditoriums or wherever they could find space. Today they have some 250 actors and stagehands who present live performances of well–known works in their own small theater on Goodlette Road. Currently anticipation of a new bigger theater by 1997 is running high. Award–winning architectural plans are ready; and the on–going funding drive has brought

Continued on next page

Mushroom Medley with Gorgonzola Polenta

The Naples Beach Hotel and Golf Club

¾ cup each of the following mushrooms, sliced:
button
cèpes
chanterelle
shiitake
½ pound bacon, diced into small pieces
1 small onion
1 crushed beef bouillon cube
1 teaspoon roux, or cornstarch dissolved in water

In a large pan over medium–high heat sauté bacon, stirring and cooking until brown. Add onions and cook until they are soft; add mushrooms and cook until tender. (If you cannot get all types of mushrooms fresh, substitute with canned, draining them and adding after the fresh are cooked). Add the crushed bouillon cube and thicken with roux or cornstarch dissolved in water. To serve, spoon over Gorgonzola Polenta.

NOTE: *Drain off some bacon fat before adding bouillon and roux, if desired.*

Preparation: 20 minutes   Easy   Serves: 6–8
Cooking: 15–20 minutes

Gorgonzola Polenta

6 Tablespoons butter
1 medium onion, chopped
2 cups milk
½ cup cream or half–and–half
½ teaspoon nutmeg
¾ cup cornmeal
5 ounces Gorgonzola or bleu cheese
salt and pepper to taste

Sauté onion in butter until transparent. Add milk, cream and seasonings and bring to a boil. Slowly stir in cornmeal to keep it smooth; reduce heat to simmer for 20 minutes, stirring frequently. Stir in cheese and pour into rectangular cake pan to cool. When cool, cut into squares and roll in more cornmeal. Pan fry squares in hot butter until golden brown and serve topped with Mushroom Medley.

Preparation: 15 minutes   Easy   Serves: 6–8
Cooking: 40 minutes

in $1.8 million – a little more than half of the $3 million that is needed.

The Naples Art Association was formed by local artists in June, 1954, with classes taught at their Fourth Avenue South headquarters. Meetings and exhibitions were held in the Naples Women's Club. That small nucleus has now grown to roughly 700 members with permanent teaching studios in the Naples Depot. New headquarters are located at 643 Fifth Avenue South, exhibitions in several places, and a scholarship program that was started in 1971.

Having only opened on November 4, 1989, the *Naples Philharmonic Center for the Arts,* located in Pelican Bay, really doesn't qualify as "history," but as the beautiful fulfillment of a long hoped–for dream we felt it should be included.

Ma–Po's Bean Curd

Shing Long Gourmet Chinese Restaurant

2 Tablespoons oil
3 ounces minced pork
1 Tablespoon minced green onion
1 teaspoon minced garlic
1 teaspoon minced fresh ginger
1 Tablespoon hot bean paste
1 cup water
1½ Tablespoons soy sauce
1 Tablespoon white cooking wine
2 squares bean curd, cut into ½–inch squares
½ teaspoon salt
1½ teaspoons cornstarch

Garnish

1–2 Tablespoons sliced green onion
½ teaspoon sesame oil
¼ teaspoon Szechwan pepper

Heat oil in a wok and stir fry pork until cooked, about 5 minutes. Remove pork and keep warm. Stir fry green onion, garlic and ginger with the remaining oil until the vegetables are fragrant. Add hot bean paste to stir fry and mix well. Add 1 cup water, soy sauce, cooking wine, bean curd and salt, if desired. Return pork to the wok; bring to a boil and then to a simmer over low heat for 3 minutes. Thicken sauce with cornstarch mixed with 1 Tablespoon water. Serve garnished with green onion, sesame oil and Szechwan pepper.

Preparation: 20 minutes   Easy   Serves: 1–2
Cooking: 15 minutes

Deep–Fried Home–Style Ribs

Golden China Chinese Restaurant

1¼ pounds spareribs
3 Tablespoons soy sauce
1 Tablespoon sugar
1 Tablespoon cooking red wine
¼ cup cornstarch
1 Tablespoon salt
¾ teaspoon black pepper
6 cups oil for frying

Cut spareribs into pieces 2 inches long, marinate in soy sauce, sugar and red wine for about 30 minutes. Mix cornstarch, salt and black pepper in a bowl and coat the spareribs. Deep–fry spareribs in oil (325°F.) over low heat for 3 minutes, remove. Reheat oil, then deep–fry again at 375°F. on high heat for 20 seconds until golden brown. Serve.

Preparation: 15 minutes   Easy   Serves: 2–3
Cooking: 10 minutes

Fettuccine Carbonara

Busghetti Ristorante

4 ounces fettuccine pasta
1 Tablespoon butter
3 slices prosciutto or pancetta
¾ cup heavy cream
¼ cup grated Romano or Parmesan cheese
pepper and minced fresh parsley to taste

Cook the fettuccine in hot boiling water for 10 minutes or until *al dente*. Drain and keep the pasta *hot*. Dice and sauté the prosciutto or pancetta in butter. Stir in the heavy cream. Add cheese; reduce heat and stir until mixture is thickened (2–3 minutes). Add pepper and fresh parsley to taste. Add hot fettuccine and toss. Serve.

Preparation: 10 minutes   Easy   Serves: 1
Cooking: 10 minutes

Tamarind

Tamarind is an integral part of Worcestershire Sauce. In Southeast Asian countries, a very liquid paste of Tamarind and water is used by the hotel cleaning staff to keep the brass door knobs clean and shining. It also does a good job of cleaning copper.

Roasted Rack of Lamb with Tamarind Barbequed Crust

The REGISTRY Resort

3 racks of lamb, split and feather bone removed
salt and pepper to taste
2 Tablespoons stone ground Dijon mustard

Season the lamb racks with salt and pepper. Sear in hot pan until brown. Finish in a 400°F. oven until medium rare (145°F. internal temperature). Remove and keep warm.

Tamarind Barbeque Crust

2 cups bread crumbs
1 teaspoon Tamarind paste
½ cup barbeque sauce
¾ cup melted butter
1 teaspoon smoked mesquite spice

Put bread crumbs in bowl and add tamarind paste, barbeque sauce, melted butter and smoke spice. Mix very well until a smooth based crust. Cover and set aside.

Just before serving, take rack of lamb, brush it with mustard and coat with barbeque crust. Put in hot oven at 450°F. to crisp the crust. Slice and serve with bean cassoulet and couscous. See recipe on page 207.

Preparation: 15 minutes   Easy   Serves: 6
Baking: 30 minutes

Spicy Orange–Flavored Lamb
Bentley Village

⅓ cup rice wine vinegar
2 garlic cloves, minced
1 Tablespoon Asian sesame oil
1 teaspoon grated orange zest
½ teaspoon crushed hot red pepper flakes
1½ pounds boneless leg of lamb, cut into 1–inch
  pieces
¼ cup orange juice
2 Tablespoons soy sauce
1 Tablespoon honey
2 teaspoons cornstarch
3 Tablespoons vegetable oil
4 scallions, sliced

In a medium bowl, combine vinegar, garlic, sesame oil, orange zest and hot pepper flakes. Add lamb pieces and toss well, set aside for a few minutes. In a small bowl combine orange juice, soy sauce, honey and cornstarch, set aside. In a wok or heavy fry pan, heat 2 Tablespoons oil over high heat, swirling to coat sides of pan. Add lamb and stir–fry until browned outside and medium–rare inside, 5 to 7 minutes. Remove and keep warm. Pour off drippings. Add last 1 Tablespoon oil to wok or fry pan and stir–fry scallions for 1 to 2 minutes until they are soft. Add the reserved sauce and lamb and continue cooking over medium–low heat, about 5 to 7 minutes more, until the sauce is thickened and the lamb is cooked through. Stir frequently to prevent sticking.

Preparation: 20 minutes   Easy   Serves: 4
Cooking: 20 minutes

Baked Lamb Shanks with Sauce

The Palm Restaurant

4 lamb shanks
2 teaspoons oregano
garlic powder to taste

Place lamb shanks in a roasting pan and sprinkle with the oregano and garlic powder. Cover roasting pan with aluminum foil and bake at 350°F. for about 2½ hours, until the meat is tender.

Preparation: 15 minutes	Easy	Serves: 4
Baking:	2½ hours	

Sauce for Baked Lamb

½ cup butter
1 teaspoon chicken bouillon
¼ cup ketchup
4 tomatoes blanched, peeled, and quartered
3 cups sliced mushrooms
1 medium onion, coarsely chopped
5 green bell peppers, seeded and sliced into 6 wedges
1 pinch oregano
1 pinch garlic powder
1 pinch white pepper
1 Tablespoon cornstarch

In a large fry pan, melt the butter, add the chicken bouillon and ketchup and stir well. Add the tomatoes, mushrooms, onion and green pepper, oregano, garlic powder and white pepper. Cover with water to a depth of 1 inch. Cover the pan and simmer over medium heat until the vegetables are softened, about 15 minutes. Mix the cornstarch with 2 Tablespoons water and add slowly to the vegetable mixture until the sauce is thickened a little. Serve baked lamb shank on plate with rice pilaf and sauce poured over.

Preparation: 20 minutes	Easy	Serves: 4–6
Cooking: 20–30 minutes		

Braised Lamb Shank Madeira Wine, Pearl Onions & Wild Mushrooms
Michael's Cafe

2 lamb shanks (10 to 12 ounces each)
¼ cup olive oil
½ cup medium diced celery
½ cup medium diced carrots
½ cup medium diced onion
1 quart veal or beef stock
2 Tablespoons Madeira wine
⅓ cup butter
⅓ cup flour
¼ cup pearl onions
½ cup shiitake mushrooms

In a hot pan with a little oil, brown lamb shanks. Place browned shanks in a roasting pan with celery, carrots and onion. Pour in the stock and cover with foil. Simmer for 1½ hours or until meat pulls away from the bone. Remove shanks when done and keep warm. Strain and simmer the pan juices until reduced by half. Skim off the grease. Make the roux by melting the butter in a small saucepan and gradually adding the flour; stirring constantly until the roux is bubbling hot but not burned. Thicken the juices with a little of this roux, stirring and adding more roux as needed, until the desired consistency is reached. Add the pearl onions, mushrooms and Madeira. Simmer for another 15 minutes. To serve, place shanks on dinner plates and pour the sauce on top of each lamb shank.

Preparation: 20 minutes   Easy   Serves: 2
Cooking: 2 hours

The Collier County Museum

In February, 1922, Dr. Earl L. Baum, a Milwaukee physician and surgeon, came to Naples for a month's vacation (complete with a well–stocked physician's bag for free emergency care for anyone who needed it, since the nearest doctor was in Ft. Myers). Like so many of us, he continued his annual visits until he moved here permanently in 1946, then wrote a booklet about those 50 years. In 1973 he offered the Historical Society 5,000 copies of the books to sell if they would agree to put every cent into a building fund for a Collier County Museum. Needless to say, they agreed and the books became available for a $10 donation to the fund.

The response was tremendous. Architect Richard Morris designed the facility to be constructed on a lot at the government complex; local builder H. L. Stoneburner bid the job at cost; and contributions continued to pour in.

Gruyère Cheese Pudding
⊶ *Wyndemere Country Club*

1 pound Gruyère cheese, sliced
16 slices whole wheat bread, toasted and cut in half
4 large eggs
2 cups heavy cream
½ teaspoon nutmeg
salt and cayenne pepper to taste
¼ cup finely chopped shallots
¼ cup fresh chopped parsley

Butter a baking dish and cover the bottom with toast; fill with alternating layers of toast and slices of cheese. Whisk the eggs with heavy cream, add nutmeg, salt and cayenne pepper to taste. Spread shallots and parsley over cheese and toast. Pour egg and cream mixture over the top. Cover and bake at 325°F. for 30 minutes. Uncover and bake an additional 15 minutes, until brown and puffed.

Preparation: 20 minutes   Easy   Serves: 6
Baking: 45 minutes

Porcini Linguini
Bon Appetit

3 Tablespoons olive oil
¼ cup chopped wild porcini mushrooms
½ Tablespoon dried pancetta or smoked bacon, chopped
1 teaspoon minced shallot
1 cup chicken stock
2 Tablespoons oven–dried tomatoes (sun–dried or fresh may be substituted)
¼ cup cream
salt and pepper to taste
¼ teaspoon fresh thyme
¼ teaspoon fresh rosemary
½ cup washed fresh spinach
linguini for one, cooked al dente

Sauté mushrooms in olive oil over high heat for 30 seconds or so, just until soft. Add pancetta and shallots, stirring 30 seconds. Add chicken stock, oven–dried tomatoes and cream. Boil and reduce until it coats the back of a spoon. Add seasonings to taste. Stir in spinach just until it wilts, then toss in linguini to thoroughly coat with sauce. Serve immediately; garnish with fresh herbs if desired.

Preparation: 30–40 minutes   Moderately difficult   Serves: 1
Cooking: 15–20 minutes   Serve immediately

Vegetables

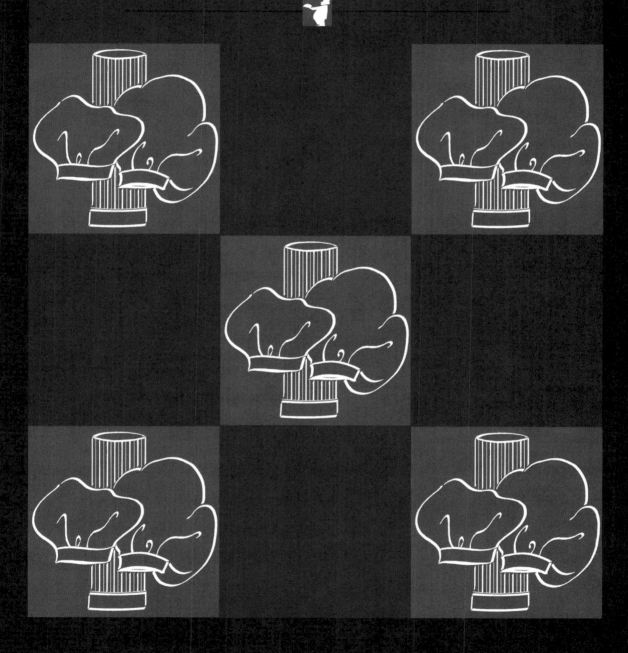

Vegetables

Asparagus Risotto with Sun–Dried Tomatoes and Mushrooms

Vineyards Country Club

1 Tablespoon olive oil
1 large onion, diced
1 large leek, white part only, washed and sliced
1 Tablespoon minced garlic
2 cups Arborio rice
¼ teaspoon fresh ground black pepper
½ cup white wine
8 cups vegetable stock
2 large pinches saffron
12 sun–dried tomatoes, thinly sliced
1 cup thinly sliced asparagus
1½ cups cremini mushrooms
½ cup fresh basil leaves, chopped
¼ cup grated Parmesan cheese

Heat olive oil in a large soup pot. Add onion and sauté 2 minutes. Add leeks and garlic, sauté 3 minutes, stirring frequently. Add rice and pepper; sauté 5 minutes. Add wine and cook until all liquid is absorbed, stirring often. In a separate pot heat vegetable stock and saffron until nearly boiling. Remove from heat. Add 7 cups of stock to rice, 2 cups at a time, stirring until almost all liquid is absorbed. In a microwave dish combine remaining 1 cup stock, tomatoes, asparagus, mushrooms, and basil. Cover loosely and microwave on High power 1½ minutes. Stir this mixture into the hot rice, add cheese and mix well. Simmer 5 minutes more and serve.

Preparation: 40 minutes
Cooking: 35 minutes
Microwave: 1½ minutes

Moderately easy
Serve immediately

Serves: 8

Swamp Buggies

Have you ever been to a swamp buggy race? Have you ever even *heard* of a swamp buggy? A swamp buggy is a home–made vehicle adapted to travel deep in the Everglades. Ed Frank, who developed the vehicle about 50 years ago, said the only rule is "Keep them short, narrow and high." All are equipped with large airplane tires and the different sized chains needed to pass over the slippery marl. Weird–looking? Absolutely; but highly prized by their owners.

The original swamp buggy race took place in the late 40s; the track was on an old potato farm in East Naples known as the "boggiest hole in the vicinity." The only race of its kind in the world, it quickly became a three–day annual event with all the trappings, including a beauty queen who ends her big day by being dunked in the deepest mud–hole by the winner of the race. Over the years changes have been made but "Swamp Buggy Days" continue to be held twice a year, drawing huge crowds of spectators from points near and far.

Risotto

Collier Athletic Club

1 Tablespoon olive oil
2 teaspoons minced garlic
2 teaspoons minced shallots
½ cup Arborio rice
1½ to 2 cups chicken stock, heated
1 Tablespoon butter
1 Tablespoon Romano cheese
1 teaspoon fresh thyme
1 teaspoon fresh oregano

Sauté garlic and shallots in olive oil over medium–low heat. Stir in rice to coat with the oil. Add ½ cup chicken stock and simmer covered over low heat, stirring occasionally, until the liquid is absorbed. Repeat this process of adding stock, ½ cup at a time, until the stock is used and the rice is soft. Stir in butter, cheese and fresh herbs.

Preparation: 10 minutes   Easy   Serves: 1–2
Cooking: 20–25 minutes

Risotto Cakes

Mangrove Cafe

½ cup unsalted butter
2 shallots, diced
½ cup Arborio rice
3 cups vegetable (or chicken) broth, heated
¼ cup Parmesan cheese
salt and pepper to taste

Sauté shallots in 2 Tablespoons butter until they are translucent and add rice; stir for 1 minute. Transfer this mixture to an ovenproof pan and add hot broth, cheese, salt and pepper to taste. Bake for 20 minutes in 400°F. oven. Cool and chill for 30 minutes. Mold into 3–inch patties. With the back of a teaspoon make a "well" in the middle of each patty. Fill the well with 1 Tablespoon of pesto and top with extra rice and press in. Dust with flour and fry patties in hot butter until golden brown.

Preparation: 15 minutes   Easy   Serves: 2
Baking: 20 minutes
Cooking: 10 minutes

Wild Mushroom Risotto
Villa Pescatore

2 Tablespoons olive oil
½ Tablespoon diced red onion
½ Tablespoon minced garlic
2 Tablespoons each of the following mushrooms,
   diced:

       Cremino
       Morel
       Black Trumpet
       Portobello

1 cup cooked risotto (rice) *al dente*
2 Tablespoons red wine
2 Tablespoons chicken stock
2 teaspoons each of the following fresh herbs:
basil
thyme
rosemary
¼ cup grated Parmesan cheese
salt and pepper to taste
¼ cup demi–glace
5 broccoli florets, steamed

Heat olive oil in sauté pan; add red onion, garlic, mushrooms and risotto. Sauté quickly on high heat, stirring, and deglaze pan with wine and chicken stock. Stir in herbs, cheese and seasonings. If sauté pan is not oven–proof, transfer to baking dish, cover and bake at 400°F. 10 to 20 minutes. Mold into a small bowl (12–16– oz.), pressing firmly, and invert onto a plate. (The risotto should hold its shape). Garnish with warm demi–glace and hot broccoli.

NOTE: demi–glace is a rich brown sauce which may be purchased already made up if you don't wish to make it at home.

Preparation: 30 minutes   Easy   Serves: 1
Baking: 10–20 minutes

Saffron Rice with Wild Mushrooms
Glenview at Pelican Bay

½ cup Chablis wine
½ ounce dried morel mushrooms
½ ounce dried cèpe mushrooms
1½ cup chicken stock
12 threads saffron
¾ cup white wine
salt to taste

Reconstitute dried mushrooms in the wine for 15 minutes or more. Drain, reserving the wine. Chop the mushrooms. Bring chicken stock, wine and saffron to a boil. Add the rice, mushrooms and salt. Cover and simmer 15–20 minutes until the rice is tender and the liquid is absorbed. To serve, mold into custard cups or rings, and unmold on serving plate.

Preparation: 15 minutes   Easy   Serves: 3–4
Cooking: 20–25 minutes

Bruschetta
Noodles Cafe Inc.

1 small eggplant (6 ounces) peeled and sliced
1 red onion, peeled, cut into 8 slices
2 large tomatoes, each cut into 4 thick slices
2 ounces sliced smoked mozzarella cheese
¼ cup balsamic vinegar
¼ cup olive oil
salt and pepper to taste
8 slices, ¾–inch thick French or Italian bread

Mix together the olive oil, vinegar, salt and pepper. Using your hands, coat the eggplant, tomato and onion slices and place the coated slices on a sprayed or oiled cookie sheet (one layer only, don't stack them). Bake at 400°F. until onions and eggplant are soft (about 15–20 minutes). Shake pan occasionally so slices do not stick. Place bread slices in oven to toast. To assemble, stack vegetables on each bread slice: eggplant, onion, tomato, and top with ¼ oz slice cheese. Serve on red leaf lettuce with shredded carrot garnish as desired.

Preparation: 10–15 minutes   Easy   Serves: 4
Baking: 20 minutes

Asian Grilled Vegetables

Collier Athletic Club

Marinade

1 finger hot pepper, seeded
¼ cup minced garlic
¼ cup peeled and sliced fresh ginger
1 Tablespoon wasabi (powdered form)
2 Tablespoons lemon zest, chopped fine
2 Tablespoons lime zest, chopped fine
¼ cup extra virgin olive oil
¼ cup fish sauce
1 Tablespoon curry powder

Purée ingredients in a blender or food processor. Pour over vegetables, turning to coat all pieces.

Vegetables

1 red bell pepper, cored, seeded, cut into ½–inch width
1 portobello mushroom, gills removed
1 red Spanish onion, peeled, cut lengthwise ½–inch width
12 scallions, roots removed, tops cut clean
1 zucchini, washed, sliced on 45° angle ¼–inch thick
1 yellow squash, washed, sliced on 45° angle ¼–inch thick
6 plum tomatoes, cored, cut in half lengthwise

Marinate vegetables in the marinade in an ovenproof pan for at least 1 hour. Grill vegetables until almost done to desired softness. Return to marinade and bake 5–10 minutes in 450°F. oven. Serve hot with rice or pasta of your choice.

Preparation: 20 minutes   Easy   Serves: 6
Marinating: 1 hour+
Grilling: 5–10 minutes
Baking: 5–10 minutes

Roast Veggie Monte Cristo
Marie–Michelle's on the Bay

1 zucchini squash, about 10" long
1½ yellow squash, each about 6" long
2 Tablespoons chopped garlic, divided
2 Tablespoons chopped basil, divided
¼ cup olive oil
24–ounce can roasted red peppers, whole
9 ounces goat's milk cheese or fresh mozzarella
1 large loaf of fresh unsliced white bread
3 eggs, whipped smooth

Slice the squash into ¼-inch thick rounds, rinse, pat dry, put into mixing bowl. Add some of the garlic, basil, and coat with olive oil; toss with hands, to coat. Lay out squash on a baking sheet and put under preheated broiler until soft, about 2–5 minutes (don't turn over). Remove and chill. To assemble the sandwiches, slice the bread into 12 double–thick slices. Beat eggs with some of the garlic and basil. Dip one side of a bread slice into egg mixture, then place egg side down on plate and layer with yellow squash, peppers and cheese, making an open–faced sandwich. Dip one side of another bread slice into egg mixture and place on plate and layer with zucchini. Brown each egg–dipped side in olive oil, using a sauté pan or griddle. Put open–faced sandwiches on a baking sheet and put into a 400°F. oven for 5 minutes, until thoroughly heated and cheese begins to melt. Gently remove cheese half from pan to plate, covering with zucchini side. Cut in half quickly with a sharp knife.

NOTE: You may wish to serve this dish with a mayonnaise that has been mixed with finely chopped garlic and sun dried tomatoes.

Preparation: 30 minutes   Moderately easy   Serves: 6
Cooking: 10 minutes

Dry Fried String Beans
Shing Long Gourmet Chinese Restaurant

1⅓ pounds string beans
3 cups oil (for frying)
⅓ cup minced pork
2 Tablespoons dried shrimp
2 Tablespoons Hoisin sauce
2 Tablespoons mustard
¼ cup water
1½ Tablespoons soy sauce
1 Tablespoon sugar

Garnish

3 Tablespoons minced green onion
1 teaspoon sesame oil

Wash string beans and discard tough fibers; drain. Heat a wok or sauté pan, add oil and heat to 320°F. (160°C.). Deep fry beans to dry (tender and shriveled slightly); lift out and drain. Remove all but 1 Tablespoon oil from wok. Stir fry the pork, dried shrimp, Hoisin sauce and mustard to "fragrant". Stir in string beans and mix evenly. Pour in a mixture of ¼ cup water, 1½ Tablespoons soy sauce and 1 Tablespoon sugar to season. To serve sprinkle with green onion and sesame oil.

Preparation: 20 minutes   Easy   Serves: 4–6
Cooking: 15–20 minutes

Green Beans

Most people believe this delicious and popular vegetable was named for its color. Wrong. It is because they are picked, marketed and consumed before they ripen – as in green tomatoes or green peppers. Green beans originated in America and were introduced into Europe early in the 16th century.

"No Taxes"

The 15 years following the war's end saw the emergence of several leading businessmen who set aside tremendous amounts of time to serve in the government of the fast–growing county. Graham Copeland, the general manager of Barron Collier's many interests, was also a county commissioner from 1929 to 1946. Ed Scott, county clerk from 1934 until his death in 1959, was well–known as one who was always willing to take on additional civic chores. Dan MacLeod served as tax assessor from 1923 until 1960 in addition to holding several other positions. Charles H. Collier, who operated a good–size insurance business, was also tax collector from 1923 to 1953. But just think how good they must have felt when they saw this screaming headline in the Collier County News dated August 8, 1946, which announced:

"No Taxes In Collier County"

The accompanying article stated that both the county and school boards' budgets had been completed and submitted for approval. It continued: "These budgets are rather unusual in that neither the county board nor the school board finds it necessary to levy any *ad valorem* taxes for the operation and maintenance of the county and its schools."

The budgets were passed and there were no taxes.

Margaux's Ratatouille
Margaux's

½ cup olive oil
1 large eggplant, peeled and cubed
1 onion, cubed
2 green bell peppers, cubed
3 medium zucchini
3 large ripe tomatoes, peeled and cubed
6 cloves of garlic, peeled and crushed
½ cup tomato paste
2 bay leaves
1 Tablespoon thyme
salt and pepper to taste

Heat olive oil in stainless steel pan or enameled pan (Do not use cast iron or aluminum). Brown the eggplant, then add the peppers, onion, zucchini, tomatoes, and finally the garlic. Cook until the onions are translucent. Stir in the tomato paste and the seasonings. Cook over low heat, covered, until desired consistency is reached (about 30–45 minutes). Remove bay leaves before serving. Serve with meat or poultry, or as a vegetarian dish.

Preparation: 20 minutes	Easy	Serves: 6–8
Cooking: 45 minutes	Can do ahead	
	Serve warm	

Sautéed Spinach
Imperial Golf Club

2 slices bacon, chopped fine
½ medium onion, diced
1 teaspoon minced garlic
4 cups washed, stemmed spinach
¼ cup white wine
salt and pepper to taste

Slowly cook the bacon in a medium sauté pan over medium heat. Add onions and garlic; cook until onions become tender and appear clear. Stir in the spinach and wine and cook for 2–3 minutes. Drain off liquid and season to taste with salt and pepper.

Preparation: 30 minutes	Easy	Serves: 4
Cooking: 20 minutes	Serve immediately	

Provençal Zucchini and Tomato Gratin

Bear's Paw Country Club

4 Tablespoons olive oil
1 medium onion, sliced
1 red bell pepper, sliced in strips
1 small eggplant, peeled and diced
1 large clove garlic, minced
1 pound zucchini
1 pound small ripe tomatoes (about 4 plum
   tomatoes)
scant ½ teaspoon thyme
¼ cup grated Parmesan cheese
¼ cup dry bread crumbs
salt and freshly ground pepper to taste

Heat 3 Tablespoons of the olive oil in large fry pan and sauté the sliced onion, bell pepper and egg plant until the vegetables are soft (about 5 minutes). Add the garlic and cook 1 minute. Pour the cooked vegetables into the bottom of an ungreased 9" x 9" baking dish. Cut the zucchini into ⅛ inch slices or coins. Core the tomatoes and slice thin. Arrange the slices of zucchini and tomato over the cooked vegetables, alternating the rows of zucchini and tomato, using all. Sprinkle the top with the thyme, salt and freshly ground pepper to taste. Cover the top with bread crumbs and Parmesan cheese; sprinkle with remaining Tablespoon of olive oil. Cover with foil and bake at 375°F. about 25 minutes. Remove foil and bake an additional 5 minutes to brown the topping. Serve piping hot.

Preparation: 15 minutes   Moderately Easy   Serves: 8
Baking: 30 minutes   Serve piping hot

Rosemary New Potatoes
Kretch's Garden Restaurant

2 cups olive oil
⅓ cup fresh rosemary leaves, chopped
1 teaspoon salt
1 Tablespoon granulated garlic
1 Tablespoon granulated onion
3 to 5 pounds New potatoes, washed, dried and
  quartered

Mix together the olive oil, rosemary, salt, garlic and onion in a bowl. Place New potatoes in a separate bowl and add enough of the olive oil mixture to coat the potatoes. Place coated potatoes on a baking sheet and roast in a 375°F. oven until brown, about 40 minutes. Turn often with spatula during roasting.

Preparation: 20 minutes   Easy   Serves: 8
Roasting: 40 minutes

Aligot—French Mashed Potatoes with Cheese and Roasted Garlic
Bear's Paw Country Club

2 pounds russet potatoes
1 teaspoon salt
3 cloves roasted garlic
¼ pound imported Swiss or Gruyère cheese,
  shredded
4 Tablespoons butter, room temperature
⅓ cup warm milk
salt and ground white pepper

Peel potatoes and rinse well. Cut potatoes into manageable chunks and place in a pot. Cover with cold water and add 1 teaspoon salt. Bring to a boil and boil until fork tender. Drain the boiled potatoes and put back into the warm cooking pot. Add the roasted, peeled garlic cloves and mash them together. Stir in the warm milk and soft butter until well mixed. Add the cheese and stir until the cheese is melted. Season to taste with salt and ground white pepper.

Preparation: 20 minutes   Moderately Easy   Serves: 6–8
Cooking: 45 minutes

HOW–TO: *Roast Garlic—Separate the cloves from a bulb of garlic but do not peel. Coat the garlic cloves with a small amount of olive oil and place in a piece of foil. Close the foil around the garlic, folding to a tight seal. Place it in a 350°F. oven for 40 minutes. The garlic should be softened. When squeezed from the skins it should have an almost buttery consistency.*

Ragoût of Red Cabbage, Apples, Fennel and Horseradish

Glenview at Pelican Bay

½ cup apple juice concentrate, no sugar added
2 Granny Smith apples, peeled, cored and diced
2 bulbs fennel, washed and diced
2 cups chopped red cabbage
1 teaspoon grated ginger
1 teaspoon ground caraway
3 Tablespoons horseradish
salt to taste

Place apple juice, apples, and fennel in a 2–quart saucepan. Simmer till the fennel is tender, 12 to 15 minutes. Add the cabbage, ginger, and caraway and simmer an additional ten minutes covered; stir frequently. Add horseradish and simmer two minutes more. Salt to taste. Remove from heat and serve.

Preparation: 30 minutes   Easy   Serves: 6
Cooking: 35 minutes   Can Do Ahead
         Serve warm

Sweet Potato and Apple Pancakes

Konrad's Seafood & Grille Room

1 red apple, peeled and cored
2 medium sweet potatoes, peeled
4 eggs, separated
¼ teaspoon salt
1 teaspoon brown sugar
6 Tablespoons flour
¼ teaspoon white pepper
3 sprigs parsley, chopped
butter for cooking pancakes

Grate the apple and sweet potatoes (in a food processor or by hand) and place in a large bowl. Stir in the egg yolks, salt, brown sugar, flour, pepper and parsley. Mix well. Whip the egg whites until frothy and slowly fold into sweet potato mixture. Spoon onto hot skillet or griddle (using butter as needed) and cook to desired color and doneness.

Preparation: 30 minutes   Yield: 14 2" pancakes
Cooking: 8 minutes   Moderately Easy

An Enduring Crop

Sweet potatoes, native to the area, were a boon for early settlers and a staple of their diet. They could be grown without fertilizer and "banked" for the next season.

Green Pea Pancakes with Mushroom and Tomato Duxelle

Vanderbilt Inn on the Gulf

Mushroom and Tomato Duxelle

2 cups chopped fresh mushrooms
¼ cup butter
2 Tablespoons finely diced shallot or onion
¼ teaspoon nutmeg
salt and pepper to taste
2 whole tomatoes, peeled, seeded and diced

In a clean cloth squeeze juice out of chopped mushrooms. Sauté in butter 5–7 minutes over medium–high heat with the shallots and seasonings. Toss in tomatoes and stir to heat, not cook. Set aside.

Green Pea Pancakes

1½ cups frozen peas
1 egg
1 egg yolk
½ cup heavy cream
¼ cup flour
3 Tablespoons sweet butter, divided
salt and pepper to taste

Garnish

½ cup butter
1–oz. truffles, chopped (fresh or canned) or
2 Tablespoons fresh herbs of your choice

Cook peas in boiling salted water until tender; drain and set aside. Combine peas, egg and egg yolk, cream and flour in a food processor until smooth. Add 3 Tablespoons melted butter, salt and pepper to taste and blend until smooth. Fry pancakes in hot buttered pan using about 1½ Tablespoons per pancake. Cook on each side until edges are golden brown. Serve 3 pancakes on a a plate with Mushroom and Tomato Duxelle in center. For garnish mix ½ cup butter with chopped truffles or fresh herbs. Serve 1 Tablespoon with each plate of Pancakes.

Preparation: 20 minutes   Easy   Serves: 4
Cooking: 20 minutes

Vegetarian Chili
Vineyards Country Club

2 Tablespoons olive oil
2 large onions, chopped
3 cloves garlic, chopped
1 carrot, diced small
3 jalapeño peppers, ribs and seeds removed, diced small
1½ teaspoons cumin
3 Tablespoons chili powder
1 28–ounce can tomatoes, chopped with juice
16–ounce can red kidney beans, drained
16–ounce can garbanzo beans, drained
16–ounce can cannellini beans, drained
½ cup bulghur wheat
1½ cups grated cheddar cheese

Heat olive oil in a heavy pot; add onions and sauté until they are soft. Add garlic, carrot, jalapeños and sauté 3 minutes. Add cumin and chili powder; sauté 2 minutes. Add tomatoes, juice and beans. Bring mixture to a simmer; add bulghur wheat. Simmer 20 minutes. Serve garnished with grated cheddar cheese.

Preparation: 20 minutes   Easy   Yield: 2 quarts
Cooking: 30–40 minutes

Vegetarian Chili
First Watch

1 Tablespoon chili powder
1 Tablespoon garlic powder
1 Tablespoon onion powder
1 Tablespoon cumin
½ cup diced onion
½ cup diced tomato
1 Tablespoon Tabasco sauce
1 Tablespoon jalapeño juice
1 cup salsa
½ cup water
2 cans (16–ounce each) black beans, drained

Garnish

¾ cup Cheddar and/or Monterey cheese, grated

In medium saucepan mix all ingredients except black beans and cheese. Bring to a boil. Add black beans and bring to a simmer. Serve in bowls; garnished with grated cheese.

NOTE: *if you wish, you may make your own jalapeño juice by blending two jalapeños with ¼ cup water in a blender.*

Preparation: 20 minutes   Easy   Serves: 4
Cooking: 20 minutes

Black Beans
Fernandez de Bull

1 pound black beans
1 teaspoon salt
1 onion, chopped
3 cloves garlic, mashed
1 teaspoon cumin
1 red bell pepper diced
2 bay leaves
2 Tablespoons olive oil

Wash beans well. Pour beans into a large pot and soak them overnight in a generous quantity of water. Add 4 cups water (or more if needed) and simmer, covered for 2 hours. Add other ingredients and continue cooking 15–20 minutes until the onion and pepper are tender and the flavors are blended.

Soaking: Overnight
Preparation: 10 minutes   Easy   Serves: 6–8
Cooking: 2½ hours

Calypso Bean Cassoulet and Golden Curry Raisin Couscous
The REGISTRY Resort

1 cup calypso beans, soaked
½ cup pancetta bacon, finely diced
½ cup celery, finely diced
½ cup carrots, finely diced
3 cups lamb stock (or beef stock)
½ teaspoon chopped rosemary
½ teaspoon chopped sage

Sauté pancetta 1–2 minutes in a large pan; add onions, celery and carrots. Sauté until vegetables are transparent; add drained soaked beans, rosemary and sage. Pour in stock and cook slowly until beans are tender; season with salt and pepper. Serve with Rack of Lamb with Tamarind Barbequed Crust. See page 186.

Preparation: 20 minutes   Easy   Serves: 6
Cooking: 40–60 minutes

Golden Curry Raisin Couscous

1 cup chicken stock
½ cup raisins
1 teaspoon curry powder
½ cup butter
2 cups couscous
salt and pepper to taste

Heat chicken stock in sauce pot; add raisins, curry and butter. Add couscous and let simmer for 5 minutes over slow heat. Season with salt and pepper to taste. Serve with Rack of Lamb with Tamarind Barbequed Crust. See page 186.

Preparation: 5 minutes   Easy   Serves: 6
Cooking: 15 minutes

Pasta Provençale

Maxwell's on the Bay

2¼ pounds pasta (linguine or fettucine)
⅓ cup olive oil
⅓ cup chopped garlic
1½ pounds fresh plum tomatoes, peeled and
   chopped
¾ cup white wine
3 cups chicken stock
¾ pound snow peas
2 Tablespoons salt (optional)
1 Tablespoon ground white pepper
½ cup chopped fresh basil
¾ cup butter
¾ cup grated Romano Pecorino Cheese

Boil the pasta in a pot of boiling water for 6–8 minutes. In a large sauté pan heat the olive oil. Add the garlic and stir to prevent burning. Add the tomatoes and stir. Deglaze the pan with the wine; add the stock, snow peas, salt, pepper, basil, butter, cheese and pasta. Mix well together and heat thoroughly. Serve hot garnished with extra cheese.

Preparation: 20 minutes   Easy   Serves: 6
Cooking: 30 minutes

Vegetarian Pasta

Mageiro

Pasta for one
1 Tablespoon olive oil
½ cup shiitake mushrooms
4 canned artichoke hearts, quartered
1 roasted red pepper, sliced thin
½ teaspoon minced garlic
½ teaspoon minced shallot
1½ cups chicken soup
a squeeze of lemon
salt and pepper to taste
½ cup snow peas (optional)

Boil the pasta when ingredients are ready to prepare the sauce. In a hot pan add the olive oil and shiitake mushrooms. When brown, add the artichoke hearts, roasted pepper, garlic and shallot (and snow peas, if desired); sauté ½ minute and add chicken stock. Simmer 2 to 3 minutes. Add a dash of lemon, with salt and pepper to taste. Serve hot over the pasta of your choice.

Preparation: 15 minutes   Easy   Serves: 1
Cooking: 15 minutes

Puttanesca Sauce

Marco Polo Restaurant

3 Tablespoons olive oil
3 cloves garlic, minced
2 medium onions, diced
10 plum tomatoes, diced
2 teaspoons capers
10–12 Greek olives, sliced
10–12 Sicilian olives, sliced
2 teaspoons fresh basil
salt and pepper to taste

Heat olive oil in a sauté pan. Add garlic and onions and sauté until the onions are transparent and the garlic is golden. Add tomatoes, capers,olives and basil; simmer for 10–15 minutes. Serve over your favorite pasta, garnished with grated Parmesan cheese.

Preparation: 15 minutes   Easy   Serves: 3–4
Cooking: 20 minutes

Beware

The word "putta", while it may be spelled differently, has the same meaning in at least three languages (Italian, Spanish, and Portuguese) –it's slang for "a lady of the evening". Perhaps this was the sauce she prepared for her customers because it is made in a hurry!

Vodka Sauce

Marco Polo Restaurant

3 Tablespoons olive oil
2 medium onions, diced
6–8 medium tomatoes, diced
¼ cup Vodka
1 quart heavy cream
1 quart tomato sauce
1 Tablespoon fresh basil
salt and pepper to taste

Heat olive oil in a sauté pan over medium–high heat, add the onions and sauté them until they are transparent. Add diced tomatoes and Vodka and continue to sauté over medium heat about three minutes. Slowly add the cream and tomato sauce and simmer for 30–45 minutes. Add basil, salt and pepper to taste. Serve over pasta of your choice garnished with grated Parmesan cheese.

Preparation: 15 minutes   Easy   Yield: 6 cups
Cooking: 45–60 minutes

Fusilli with Vodka

Asti Ristorante

1 small dried red chili, halved
¾ cup vodka
2⅔ cups heavy cream
⅔ cup unsalted butter
2 medium tomatoes, peeled, seeded and chopped
1 pound fusilli (corkscrew) pasta
salt
¾ cup Parmesan cheese
3 Tablespoons fresh minced parsley
freshly grated Parmesan cheese
freshly ground pepper

Marinate chili in vodka 24 hours. Remove chili from vodka and discard chili but save the chili flavored Vodka. In large heavy saucepan combine cream, butter and tomatoes. Bring to a boil and simmer until reduced by one third, about 12 minutes. In a large pot bring 3 quarts water to a boil. Add pasta, stirring to prevent sticking. Cook until just tender but still firm to the bite. Drain well. Add pasta to sauce and boil 1 minute, stirring constantly. Add chili flavored Vodka to pasta and simmer until sauce thickens, stirring constantly about 3 minutes. Mix in ¾ cup Parmesan cheese and parsley. Serve immediately with additional freshly grated Parmesan and ground pepper.

Marinating: 24 hours
Preparation: 20 minutes   Easy   Serves: 4–6
Cooking: 20 minutes

Condiments

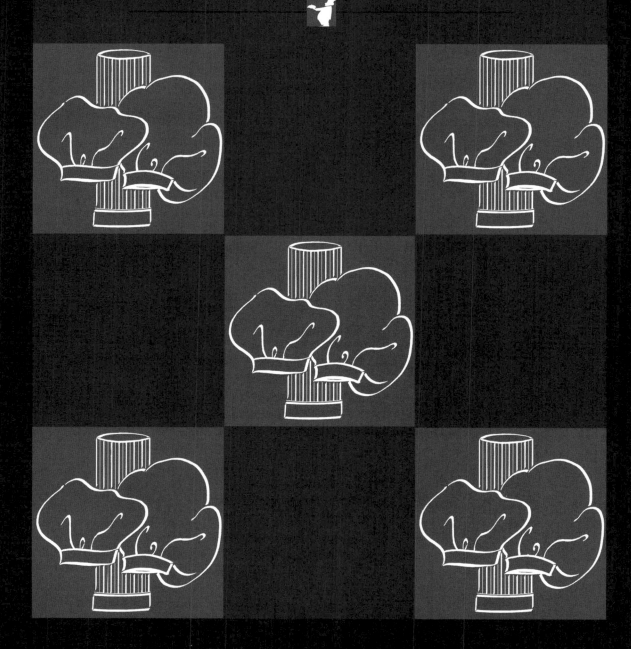

Condiments

Mango and Avocado Salsa
Royal Poinciana Golf Club Inc.

1 cup diced mango (peeled, seeded, cut into ¼ inch dice)
1 cup diced avocado (¼ inch dice)
½ cup diced red onion (¼ inch dice)
2 Tablespoons chopped fresh cilantro
2 Tablespoons fresh lime juice
½ teaspoon lime zest
½ cup olive oil
½ teaspoon salt
½ teaspoon pepper

Combine all ingredients; mix well. Refrigerate 2–3 hours or overnight. Serve with grilled fish.

Preparation: 45 Minutes   Easy   Yield: 2½ cups
Chill: 2–3 hours or overnight

Pineapple, Mango, Papaya Salsa
The Club Pelican Bay

¼ fresh pineapple, peeled, cored, cut into small chunks
1 small fresh mango, peeled, seeded, and diced
1 small fresh papaya, peeled, seeded, and diced
½ small green bell pepper, seeded and diced
½ small red bell pepper, seeded and diced
1 small jalapeño pepper, seeded and diced
¼ small red onion, peeled and diced
2 Tablespoons rice vinegar
juice of ½ lime
juice of ½ lemon
1 Tablespoon chopped fresh cilantro

Mix all ingredients together in a mixing bowl. Serve with grilled chicken or swordfish.

Preparation: 30 minutes   Easy   Yield: 2–3 cups
Can store in refrigerator 1 month

Mangoes

The mango is the apple of the tropics and one of the world's finest fruits. They are grown in tropical and subtropical lowlands throughout the world. Their first recorded introduction into Florida was in 1833 at Cape Sable.

The tree itself grows quite large, with attractive green leathery leaves. The fruit runs the gamut of color from greens to yellow, red, orange and purple, and can weigh up to four pounds. Some mangoes have a turpentine scent but the Haden, which is the most popular, does not. Mangoes can be peeled and sliced, or eaten like peaches, but for first–timers there is a caution: some people break out in a rash after touching or eating the rich fruit.

Papaya

Once used as food for chickens and pigs, the papaya has become a favorite fruit. It looks like a melon but grows on a tree. Green un-bruised papaya will ripen at room temperature in about 3 to 5 days. Use lemon or lime juice to intensify its flavor, as papaya lacks acidity. It contains an enzyme believed to aid in digestion and is a great meat tenderizer, which is why it is added to marinades. Like uncooked pineapple and kiwi, you cannot use it in gelatin but that doesn't limit its participation in many desserts and salads. See for yourself!

Everglades Honey

Honey has had better days in southwest Florida. Until relatively recently an educational apiary on SR 41 at Estero was a popular attraction for passing motorists. In Marco in the 1930's Tommy Barfield and George Lowe operated the largest apiary in South Florida, shipping 60,000 pounds of honey in 1942. Bring back the bees!

Fresh Mango and Papaya Relish
Bayside

½ red onion, chopped
½ inch fresh ginger, minced
1 jalapeño, seeded and chopped
½ red bell pepper, seeded and chopped
4 cloves garlic, chopped
¼ cup cider honey vinegar
2 ripe papayas, peeled, seeded and diced
1 ripe mango, peeled, seeded and diced
½ teaspoon allspice
¼ teaspoon cinnamon
¼ cup fresh mint leaves, chopped
2 Tablespoons fresh cilantro leaves, chopped
salt and cayenne pepper to taste

Sauté onion, ginger and peppers until soft. Add garlic and toss. Deglaze pan with cider honey vinegar. Add papaya and mango. Remove from heat. Gently stir in seasonings and herbs. Taste and add salt and cayenne pepper if needed. Serve with grilled fish, chicken or lamb.

NOTE: *If you can't find honey cider vinegar, substitute 1 Tablespoon honey and 3 Tablespoons cider vinegar for the ¼ cup honey cider vinegar.*

Preparation: 30 minutes | Moderately Easy | Yield: 1 quart
Cooking: 15 minutes | Can store in refrigerator for 1 month

Mango–Pineapple Salsa
Naples Beach Hotel and Golf Club

½ ripe pineapple, peeled, cored and finely chopped
1 ripe mango, peeled and finely chopped
½ red bell pepper, seeded and finely chopped
½ green bell pepper, seeded and finely chopped
1½ teaspoons grated fresh ginger
1 clove garlic, minced
1 small jalapeño pepper, seeded and chopped fine
2 teaspoons chopped cilantro (optional)
2 teaspoons chopped basil
2 teaspoons chopped mint
1 Tablespoon cider vinegar
1 Tablespoon rice wine vinegar
1 teaspoon soy sauce
1 teaspoon sesame oil
juice of 1 lime
salt to taste

Mix all ingredients together, cover and chill. Serve with grilled chicken or seafood.

Preparation: 30 minutes | Easy | Yield: 3 to 4 cups
Can store in refrigerator for 1 month

Cranberry Chutney
Alexander's

1 pound bag cranberries
2 large apples, peeled, cored, and diced
2 cinnamon sticks
4 whole cloves
1 jar Major Grey Chutney
3 Tablespoons sugar (optional)

Mix cranberries, apples, cinnamon and cloves in a sauce-pan. Sprinkle with sugar and simmer for 15 minutes; cool. Stir in the chutney; serve. Refrigerate the leftovers.

Preparation: 15 minutes   Easy   Serves: 6–8
Cooking: 15 minutes

Cilantro Pesto
O━━┳ *Countryside Country Club*

2 Tablespoons slivered almonds
2 cloves garlic, crushed
2 cups lightly packed cilantro leaves
¼ teaspoon salt
¼ teaspoon cracked black pepper
2 Tablespoons canola or olive oil
2 Tablespoons nonfat plain yogurt
1 Tablespoon fresh lime juice

Toast almonds. With motor running, drop garlic into food processor or blender. Add the toasted almonds and process until ground. Add cilantro, salt and pepper; process until ground. While motor is still running, gradually add oil, yogurt and lime juice; process until mixture becomes a paste. Serve with pasta or grilled fish.

Preparation: 10 minutes   Easy   Yield: ⅔ cup

Kretch's Blackened Seasoning
Kretch's Garden Restaurant

¼ cup salt
¼ cup granulated garlic
¼ cup ground black pepper
2 Tablespoons cayenne pepper
2 Tablespoons thyme
2 Tablespoons oregano
⅓ cup paprika
3 Tablespoons granulated onion

HOW-TO: *Blacken Fish—Heat vegetable oil (¼" deep) in a cast iron skillet until extremely hot—450°F. Coat fish fillets with blackening seasoning and cook on both sides until done. The pan may be covered when cooking thick fillets. Seasoning can be sprinkled on when barbecuing or broiling in the oven.*

Combine all ingredients and place in an air–tight container. May be used with fish, shrimp, beef, chicken, etc.

Preparation: 10 minutes   Easy   Yield: 2 cups

Ginger

Ginger has been cultivated in tropical Asia for more than 3,000 years and was one of the first spices to reach the Mediterranean. The first–century Roman epicure, Apicius, recommended it in sauces for meat and chicken, with dried peas and lentils, and in aromatic salt. By the ninth century it was set on the table as commonly as we use salt and pepper in our homes today. Since the rhizomes are easy to transport, it was the first Oriental spice to be widely introduced elsewhere and today it grows almost everywhere in tropical regions.

Ketchup

Ketchup, the anglicized version of the Chinese word for a spicy pickled–fish condiment used in the 17th century. In the late 1700's tomatoes were added to the mixture. As the recipe for this condiment traveled with the Chinese overseas it made its way to Malaysia. To this day the word "Ketchup" is one of only two Malay words in the English language (the other being "amok").

Ginger Teriyaki Sauce or Marinade
Kretch's Garden Restaurant

1 cup soy sauce or lite soy sauce
½ cup cream sherry
1 cup honey
2 Tablespoons minced fresh ginger
2 Tablespoons minced fresh garlic
½ cup frozen pineapple juice concentrate, thawed

Place all ingredients in a bowl and mix. Store in refrigerator and use as needed. To marinate meat, chicken, fish, and shellfish: Place meat, chicken, fish, or shellfish in a shallow dish or large zip closure plastic bag with sufficient marinade. Let marinate in refrigerator for one hour but do not over marinate. Char–broil or bake food in oven, basting frequently with melted butter and Teriyaki Sauce. ALWAYS use fresh sauce for dipping. Discard leftover marinade that doesn't get used up in the cooking and basting process.

NOTE: When using this marinade watch food carefully as it broils or bakes, turn pieces often so they don't burn. The honey in the sauce burns easily.

Preparation: 10 minutes   Easy   Yield: 3 cups

Balsamic Ketchup
Pazzo!

3 ripe tomatoes, large dice
¼ cup sugar
3 Tablespoons balsamic vinegar
salt and pepper to taste
extra sugar if needed
1 Tablespoon cornstarch
2 Tablespoons water

Place tomatoes, ¼ cup sugar and vinegar in a saucepan and bring to a boil, reduce heat and simmer uncovered 15 to 20 minutes. Remove from heat. Purée mixture in blender or processor and strain through cheese cloth. Return to saucepan and season to taste with salt, pepper and extra sugar if needed. Return to simmer. Blend cornstarch and water; stir into simmering liquid and boil 1 minute to thicken. Cool and use for a unique ketchup!

Preparation: 10 minutes   Easy   Yield: 3 cups
Cooking: 25–30 minutes

Paula A. Malone ©1988

Desserts

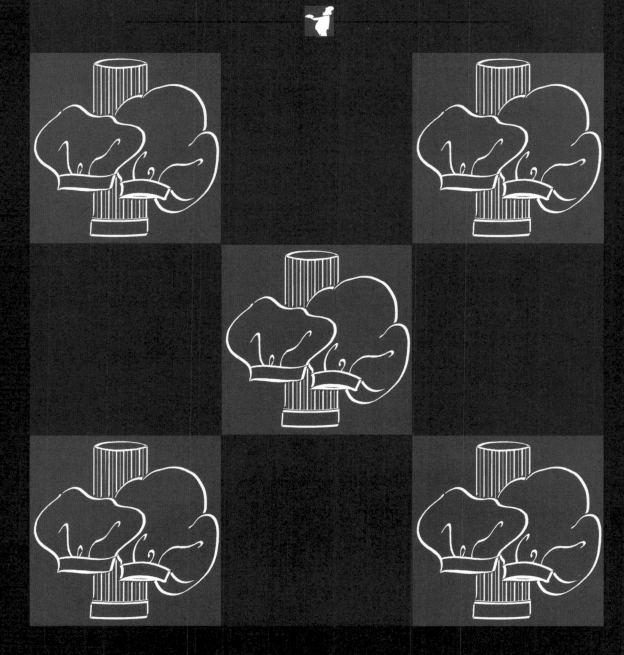

Desserts

Warm Chocolate Cake

The Ritz–Carlton Naples

4 Tablespoons butter
4 ounces bittersweet chocolate
½ cup powdered sugar
¼ cup flour
2 whole eggs
2 egg yolks
2 teaspoons dark rum

Melt chocolate and butter together in a double boiler or in the microwave. Sift flour and sugar. Carefully stir in whole eggs and egg yolks. Fold in flour and sugar and then add the rum. Pour into a small 3–inch by 1–inch ramekin that has been lightly buttered and dusted with sugar. Chill for 2 hours and then bake in a 400°F. oven for 7 minutes. Turn cake out of mold and serve warm.

Preparation: 20 minutes	Easy	Serves: 1
Chilling: 2 hours	Serve warm immediately	
Baking: 7 minutes		

Chocolate Sorbet

The Ritz–Carlton Naples

4 cups water
⅔ cup sugar
⅓ cup corn syrup
10 ounces bitter chocolate, chopped

Bring water, sugar and corn syrup to a boil in a saucepan. Remove from heat and stir in the chocolate. Allow to cool for 4 hours and freeze according to your ice cream machine's instructions or pour into ice cube trays and freeze.

Preparation: 10 minutes	Easy	Serves: 4–6
Cooking: 10 minutes	Must do ahead	
Cooling: 4 hours		
Freezing: 6 hours or overnight		

Chocolate Coriander Sauce

The Ritz–Carlton

1¼ cups milk
¼ cup corn syrup
1 teaspoon coriander
8 ounces bittersweet chocolate

Bring the milk, corn syrup and coriander to a boil in a saucepan. Pour over chopped chocolate and stir until it is of sauce consistency. Serve warm.

Preparation: 10 minutes	Easy	Yield: 1½ cups
Cooking: 10 minutes		

Palm Cottage

About 1895, William Haldeman built a prestigious home one block south of the pier. His good friend and distinguished editor of the Louisville Courier–Journal, Henry Watterson spent each winter at this house. Now known as Palm Cottage (home to the Collier County Historical Society) it was constructed of tabbie mortar with 12–inch thick walls and 12–foot high ceilings. The parlor was heated by a fine fireplace and the library provided him with a large space for writing. His completed work was sent to Ft. Myers then forwarded by telegraph to the newspaper.

The house was later purchased by Lawrence and Alexandra Brown, a fun–loving couple who were known for their many parties, attended by a wide assortment of celebrities and local friends. Following the death of Mrs. Brown, the house was sold to The Historical Society, which was then faced with paying off the mortgage and raising funds for the complete restoration. As always, a corps of volunteers went to work – to clean up the house inside and out, and then to refurbish and add to the Victorian furnishings that came with the house. By April, 1981, the Society had received enough donations to pay off the mortgage and begin renovation, which was completed about a year later.

Today a massive restoration is underway to preserve Palm Cottage for future generations to enjoy.

Flourless Chocolate Cake
The REGISTRY Resort

1 pound semi–sweet chocolate chunks or morsels
4 ounces unsalted butter
10 large eggs, separated
1½ cups sugar, divided

In a water bath, double boiler, or microwave melt the chocolate and butter together. In a large bowl whip the egg whites adding ¾ cup sugar very gradually until meringue peaks softly. In another bowl whip the egg yolks together with ¾ cup sugar until they triple in volume. Pour the chocolate mixture into the egg yolk mixture on slow speed until the mixture comes together. Fold the chocolate–egg yolk mixture into the egg whites slowly and carefully blend together. Pour into a 9 inch by 1½ inch cake pan about ½ to ¾ full. Any extra can be poured into another pan. Bake at 350°F. 20–30 minutes or until an inserted toothpick comes out clean. Remove from oven. Let cool in pan briefly then remove. Can also be chilled for an hour before serving.

Preparation: 20 minutes   Easy   Serves:6–8
Baking: 20–30 minutes
Chilling: 1 hour or more as desired

Chocolate

The Latin name for the chocolate plant means "Food of the Gods" because Indians thought that it had a divine origin.

Kahlúa Chocolate Cake
The Moorings Country Club

2 cups all–purpose flour
1½ cups granulated sugar
1 cup unsweetened cocoa
1½ teaspoons baking soda
1½ teaspoons salt
1½ cups buttermilk
1 cup vegetable oil
1½ teaspoons pure vanilla extract
3 eggs
½ cup Kahlúa liqueur

Grease and flour two 9–inch cake pans. Preheat oven to 300°F. In a large mixing bowl sift together flour, sugar, cocoa, baking soda and salt. Whisk together in a separate bowl the buttermilk, oil, vanilla and eggs. Pour liquid into flour mixture, mixing well. Pour batter into prepared pans and bake at 300°F. for 35 to 40 minutes. Remove from oven and let cool for 10 minutes. Invert cakes onto cooling racks and let cool completely. When cool, brush Kahlúa evenly on each layer. Fill, assemble and frost as desired.

Preparation: 15 minutes   Easy   Serves: 10–12
Cooking: 35–40 minutes

Flourless Double Chocolate and Espresso Tart (Torta alla Sanna)

Bay Colony Club

1¼ **pounds semi–sweet dark chocolate**
1¼ **pounds unsalted butter**
1 **cup heavy whipping cream**
½ **cup strong espresso**
⅔ **cup sugar**
10 **large eggs**

Using a knife or food processor, finely chop the chocolate. In a saucepan over medium heat bring the butter, sugar and cream to a boil. Pour the hot cream mixture over the chocolate and stir until the chocolate is smooth and creamy in texture. Stir in the espresso, and then the eggs, one at a time, until fully combined. Pour into a 10" cake pan, which has been buttered, sugared, and lined with baking or waxed paper. Set this batter–filled pan into a water bath [a larger pan with water that comes halfway up the sides of the cake pan]. Bake in a 350°F. oven 1 hour and 15 minutes. Let cool – it will harden; refrigerate to speed cooling if desired. To serve, garnish with whipped cream and fresh raspberries.

Preparation: 20 – 30 minutes   Easy   Serves: 14–16
Baking: 1 hour 15 minutes   Must do ahead, Must cool

Chocolate

If you fall into the category of "Chocoholic" give thanks to the Spanish explorers and the Americas for your pleasant addiction.

Columbus, after his second voyage, brought plants and pods of cocoa to King Ferdinand. Cortez, in 1528, returned to Spain not only with the pods but also the "know–how" in preparing cocoa drinks, having enjoyed them in Montezuma's court.

Hazelnut and Cream Cheese Pound Cake with Orange Chocolate Sauce

Bay Colony Club

Orange Chocolate Sauce

½ pound semi–sweet dark chocolate
1½ cups heavy whipping cream
½ cup orange juice

Using a knife or food processor, finely chop the chocolate. In a small saucepan bring the cream to a boil; pour over the chocolate and stir until melted smooth. Stir in the orange juice and chill.

Preparation: 10 minutes   Moderately Easy   Yield: 2 cups
Cooking: 10 minutes   Must chill, Must do ahead

Cake

1 cup unsalted butter
6 ounces cream cheese
⅔ cup toasted, ground hazelnuts
2 cups sugar
pinch salt
1 teaspoon vanilla
4 large eggs
2 cups sifted cake flour
fresh mint leaves

In a large mixing bowl, cream the butter, cream cheese, hazelnuts, and sugar until smooth and creamy. Add the salt and vanilla. Add the eggs, one at a time, beating well after each one. Add the flour and mix until combined. Spread evenly into a buttered and floured 8–inch bundt pan and bake at 350°F. 1½ hours or until a wooden pick comes out clean. Cool at room temperature for 45 minutes and remove from pan. To serve: spoon chilled Orange Chocolate Sauce over or around each slice of cake and garnish with orange segments and fresh mint.

Preparation: 30 minutes   Moderately Easy   Serves: 16
Baking: 1½ hours   Must cool, Must do ahead

Chocolate–Pecan Coffeecake
The Moorings Country Club

Streusel Topping

1 cup light brown sugar
1 Tablespoon cinnamon
¾ cup miniature chocolate chips
¾ cup chopped pecans

Mix the cinnamon and sugar well; add the chocolate chips and pecans, mix thoroughly and set aside.

Cake

2 cups flour
½ teaspoon baking powder
¾ teaspoon baking soda
½ teaspoon salt (optional)
1 cup butter
½ cup light brown sugar
½ cup sugar
½ teaspoon cinnamon
2 eggs, room temperature
½ cup sour cream, room temperature
¾ teaspoon vanilla
1 cup buttermilk (or ½ cup whole milk)

Butter and flour a 9" x 13" pan or a bundt pan. Sift the flour, baking powder, baking soda, and salt. Cream together the butter and sugars in a large mixing bowl until fluffy. Add the cinnamon to the butter mixture and blend well. In a separate bowl combine the eggs, sour cream, vanilla and buttermilk, whisking to blend well. Add the flour mixture to the butter mixture alternately with the egg mixture, blending well after each addition. Pour half the batter into the bottom of baking pan then half the streusel followed by the remaining batter. Top with the remaining streusel. Bake at 350°F. for 30–45 minutes, or until a toothpick inserted comes out clean. Let cool 15 minutes before cutting to serve.

Preparation: 15 minutes
Baking: 30–45 minutes
Cooling: 15 minutes

Easy
Can be made ahead
Can freeze

Serves: 16

HOW–TO: *Add Spices—Always add spices with the shortening, butter or oil so they can be better absorbed into the batter. When you mix the spices with the flour you coat the spices and they do not release their flavor as they should.*

Naples Golf and Beach Club

In 1946 Henry Watkins Sr., William McCabe and Darold Greek of Columbus, Ohio purchased all the holdings of the original Naples Improvement Realty Company and placed them under one umbrella called The Naples Company. Almost immediately they announced plans for 12 new homes, the renovation/redecoration of the Naples Hotel and the construction of a 20 room annex on adjoining ground.

Early in 1948 they purchased the relatively new rental golf apartments adjacent to the Naples Golf and Beach Club hotel, remodeled the main wing of the 1930s club to provide eating facilities and reopened as the 70–room Naples Beach Hotel and Golf Club in November, 1948. Over the next 20 years, Watkins bought out his

Continued on next page

Amaretto Cheesecake
The Fifth Season Restaurant

2½ pounds cream cheese
1¾ cups sugar
5 eggs
2 egg yolks
1 teaspoon almond extract
3 Tablespoons Amaretto
1 cup heavy cream

Prepare a 10–inch spring form pan with graham cracker crust and set aside. Using electric mixer whip cream cheese in a large mixing bowl until it is smooth. Add sugar and whip; scraping sides of bowl as you mix the sugar into the cream cheese. With mixer going, gradually add eggs and egg yolks. Fold in almond extract, amaretto, and heavy cream. Pour mixture into the springform pan. Place on a tray or in a roasting pan; add water to surround cake pan, ½ inch deep. Bake at 375°F. for 1 hour. Cool and refrigerate until serving.

Preparation: 25 minutes   Easy   Serves: 12
Baking: 1 hour   Can freeze, Can do ahead

Cookie Crumb Crust

1½ cups graham cracker crumbs, or shortbread
   cookie crumbs
3 Tablespoons sugar
⅓ cup melted butter

Mix all ingredients together with a fork. Pour mixture into pie pan and press into place easily by placing another pie pan of the same size on top of mixture and pressing. Turning around the upper pan forms and smooths the crust in the bottom pan. Bake 10 minutes in a 350°F. oven. Cool. (may be used unbaked but MUST be thoroughly chilled first!)

Preparation: 10 minutes   Easy   Yield: 1 pie crust
    Must chill

Almond Meringue Topping

2 egg whites
2 Tablespoons confectioners sugar
½ cup sliced almonds

Beat egg whites until stiff. Add sugar and almonds. Spread over baked cheesecake and broil until light brown—do not burn.

Amaretto Cheesecake
Naples Beach Hotel and Golf Club

Crust

1 cup finely ground graham cracker crumbs
½ cup finely ground almonds
6 Tablespoons sugar
6 Tablespoons butter, melted

Prepare a 10–inch springform pan by buttering and flouring the bottom and sides. In a small bowl, combine crumbs, almonds and sugar, stirring until well blended. Stir in melted butter until well combined. Firmly press crumb mixture evenly into bottom of pan. Refrigerate.

Filling

1½ pounds cream cheese, softened
1 pound unsalted butter, softened
½ pound salted butter, softened
4 whole eggs
2 egg yolks
½ cup sour cream
½ teaspoon vanilla
¼ cup Amaretto di Saronno
grated zest from one lemon

Preheat oven to 375°F. In large mixing bowl cream the cheese and butters. Add sugar and blend well. Add eggs and egg yolks, one at a time, beating well after each addition. Stir in remaining ingredients and beat until well combined. Remove crust from refrigerator. Spoon cheesecake filling over crust and smooth top. Place cheesecake on the upper rack of the preheated oven. On lower rack of oven, place a roasting pan filled with approximately 1 inch of water (to keep cheesecake from becoming dry). Bake for 50 minutes. Do not remove cheesecake from oven, just turn off oven and wait 1 hour before removing the cheesecake and the pan of water. This helps the center of the cake hold its height. Let cool and refrigerate overnight.

Preparation: 30 minutes   Moderately Easy   Serves: 12
Baking: 50 minutes +   Must make ahead
  1 hour wait in the oven
Chilling: 4 hours or more

partners' share in the hotel and golf course and, as the demand grew, began adding rooms to the contemporary hotel.

Mr. Watkins, an astute businessman, contributed so much to the community in so many ways that he was honored as the first recipient of the *Naples Daily News* Outstanding Citizen award in 1956 – and he continued to remain very active until his death at the age of 91, in 1981.

One of his less–known, kind legacies is a special recognition to the graduating class of Naples High School, established many years ago. Shortly before the close of school, the entire senior class is invited to be the guests of the Naples Beach Hotel and Golf Club for what is known as "Senior Skip–Day."

New York Style
White Chocolate Cheesecake
Bistro 821

1½ pounds cream cheese, room temperature
¼ cup sugar
4 large eggs, room temperature
2 teaspoons vanilla
⅛ teaspoon salt
2½ pounds sour cream, room temperature
12 ounces white chocolate melted, cooled slightly

Prepare a 10–inch spring form pan with buttered parchment or waxed paper on the bottom. In mixer bowl whip the cream cheese and sugar with paddle attachment for 3 minutes on medium speed. Add eggs, one at a time, mixing until blended. Blend in vanilla and salt; blend in sour cream. Add white chocolate and blend. Place pan in a hot water bath (larger roasting pan with enough hot water in it to go half–way up the sides of the spring form pan). Make sure your spring form pan is watertight. Bake at 350°F. for 1 hour until set. Chill thoroughly before unmolding and serving.

NOTE: Chocolate may be melted in double boiler, or in a glass mixing cup in the microwave. Stir often and do not cook too long as the chocolate will toughen in the microwave—1–1½ minutes should be enough time.

Preparation: 30 minutes   Easy   Serves: 16
Baking: 1 hour
Chill : 2 hours

Mango Cheesecake with Anglaise Sauce

Trio's

Crust

½ cup butter, melted
2 cups cinnamon graham cracker crumbs

Mix graham cracker crumbs with melted butter in a mixing bowl until they are moist (you may not need all the butter). Press crumb mixture into a buttered or sprayed 11–inch springform pan, forming a ½–inch edge up the sides as well.

Cheesecake Filling

1 cup orange juice
2 large mangoes
2 pounds cream cheese (4 8–ounce packages)
½ cup sugar
⅛ teaspoon salt (optional)
1 teaspoon cinnamon
4 eggs

In a small saucepan, over moderate heat, reduce orange juice by half. Peel mangoes and cut into ½ inch cubes; add to orange juice. Cook on medium to low heat, stirring occasionally, until mixture begins to thicken, about 10 minutes. With electric mixer, beat cream cheese, sugar, salt and cinnamon until smooth. Scrape sides of bowl. Beat in eggs, one at a time; add mango mixture and blend well. Pour into prepared graham cracker crust lined spring form pan and bake at 350°F. for 45–60 minutes or until toothpick comes out clean. Cool.

Preparation: 30 minutes   Easy   Serves: 12
Baking: 1 hour   Cool before serving

Anglaise Sauce

2 cups light cream
1 teaspoon vanilla
½ cup sugar
6 egg yolks
⅛ teaspoon salt (optional)

Bring cream, vanilla, and ¼ cup of the sugar just to a boil. In metal mixing bowl, mix egg yolks with remaining ¼ cup sugar. Temper eggs with ¼ cup hot cream, whisking quickly. Then whisk egg mixture into the cream mixture in the pot, stirring constantly, heating to 185°F. or until sauce coats the back of a spoon. DO NOT BOIL. Strain and cool.

Preparation: 10 minutes   Moderately Easy   Yield: 3 cups
Cooking: 10–15 minutes   Cool before serving

The "Naples Plan"

Henry B. Watkins, Sr. has been credited with initiating the unique, tax–deductible "Naples Plan" in 1947, when he and his partners, William McCabe and Darold Greek, volunteered to contribute $10,000 apiece plus 10 acres of land to the City of Naples for a park – if the plan was approved by the revenue department. Subsequently approved, the Plan provided for the raising of $300,000 in cash and pledges from local citizens, to be used for new streets, a park/playground, groins to restore the beach, and a mosquito control program – improvements that were badly needed but could not be funded by the city at that time.

The Plan was a huge success. Pledges were made and kept; the money came in on time. On July 5, 1949 the park, named in honor of William Cambier, the town engineer, was officially dedicated, and the remaining work was already well underway. But even more important, its established success let to other projects, such as the drive to raise $108,000 for a new hospital and other improvements.

Vanilla

For centuries vanilla was used as a flavoring and the Aztec Indians in Mexico offered it as a tribute to their emperor. In 1520 Bernal Diaz, a Spanish conquistador, recorded that ground vanilla was added to the emperor Montezuma's chocolate drink. Although vanilla was being used in Europe to flavor chocolate, Mexico kept a monopoly on its product until 1841, when a method of artificial fertilization made it possible to grow vanilla elsewhere.

Chocolate Bread Pudding
Truffles

12 6–ounce custard cups
small amount of butter and sugar to prepare custard cups
1 large croissant, sliced
1 quart heavy cream
¾ cup sugar
1 vanilla bean, split or 1 teaspoon vanilla extract
pinch salt
8 egg yolks
1 pound semi–sweet chocolate, chopped

Prepare the custard cups by buttering and dusting with sugar. Divide croissant slices evenly among the cups. In a heavy-bottomed saucepan, combine the cream, sugar, vanilla bean and salt. Scald but do not boil. Lightly whip egg yolks in a bowl and add half of the scalded cream mixture, whisking vigorously, to avoid breaking. Pour mixture back into the saucepan with reserved cream. Add the chocolate and stir until melted. Do not let it boil! Strain the mixture to remove the vanilla bean. Divide the mixture evenly among the custard cups, making sure all the croissant slices are covered. Bake in a water bath at 325°F. until the custard is set, about 35 minutes.

Preparation: 20 minutes   Moderately easy   Serves: 12
Baking: 35 minutes

French Bread Pudding with Rum Sauce
Kretch's Garden Restaurant

1 cup sugar
¼ pound butter
5 eggs, beaten
2 cups whipping cream
1 teaspoon cinnamon
½ cup raisins
1 Tablespoon pure vanilla
2 cups packed, diced (½–inch size) French bread
   with crust

Cream butter and sugar until light and fluffy. Add eggs, cream, cinnamon, raisins, vanilla. Mix well. Pour into a greased 8–inch square baking pan. Place French bread cubes on top of mixture and stir. Let stand for 30 minutes, pressing French bread into mixture. Cover baking pan with aluminum foil. Place in a larger pan with 1 inch of water. Bake at 350°F. for 40 minutes. Uncover and bake until brown on top. Cut into squares and serve warm with rum sauce.

Preparation: 20 minutes   Easy   Serves: 8
Baking: 40 minutes

Rum Sauce

1 cup sugar
1 cup water
1 teaspoon cinnamon
2 Tablespoons butter
1 cup light rum
2 Tablespoons cornstarch
¼ cup water

Bring first five ingredients to a boil in a saucepan. Mix 1 Tablespoon cornstarch with ¼ cup water. Add to boiling mixture to thicken. Serve warm over pudding topped with whipped cream.

Preparation: 10 minutes   Easy   Yield: 3 cups
Cooking: 10 minutes

Naples Community Hospital

The Naples Community Hospital was originally planned as an emergency clinic–infirmary, but a growing conviction that a more complete service was essential in order to attract highly skilled physicians and surgeons, led to the severing of the hospital project from the other parts of the "Naples Plan." It then became the principal activity of a large number of people who, in a one–week kickoff drive, raised cash and two–year pledges in the amount of $381,999., with more than $4000 of which was contributed by the very small black community.

Two years later, (1956) Naples had a $750,000 fully equipped and accredited 52–bed hospital, all paid for by public subscription.

Chocolate Pots Du Crème
Bear's Paw Country Club

¾ cup milk
¾ cup heavy cream
2 egg yolks
1 whole egg
⅔ cup granulated sugar
3 ounces semi–sweet chocolate, melted
¼ teaspoon vanilla extract

Combine the milk and cream and heat until warm. Combine the egg yolks, whole egg, and scant ¼ cup of the sugar, whisking well. Place the remaining sugar in the bottom of a deep pot. (This pot should be considerably deeper than you think you will need it to be.) Cook the sugar over high heat until the sugar forms a dark amber color. The pot and spoon should be very clean to prevent crystallization. Carefully add the cream to the caramel. The need for the deep pot will now become clear as it will boil furiously (beware of the steam.) Boil this mixture until the caramel is entirely dissolved. Remove from heat. Pour one third of the milk mixture into the eggs and whisk well. Whisk in the melted chocolate and vanilla, mixing well. Strain the custard into a clean container and then divide into 4 custard cups. Bake in a water bath, covered with foil at 325°F. for 20 – 30 minutes, until barely set. Cool and wrap, then refrigerate overnight before serving.

Preparation: 30 minutes   Moderately easy   Serves: 4
Baking: 20–30 minutes   Must make ahead
Chill: overnight

White Chocolate Crème Brûlée

Blue Heron Inn

5 large egg yolks
2 cups cream
½ cup sugar
3 ounces white chocolate, broken up
¼ teaspoon vanilla
2 Tablespoons sugar for topping

Whisk egg yolks and ¼ cup sugar until smooth. In a sauce-pan bring cream and ¼ cup sugar to simmer, reduce heat and add chocolate, whisking until melted. Remove from heat. While vigorously whisking yolks, add cream mixture then vanilla. Pour into four buttered and sugar–dusted soufflé or custard cups, and place in large baking pan. Sprinkle ½ Tablespoon sugar on each cup. Surround with hot water, half–way up the sides of the baking cups. Bake at 300°F. about 1 hour. Serve chilled.

Preparation: 15 minutes   Easy   Serves: 4
Baking: 1 hour   Chill before serving

Crème Caramel

L'Auberge on Fifth Restaurant Français

1 quart whole milk
zest of 1 orange
½ teaspoon vanilla
6 whole eggs
3 egg yolks
1½ cups sugar

Scald milk, orange zest, and vanilla in a large saucepan over medium heat. Do not boil! Beat 6 eggs and 3 yolks in a large mixing bowl. Gradually add 1 cup of sugar. While milk mixture is still hot, slowly beat into egg mixture. Strain and let cool 6 hours in refrigerator. To caramelize the ½ cup sugar, heat it in a saucepan over very low heat. Stir only after the sugar begins to melt. Cook until smooth; do not burn! Pour hot caramelized sugar into 8 six–ounce custard cups, tilting to coat the bottom of each one. Place custard cups into a baking pan with 1 inch deep hot water. Pour egg mixture into cups until cups are almost full. Bake at 375°F. for 40 minutes or until custards are firm.

Preparation: 30 minutes   Moderately Easy   Serves: 8
Chilling: 6 hours before baking
Baking: 40 minutes

Oranges

The first oranges in England were brought by Spanish ships and quickly became popular with royalty. In 1805 orange orchards were started in California, soon followed by orange groves in central and northern Florida. In the past decade much of the industry has moved to Collier County where there is far less likelihood of killer freezes. Collier's warm, humid climate helps to grow a juicy orange and, as a result, the bulk of the County's oranges are grown for processing.

The Conservancy

In 1964, when Rookery Bay and outlying islands were threatened by development, a group of prominent residents met to decide on a strategy to halt it. They planned and carried out a 50–foot petition signed by more than 1,000 opponents and presented it to the County Commissioners which eventually led to denial of such a development. From that meeting an organization was formed, dedicated to the protection of natural resources through preservation of ecologically sensitive areas – *The Conservancy.*

Their first goal was the purchase of the Rookery Bay area, but when their offers were accepted they requested and received an adjacent area – a total of 2600 acres which meant they had to raise $400,000. Part of it was met when the National Audubon Society agreed to manage the sanctuary and match donations with $150,000 from their own funds. Just seven months later, on April 1, 1966, contributions from some 1,400 individuals and 20 civic organizations retired the debt and the deed was turned over to the Audubon Society at a huge environmental rally on January 12, 1968. With dynamic Willard Merrihue at the helm, in 1981 The Conservancy moved its administration offices to a beautiful new facility on Merrihue Drive, which includes the Naples Nature Center as well as a peaceful, beautiful pavilion on the water.

Sticky Coconut Date Pudding with Rum Toffee Sauce
Bon Appetit

Pudding

4 ounces dates, pitted and finely chopped (½ cup)
⅓ cup unsweetened coconut flakes
1 cup water
1 teaspoon baking soda
¼ cup butter
¾ cup sugar
2 eggs
¾ cup self–rising flour
1 teaspoon vanilla

In a small pan combine dates, coconut and one cup water. Bring to a boil. Remove from heat and stir in baking soda; set aside. In mixer bowl cream butter, adding sugar a small amount at a time. Add eggs one at a time, beating well. Carefully fold in flour. Stir in date coconut mixture and vanilla. Pour into two buttered 7" cake pans with removable bottoms. Bake in 350°F. oven for 30 to 40 minutes, adding sauce last 5 minutes.

Preparation: 30 minutes   Moderately easy   Serves: 12
Baking: 30–40 minutes

Rum Toffee Sauce

¾ cup firmly packed light brown sugar
½ cup heavy cream
⅓ cup butter
3 Tablespoons dark rum
¼ cup chopped toasted macadamia nuts

In a small saucepan bring sugar, cream and rum to boil; boil 3 minutes and set aside. Five minutes before pudding is done, pour sauce over the pudding and return to oven. Bake until sauce has soaked in and bubbles down.

Preparation: 10 minutes   Easy   Yield: 1½ cups
Cooking: 10 minutes

Chocolate Decadence with Passion Fruit Sauce

Bon Appetit

5⅓ ounces semi–sweet chocolate
11 Tablespoons butter
3 eggs
3 egg yolks
⅓ cup sugar
⅓ cup flour

Melt chocolate and butter together. In mixer bowl beat eggs, egg yolks and sugar until they are thick and fluffy, or when the beater is lifted out, a ribbon forms on the batter as the egg mixture drops off the beaters. Add flour and chocolate butter mixture. Beat for 2 minutes. Pour batter into buttered and floured 8 or 10–ounce custard cups. Bake at 375°F. for 25 minutes. Serve warm or cold; turn out on plate with Passion Fruit Sauce spooned around, drizzled, or covering the Chocolate Decadence.

Preparation: 20 minutes   Moderately Easy   Serves: 6
Baking: 25 minutes   Serve warm or cold

Passion Fruit Sauce

8 fresh passion fruit
1 vanilla bean, split or 1 teaspoon vanilla extract
1 cup sugar
1 cup water
1 cup fresh raspberries
juice of 1 lemon

Cut the passion fruit in half and scoop out the pulp into a heavy stainless or non–reactive saucepan. Add the vanilla bean, sugar and water. Bring to a boil and remove from heat. Remove the vanilla bean. Purée the raspberries with the lemon juice in a blender or food processor. Strain the raspberry purée into the passion fruit mixture and let cool completely.

NOTE: Some speciality stores have passion fruit purée.

Preparation: 10 minutes   Easy   Yield: 1½ cups
Cooking: 10 minutes   Cool before serving

Passion Fruit

Passion fruit was so named by Spanish Missionaries to South America. The complex flower of the fruit represented, to them, the crown, the nails, and the wounds of the crucifixion of Christ. It is a juicy, tart fruit used to add zip to fruit salads, tropical drinks, desserts and sauces. Hint: Select the heaviest, smoothest fruit although even the wrinkled fruit remains fresh and juicy inside.

Julius Fleischmann

Julius Fleischmann, a wealthy man of many interests, with an amazing background and a great love of beauty and the arts, came to Naples in 1946 as a visitor from Cincinnati but soon became an investor and developer of the finer things of life. His innate good taste was tempered only by his practical business sense, which earned him the admiration and respect of all who knew him.

Fleischmann's first project was the development of Naples' elegant Third Street South shopping mecca, started at a time when the street was barely paved and had a half dozen unlovely structures sprawled along its length. In 1950 he opened the Brae–Bedell Patio which offered beautiful, luxury resort wear to a population of less than 1,200; followed by a store that sold fine furniture and antiques. Gradually, others opened interesting shops stocked with fine wares that appealed

Continued on next page

Lemon Mousse
Imperial Golf Club

1 pint heavy cream
3 Tablespoons liqueur, such as Grand Marnier
1 envelope unflavored gelatin
¼ cup hot water
1 cup lemon juice
¾ cup sugar
4 ounces semi–sweet chocolate
4 flat chocolate cookies, such as Famous Chocolate
2 teaspoons orange marmalade
1 Tablespoon whipped topping (or reserved whipped cream)

Whip cream until soft peaks form, adding liqueur slowly as you whip. Hydrate gelatin in 2 Tablespoons cold water and then dissolve in 2 Tablespoons hot water. Add sugar and lemon juice. Gently fold whipped cream into the lemon liquid mixture with a spoon, a little at a time until fully incorporated. Spoon into biscuit rings (or other molds) and set on a cookie sheet. Freeze for 2 hours. Remove from ring or mold and set aside. To serve, melt chocolate and put in pastry bag with small tip. Place cookie off center on plate and outline with chocolate, drawing a stem and two leaves from it. Put mousse on top of cookie. Fill leaf outlines with marmalade. Top mousse with a dab of whipped topping and decorate with lemon skin.

Preparation: 45 minutes   Serves: 4
Freezing: 2 hours

Brownies
Hilde's Tea Room

4 eggs
2 cups sugar
1 cup butter, melted
4 ounces unsweetened chocolate, melted
1 cup flour

Beat eggs and sugar together until light and fluffy. Add melted butter and chocolate, mixing well; add flour and mix. Butter or spray a 7–inch by 11–inch pan. Pour batter into pan. Bake at 350°F. for 30 minutes.

Preparation: 15 minutes   Easy   Serves: 8–10
Baking: 30 minutes   Can freeze

Raspberry Brownies with Velvet Chocolate Glaze

Moorings Park

3 ounces unsweetened chocolate
½ cup shortening
3 eggs
1½ cups sugar
1½ teaspoons vanilla
¼ teaspoon salt
1 cup flour
1½ cups chopped walnuts
⅓ cup raspberry jam

Melt chocolate with shortening over warm water; cool slightly. In mixing bowl blend together the eggs, sugar, vanilla and salt. Stir in the chocolate mixture, then flour. Fold in walnuts and turn into a well–greased (or sprayed) 8–inch square pan. Bake at 325°F. for 35 to 45 minutes. Carefully spoon raspberry jam over the hot brownies, spreading evenly. Let cool.

Preparation: 30 minutes	Moderately Easy	Serves: 12
Baking: 40 minutes	Can do ahead, Can freeze	

Velvet Chocolate Glaze

1 ounce unsweetened chocolate
2 Tablespoons butter
2 Tablespoons light corn syrup
1 cup powdered sugar
1 Tablespoon milk
1 teaspoon vanilla

Melt chocolate, then blend in the butter and corn syrup. Stir in powdered sugar, milk and vanilla. Mix well and spread over the cooled raspberry topping on the brownies. Let glaze cool, then cut into 12 delicious bars.

Preparation: 15 minutes	Easy	Yield: 1 cup

to more cultivated tastes. With his 1961 transformation of the old Naples Company building and the Seminole market into specialty shops, the future of the area was assured.

In 1951 Fleischmann bought the home and grounds of Dr. Henry Nehrling, a famous botanist who lived and worked in Naples until 1929. After years of neglect, the grounds were a disaster. Once Fleischmann had their former beauty restored, they were opened as a local attraction called Caribbean Gardens, eventually boasting more than 5,000 orchids and the world's largest collection of free–roaming waterfowl.

At the time of Mr. Fleischmann's death in 1968, his plans for the area's first shopping mall – Coastland Center – were underway. Today, with his daughter at the helm of the family's Neapolitan Enterprises, the contributions to the area continue.

Plantain

The plantain, which looks like a large banana, has three stages. Unripe and green, it is starchy and rather bland, similar to a potato. Half–ripe, it has a creamier texture and tastes something like a sweet potato. Ripe and cooked, its sweet-ness outshines a banana, which is why it is used in so many desserts. Hint: Select plantains with a dark (brown to black) skin for best flavor.

HOW–TO: *Flambé—Add the liqueur to the mixture in the sauté pan slowly and care-fully. When it is heated, ignite the liquid and let it burn. Be careful not to get burned when it flames.*

Soft Tortilla with Plantains and Caramel Sauce

Mangrove Cafe

6 plantains
2 Tablespoons butter
2 Tablespoons orange juice
2 Tablespoons rum
½ cup brown sugar
6 flour tortillas

Garnish

strawberry and papaya purée
sweetened whipped cream

Cut plantains into ¼–inch dice and sauté in butter for 3 minutes. Add orange juice and rum, and cook for 5 minutes. Add brown sugar and stir until melted (1 minute). Spoon plantains onto tortilla, roll up and ladle sauce over top. To serve, garnish with fruit purée and sweetened whipped cream.

Preparation: 15 minutes	Easy	Serves: 6–8
Cooking: 5 minutes	Must do ahead	

Bananas Foster á la Calella

Calella's Bistro Inc.

¼ cup maple syrup
¼ cup dark brown sugar
2 Tablespoons butter
4 ripe medium bananas, cut into 1–inch thick slices
1 dash cinnamon
2 Tablespoons Grand Marnier liqueur
2 Tablespoons Triple Sec liqueur
4 scoops vanilla ice cream (or favorite flavor)

Pour maple syrup and brown sugar into a 12–inch, non–stick sauté pan and place over medium–high heat. Add butter and blend together until a froth occurs. Add bananas and sauté about 1 minute. Add cinnamon to taste. Flambé with Grand Mariner and Triple Sec. Scoop ice cream into dessert dishes and spoon bananas over ice cream.

Preparation: 5 minutes	Easy	Serves: 4
Cooking: 10 minutes		

Florentine Bowl with Berries and Cream

⌐━━ *Country Club of Naples*

6 Tablespoons butter
¾ cup sugar
1 cup crushed almonds
2 Tablespoons flour
2 Tablespoons milk

Cream together softened butter and sugar. Add crushed almonds, flour and milk, mixing thoroughly. Chill 2–3 hours. Shape chilled dough into 1½ inch balls and space 6 inches apart on large buttered cookie sheets. Bake at 375° to 400°F. for 10–14 minutes or until golden brown. Remove from oven and let rest 30 seconds to 1 minute but NOT till hardened. Working quickly, remove round from cookie sheet and press and form each round over an upside down buttered bowl. When hardened, gently remove and keep in a cool, dry place. (Make early in the day you want to serve them.)

Chilling: 2-3 hours   Moderately Difficult   Serves: 10–12
Preparation: 20 minutes
Baking: 10–14 minutes

Berries and Cream

2 cups heavy cream
¼ cup sugar
1 teaspoon vanilla
1 Tablespoon Grand Marnier (optional)
1 pint fresh berries, or more if desired

In mixing bowl whip heavy cream, sugar, vanilla, and Grand Marnier until cream is stiff, but still smooth. Rinse and hull berries, pat dry then gently toss with whipped cream until evenly coated. Refrigerate unless using immediately. Spoon berries and cream into Florentine Bowls just before serving. Garnish with mint leaves or fanned strawberry.

Preparation: 20 minutes   Easy   Serves: 10–12

Banana

The banana, a main–stay of any tropical diet, actually means "fruit of the wise man". It is the largest herb in the world. It has been called many things and has symbolized many things. The Hindus regard it as a symbol of fertility and prosperity. Hence it is given as a gift of marriage.

Siesta Key Cocktail
First Watch Restaurant

¼ cup granola
¼ cup plain or vanilla yogurt
¼ cup diced fresh fruit
2 Tablespoons mixed raisins and walnuts
¼ cup strawberry yogurt
¼ cup diced fresh fruit
powdered sugar, sprinkled
cinnamon, sprinkled

In two parfait glasses or two 10–ounce glasses layer the items in the order listed. The sugar and cinnamon may be sprinkled separately (or mixed together and kept in a small shaker for convenient sprinkling on this and other items). This makes a lovely light meal, dessert or snack.

Preparation: 10 minutes   Easy   Serves: 2
                    Serve immediately

Granny Puff Pastry
Olde Marco Inn

2 sheets puff pastry, 12 inches by 20 inches
3 large Granny Smith apples
½ cup sugar
1 teaspoon cinnamon
6 scoops vanilla ice cream
6 Tablespoons apple jack schnapps (optional)
1 cup raspberry sauce (sold in speciality shops)
confectioner's sugar for dusting

Cut six circles (5 to 6 inches in diameter) from the sheets of puff pastry. Place pastry on well–buttered cookie sheet. Clean, core, and thinly slice the apples, fanning ½ apple on each circle. Mix the sugar and cinnamon together and sprinkle over the apples. (Add more sugar to taste, if the apples are very tart.) Bake at 350°F. for 15 minutes or until apples are tender. Remove from oven and place on 6 plates. To serve: place a scoop of vanilla ice cream on top of each puff, pour 1 Tablespoon of apple jack schnapps over ice cream (if desired), and garnish with powdered sugar and raspberry sauce.

Preparation: 20 minutes   Easy   Serves: 6
Baking: 15 minutes

Coconut Pineapple Pudding with Roasted Banana Rum Sauce
Savannah a Fine Traditional Restaurant

¼ cup butter
¾ cup sugar
1 teaspoon vanilla
2 eggs
¾ cup flour
⅛ teaspoon salt (optional)
1 Tablespoon baking soda
1 cup finely diced fresh pineapple, firmly packed
1 cup shredded coconut
1 cup water

Cream butter and sugar until light and fluffy; add vanilla and blend. Add eggs, one at a time, blending well, scraping sides of bowl. Combine flour, salt and soda; blending into butter mixture. Thoroughly blend in rest of ingredients. Pour into well-greased molds, cups or ramekins. Bake at 350°F. until dark brown, 30–40 minutes. Serve unmolded with Roasted Banana Rum Sauce around it.

Preparation: 30 minutes   Easy   Serves: 8
Baking: 30–40 minutes

Roasted Banana Rum Sauce

2 bananas, peeled
½ cup firmly packed light brown sugar
¼ cup dark rum
3 ounces pineapple juice
juice of 1 lemon
1 cup half–and–half

Roast bananas whole in 350°F. oven until mushy, 15–20 minutes. In a saucepan melt the light brown sugar until caramelized (dark brown). CAREFULLY add the rum, letting the alcohol cook off. *Watch for flaming!* Remove from heat to cool. Place banana, sugar and rum mixture in a blender; blend well. Add fruit juices; blend. Add just enough half–and–half so mixture is pourable but slightly thick.

Preparation: 5 minutes   Easy   Yield: 1½ cups
Baking: 15–20 minutes
Cooking: 15–20 minutes

Coconut

"He who plants a coconut tree, plants vessels and clothing, food and drink, a habitation for himself and a heritage for his children."
An old saying

Coconut Palms

Because the markings on the stem have a strong resemblance to a monkey, the Portuguese termed them "coco."

It supplies us with oil, fiber, lumber, charcoal as well as food!

Here in Collier County we have hundreds of these helpful trees, whose fronds do a soft ballet on a breezy day.

Almond Crescents
Graf Rudi Restaurant

1 cup butter
½ cup powdered sugar
1 teaspoon vanilla
¼ teaspoon almond flavoring
1 Tablespoon water
1¾ cups flour
¾ cup very finely chopped almonds

Cream butter with sugar. Beat in flavorings and water. Blend in flour and almonds. Chill. Shape into small crescents, about 2" across; place on ungreased baking sheets. Bake in a pre–heated 300°F. oven for 25–30 minutes or until lightly browned.

Preparation: 15 minutes	Easy	Yield: 4 dozen
Baking: 25–30 minutes	Must chill before baking	

French Almond Macaroons
Glenview at Pelican Bay

1 pound confectioners sugar
1 pound almond paste
1 Tablespoon flour
5 egg whites

In a mixer bowl combine sugar, almond paste and flour; mix on low speed until crumbly. Add egg whites. Blend thoroughly until smooth. Using a pastry bag or 1–ounce scoop (2 Tablespoons), drop cookies on parchment–lined cookie sheet, 2 inches apart. Bake at 350°F. oven for 10–12 minutes. Cool. Remove from paper and store in resealable bags. These cookies freeze very well.

NOTE: *Almond paste is available at speciality stores, bakeries and grocery stores.*

Preparation: 10 minutes	Easy	Yield: 36 cookies
Baking: 15 minutes	Can freeze	

Off-Season Naples

With fewer than 13,000 people in 1970, the little city of Naples was still a place where specialty shops closed their doors and their owners left town from May 15 to October 15. Streets were deserted after 9 p.m. and, aside from two drive–ins on the outskirts, the only movie was in the new Coastland Canter mall. Except for a couple of small taverns, there were no night–spots. Golf and country clubs had begun to appear (Hole–in–the–Wall in 1957, Moorings Country club in 1963, Country Club of Naples in 1966, Royal Poinciana in 1969) but most were available to members only.

But the residents didn't lead a monastic life by any means. They

Continued on next page

Cashew Coffee Biscotti
Asti Ristorante

1½ **cups unsalted cashews**
1¾ **cups flour**
½ **teaspoon baking powder**
¼ **teaspoon salt**
¾ **cup sugar**
¼ **cup cold unsalted butter**
2 **Tablespoons instant coffee or espresso granules**
2 **large eggs**
½ **teaspoon vanilla**

Preheat oven to 350°F. Spread cashews on large baking sheet; toast for 10–12 minutes, until golden brown. Cool. Combine flour, baking powder, salt and ⅔ cup sugar in a food processor. Add cold butter and pulse until mixture resembles coarse meal. In a large mixing bowl combine the flour mixture and the cashews. Mix in the coffee granules. In a small bowl, using a fork, lightly beat the eggs with the vanilla. Stir the egg mixture into the flour mixture, then mix with your hands until just blended. Pat into a disk. On a lightly floured work surface cut the disk into quarters. Using your hands, roll each quarter into an 8–inch log. Place the logs 2 inches apart on lightly greased baking sheet, and flatten each log to a width of 2 inches with the heel of your hand. Sprinkle the tops of each log with the remaining sugar. Bake for 20 minutes or until golden brown. Carefully transfer the logs to a wire rack for cooling, 5–10 minutes. Place logs on a cutting surface, and using a sharp knife in a quick motion, slice each log on the diagonal ¾–inch thick (biscotti shaped). Place the cut biscotti on a baking sheet and bake for an additional 5–7 minutes, just until they begin to color on all sides. Cool and store in airtight container for up to one month.

Preparation: 1 hour   Moderately Easy   Yield: 3 dozen
Baking: 30 minutes

simply shifted to informal cocktail and dinner parties with neighbors and local friends. Families would build a fire, cook dinner and eat it on the beach (no longer allowed). The Gulf invited everyone to swim, sail or fish; relaxing on the beach while watching the gorgeous sunsets was a good way to start the evening. Their small town lifestyle was very important to them. Most of the full–time residents were known by name; service in familiar stores was personalized and caring; everyday civility included pleasantly greeting the passing stranger on the beach.

And by the end of the hot, lazy summer, everyone was looking forward to the return of our guests, visitors...and a very different lifestyle!.

Turtle Eggs for Breakfast?

An early Naples recipe talks of turtle egg omelet with rum. Turtle soup and turtle eggs were once big seafood items in Collier County. Turtle nests were easy to find by following the heavy trails the turtles made when coming ashore to lay their eggs. In 1882 Chokoloskee's Adolphus Santini, who regularly shipped such produce as cabbages, pumpkins, potatoes, melons, peppers, eggplant, sugar cane and bananas across the water to Key West, added a profitable haul of turtle eggs, after gathering over 1,000 eggs from fourteen nests. Today nests are hunted to be marked and protected and the human threat is not from hunters but from those who let the lights from cars or homes shine near the seashore at night.

Aunt Jo's Glazed Cookies
Mageiro

6 eggs
1 cup baking shortening
1 cup sugar
2 teaspoons flavoring (vanilla, almond,or lemon extract)
4 cups flour
2 Tablespoons baking powder
½ teaspoon salt (optional)

In a large mixing bowl blend the eggs, shortening, sugar, and flavoring of your choice until fluffy. Combine flour, baking powder, and salt; add to egg mixture, blending well without over–beating. Refrigerate one hour. Roll into 1–inch balls and place on greased cookie sheet. Bake at 375°F. 6–10 minutes until slightly browned on the bottom. Cool and glaze.

Preparation: 30 minutes	Easy	Yield: 6 dozen
Baking: 10 minutes	Can freeze	
Chilling: 1 hour		

Glaze

1 pound confectioner's sugar
1 Tablespoon flour
1 teaspoon vanilla
Milk, 1 Tablespoon at a time until dipping consistency
A Few drops of food coloring, optional

Blend sugar, flour and vanilla, adding milk to desired consistency. Dip cookie in glaze. For variety divide glaze into smaller bowls, tinting each a different pastel color. Store tightly covered.

Preparation: 15 minutes	Easy	Yield: 1½ cups

Lace Cup
Royal Poinciana Golf Club Inc.

½ **cup butter**
½ **cup sugar**
¼ **cup molasses**
¼ **teaspoon cinnamon**
½ **cup flour**
½ **cup chopped pecans**

Line cookie sheets with parchment paper or grease very well. Over medium heat melt the butter, sugar, molasses and cinnamon, stirring well. Add the flour and pecans to blend well. Use 2–3 rounded Tablespoons of batter for each Lace Cup, depending on the size you want. Cookies will triple in size during baking. (Make 3 on the first sheet, then adjust amount to size or cup you want.) Bake at 350°F. for 8–10 minutes, or until dark around edges. Working quickly, as soon as you can handle the cookies, use a spatula to lift the cookies off the cooking surface and invert them over well–buttered upside down bowls or custard cups and shape as you wish. Let air cool, do not refrigerate! Remove when hardened; fill with ice cream and sauce of your choice.

Preparation: 10 minutes	Moderately Easy	Serves: 8
Baking: 8–10 minutes	Must make ahead	

Creamsicle Pie
Countryside Country Club

1 **9–inch chocolate pie shell**
2 **pints vanilla ice cream**
½ **pound Oreo cookie pieces**
2 **pints orange sherbet**

Slightly soften vanilla ice cream, then beat with a paddle until smooth. Gently fold in cookie pieces, and spread into the pie shell. Beat orange sherbet with paddle until smooth and spread over the pie. Freeze until firm (about 4 hours). To serve, remove from freezer and let stand about 5 minutes. Slice and serve.

Preparation: 15 minutes	Easy	Serves: 8
Freeze: 4 hours	Must make ahead	

To make your own crust:

½ **pound Oreo cookie crumbs**
¼ **cup butter, melted**

Mix the crumbs together with the melted butter and line a 9–inch deep–dish pie pan. Bake at 325°F. for 20 minutes. Remove and let cool while you prepare the filling.

Preparation: 5 minutes	Easy	Serves: 8
Baking: 20 minutes		

Naples Community Hospital #2

When the Community Hospital began to burst out of its seams in 1964, a 14–bed addition helped, but did not solve the problems – and another drive for funds was underway the following year. This newest project was to cost $2,500,000. By September, pledges had been received for $1,750,000, and anticipated federal funds left only a little more than $500,000 to be financed.

In the late summer of 1966 the new tower and additions to the standing buildings provided 50 medical–surgical beds and better quarters for the expanding services and administration of the hospital.

Currently a new heart wing is under construction.

Key Limes

If you live in or come from Florida, you no doubt already have a passion for Key Lime Pie; if you are a visitor, don't leave town until you try it. Most Collier County residents who do not have a Key Lime tree in their own backyard seek a friend who does because the fruits are seldom available in the market-place and a Persian lime simply doesn't have the same zip. How can you tell the difference? Persian limes can be the size of a lemon; Key limes are quite small, yellow when ripe, have a thin skin, and are full of juice.

Persian Lime Pie with Chocolate – Coconut Crust

Glenview at Pelican Bay

1¼ cups coconut flakes, lightly toasted and chopped
2 Tablespoons soft butter
1 cup semi–sweet chocolate morsels, melted
1 (14–ounce) can sweetened condensed milk
4 Persian limes, zest and juice
1 cup heavy cream, whipped to soft peaks

Rub the interior of a 9" pie pan with the soft butter. Mix the coconut and chocolate together and mold into the pie pan, forming a thin bottom and side. Chill. Pour the sweetened condensed milk into a bowl and thoroughly mix in the lime juice and zest. Fold in the whipped cream. Pour into prepared pie shell and chill until set (1 hour), or freeze. Serve either chilled or frozen with raspberry sauce. Use a very sharp knife to cut through the crust.

Preparation: 30 minutes   Easy   Serves: 8
Must chill or freeze: 1 hour

Easy Key Lime Pie

Island Club of Naples Inc.

½ cup key lime juice
1 can sweetened condensed milk
1 cup heavy whipping cream
1 8–inch graham cracker pie shell

Mix the lime juice and condensed milk until smooth and blended. Whip cream and fold into key lime mixture. Spoon mixture into pie shell and chill overnight. To serve, garnish with key lime slices and dollops of whipped cream.

Preparation: 15 minutes   Easy   Serves: 6
Chill: overnight

Key Lime Pie
Maxwell's on the Bay

1 unbaked pie shell
2¼ cups (18 ounces) sweetened condensed milk
6 egg yolks (from large eggs)
6 Tablespoons key lime juice
Garnish:
1 cup whipped cream

Preheat oven to 400°F. Bake the pie shell for 10 minutes or until golden. In a mixing bowl combine the condensed milk and egg yolks. Blend well. Add the lime juice, slowly mixing together. Pour into baked pie shell and bake 10 minutes at 300°F. Remove from oven and let cool. Serve with whipped cream. Refrigerate leftovers.

NOTE—*the amount of sweetened condensed milk is greater than 1 can, so measure carefully!*

Preparation: 10 minutes   Easy   Serves: 8
Crust Baking: 10 minutes
Pie Baking: 10 minutes

Key Lime Pie
Marco Polo Restaurant

1 graham cracker crust
2 cups heavy cream
10 ounces sweetened condensed milk
⅔ cup key lime juice

Whip cream until stiff, slowly add condensed milk and blend in lime juice. Freeze 30 minutes to 1 hour before serving.

Preparation: 10 minutes   Easy   Serves: 4–6
Freezing: 30 minutes to 1 hour   Must do ahead

Limes

In England, during the 18th century, limes were issued to British sailors with their rum ration to prevent scurvy—which is how the sailors came to be called "limeys." About half the size of a lemon, limes contain one–third more citric acid.

Key Lime

The Key Lime is neither a native of Florida nor of the Keys, but is thought to be a cross between the Persian lime and the northern Indian lime trees. With established trade routes between India and North America, Spain and Portugal, it could easily have been carried there and eventually to the Americas, where it became naturalized in the West Indies and the Florida Keys. Thus its present day name: Key or West Indian Lime. The tree flowers throughout the year and bears some fruit most of the year.

Education

Records indicate that makeshift schools held classes in private kitchens, tin sheds, palmetto shacks and even, in one instance, an old out–house. Later the lumber for schoolhouses was provided by the county. Schools of record existed near what is now Port of the Islands, Chokoloskee, Everglade (the original spelling of Everglades City), Marco Island, Belle Meade, and on Pig Key Island (south of Marco).

Naples first public school was built in 1900 by Capt. Charles W. Stewart and Andrew Weeks, who also shared construction costs and paid the teacher's salary until the county took over. Stewart's son Arthur attended the school in 1915 and became the first graduate of the new Naples High School in 1928. Earlier high school students had to travel to Everglades City or Fort Myers.

Paradise Peanut Butter Pie

Lakewood Country Club

1 8–or 9–inch graham cracker (or cookie crust) pie shell
4 ounces cream cheese, softened
⅓ cup powdered sugar
½ cup peanut butter
3 Tablespoons vanilla instant pudding
12 ounces non–dairy whipped topping

Mix together the cream cheese, powdered sugar, peanut butter and instant pudding until well blended. Mix in the whipped topping and carefully spoon into the pie shell, being careful not to crack the pie shell (the mixture is very thick). Chill at least 1 hour. Serve with a dollop of whipped cream and drizzle chocolate syrup over the top of each slice.

Preparation: 20 minutes   Easy   Serves: 6–8
Chill: 1 hour

Pecan Pie

Countryside Country Club

1 9–inch unbaked pie shell
6 eggs
1¼ cups brown sugar
3 Tablespoons melted butter, cooled
1 cup dark corn syrup
1 teaspoon vanilla
¼ teaspoon salt
1 cup pecan halves

Mix all ingredients together, stirring after each addition. Pour into an unbaked 9–inch pie shell. Bake at 375°F. until done, about 1 hour.

Preparation: 15 minutes   Easy   Serves: 6–8
Baking: 1 hour

Measurements and Useful Cooking Terms

Dash – less than ⅛ teaspoon
Trace – less than ⅛ liquid teaspoon
3 teaspoons – 1 Tablespoon
2 Tablespoons – 1 liquid ounce – ⅛ cup
4 Tablespoons – 2 liquid ounces – ¼ cup
5 Tablespoons plus 1 teaspoon – ⅓ cup

8 Tablespoons – 4 liquid ounces – ½ cup
16 Tablespoons – 8 liquid ounces – 1 cup
2 cups – 16 liquid ounces – 1 pint
2 pints – 32 liquid ounces – 1 quart
2 quarts – 64 liquid ounces – ½ gallon
4 quarts – 128 liquid ounces – 1 gallon

Blanch – An item is blanched when it is plunged into boiling water for a brief time and then placed in cold water to stop the cooking process

Clarified Butter – or drawn butter is made by slowly melting unsalted butter and letting the milk solids sink to the bottom of the pan. The clear, golden liquid on the surface is the clarified butter. (**Hint** – be sure to skim off any foam floating at the top.)

Deglaze – A technique accomplished by removing sautéed meat from pan, draining off excess fat, returning pan to heat and adding a small amount of liquid, usually stock or wine, to loosen the browned bits remaining in pan. This seasoned liquid serves as a base for an accompanying sauce or gravy.

Pot – A round deep container with a lid and usually two handles, used for soups and such.

Roux – A mixture made by melting butter and stirring in flour over low heat until golden or beige. Used to thicken mixtures such as soups or sauces.

Saucepan – A round pan with a fairly long handle, straight, deep sides and a tight fitting cover.

Sauté – To cook meat or fish in a small amount of oil or butter over direct, usually high heat.

Sauté Pan – A flat pan with straight or slightly curved sides higher than that of a frying pan.

Simmer – Cooking at a low enough temperature that tiny bubbles just begin to break the surface.

Skillet – A long–handled frying pan with sloping sides to collect the steam that arises from foods being cooked over high heat.

Zest – The colorful outer layer of citrus fruit which is removed for flavor. (**Hint** – only the colored portion of the skin is considered the zest of the fruit.)

Hints on How Much to Buy

Item	Amount to Buy	For Prepared Amount
Bacon	8 slices	½ cup crumbled
Beans, dried	½ pound	1 cup
Bell peppers, all colors	1 large	1 cup chopped
Bibb Lettuce	1 medium head	3 cups torn
Boston Lettuce	1 medium head	5 cups torn
Broccoli	1 pound	3½ cups flowerets
Cabbage	1 small head (1 pound)	5 cups shredded
Carrots	2 medium	1 cup sliced
Cauliflower	1 medium head (1½ pounds)	4 cups flowerets
Celery	1 stalk	½ cup sliced
Cheese, Cheddar	4 ounces	1 cup shredded
Cheese, Parmesan	¼ pound (4 ounces)	1¼ cup grated
Chicken	1 large, boned breast	2 cups cooked
Green onions with tops	1 bunch of 7	½ cup sliced
Herbs, fresh	1 Tablespoon	1 teaspoon dried
Iceberg lettuce	1 small head	7½ cups torn
Meat, cooked	1 pound	3 cups chopped
Mushrooms	¾ pounds	3 cups sliced
Onion	1 medium	½ cup chopped
Pasta	¼ pound, uncooked	2-2½ cups cooked
Rice	1 cup raw, long-grain white	3 cups cooked
Romaine	1 medium	10 cups torn
Shrimp	1 pound raw in shell	½ pound, cleaned
Spinach	1 pound	12 cups torn
Tomato	1 medium	1 cup chopped

Metric Conversion Information

IF YOU HAVE	MULTIPLY BY	TO EQUAL
teaspoons	5	milliliters
Tablespoons	15	milliliters
fluid ounces	30	milliliters
cups	.24	liters
pints	.47	liters
quarts	.95	liters
ounces	28	grams
pounds	.45	kilograms
inches	2.544	centimeters

LIQUID MEASURE TO MILLILITERS

¼ teaspoon	=	1.25 milliliters
½ teaspoon	=	2.50 milliliters
¾ teaspoon	=	3.75 milliliters
1 teaspoon	=	5.00 milliliters
1¼ teaspoons	=	6.25 milliliters
1½ teaspoons	=	7.50 milliliters
1¾ teaspoons	=	8.75 milliliters
2 teaspoons	=	10 milliliters
1 Tablespoon	=	15 milliliters

LIQUID MEASURE TO LITERS

¼ cup	=	.06 liters
½ cup	=	.12 liters
¾ cup	=	.18 liters
1 cup	=	.24 liters
1¼ cups	=	.30 liters
1½ cups	=	.36 liters
2 cups	=	.48 liters
2½ cups	=	.60 liters
3 cups	=	.72 liters

FARENHEIT TO CELSIUS

°F	°C
275	135
300	149
325	163
350	177
375	191
400	205
425	218
450	232
475	246
500	260

Participating Businesses

Restaurants, Hotels, Resorts, Private Clubs, and Retirement Resorts participating in this cookbook:

Restaurants—

Alexander's
4077 Tamiami Trail N.
Naples, FL

Apollo's Oceanview Restaurant
900 S. Collier Boulevard
Marco Island, FL

Asti Ristorante
886 Neapolitan Way
Naples, FL

Bayside
4270 Gulfshore Boulevard N.
Naples, FL

Bistro 821
821 Fifth Avenue S.
Naples, FL

Blue Heron Inn
387 Capri Boulevard
Marco Island, FL

Bon Appetit
3126 Ninth Street N.
Naples, FL

Busghetti Ristorante
155 First Avenue
Marco Island, FL

Cafe de Marco
244 Palm Street
Marco, Island, FL

Calella's Bistro Inc.
368 Fifth Avenue S.
Naples, FL

The Chef's Garden
1300 Third Street S.
Naples, FL

The Dock Restaurant at Crayton Cove
Twelfth Street S.
Naples, FL

Fernandez de Bull
4951 Tamiami Trail N.
Naples, FL

The Fifth Season Restaurant
4947 Tamiami Trail N.
Naples, FL

First Watch Restaurant
1400 Gulfshore Boulevard N.
Naples, FL

Frascati's Italian Restaurant
1258 Airport Pulling Road
Naples, FL

Golden China Chinese Restaurant
1831 San Marco Road
Marco Island, FL

Graf Rudi Restaurant
870 Neapolitan Way
Naples, FL

Hilde's Tea Room
336 Thirteenth Avenue S.
Naples, FL

Il Posto Restaurant
1170 Third Street S.
Naples, FL

Island Club of Naples Inc.
600 Neapolitan Way
Naples, FL

Kelly's Fish House Dining Room
1302 Fifth Avenue S.
Naples, FL

Key Wester Fish & Pasta House
1001 Tenth Avenue S.
Naples, FL

Konrad's Seafood & Grille Room
599 S. Collier Boulevard
Marco Island, FL

Kretch's Garden Restaurant
527 Bald Eagle Drive
Marco Island, FL

L'Auberge on Fifth Restaurant Français
602 Fifth Avenue S.
Naples, FL

The Little Bar
205 Harbor Drive
Marco Island, FL

Mageiro Restaurant & Bar
2840 Ninth Street N.
Naples, FL

Mangrove Cafe
878 Fifth Avenue S.
Naples, FL

Marco Polo Restaurant
30 Marco Lake Drive
Marco Island, Fl

Margaux's
3080 Tamiami Trail N.
Naples, FL

Marie Michelle's on the Bay
Village on Venetian Bay
Naples, FL

Maxwell's on the Bay
4300 Gulf Shore Boulevard N.
Naples, FL

Merriman's Wharf
1200 Fifth Avenue S.
Naples, FL

Michael's Cafe
2950 Ninth Street N.
Naples, FL

Noodles Cafe Inc.
2059 Pine Ridge Road
Naples, FL

Olde Marco Inn
100 Palm Street
Marco Island, FL

The Palm Restaurant
754 Neapolitan Way
Naples, FL

Pazzo!
853 Fifth Avenue S.
Naples, FL

Plum's Cafe
8920 Ninth Street N.
Naples, FL

Ridgeport Pub
5425 Airport Pulling Road N.
Naples, FL

Savannah a Fine Traditional Restaurant
5200 Tamiami Trail N.
Naples, FL

Shing Long Gourmet Chinese Restaurant
3615 Ninth Street N.
Naples, FL

Trio's
1170 Third Street S.
Naples, FL

Truffles
1300 Third Street S.
Naples, FL

Villa Pescatore
8900 Tamiami Trail N.
Naples, FL

Vito's Restaurant
1079 Bald Eagle Drive
Marco Island, FL

Voilà! Wine Bar & Brasserie
590 Ninth Street N.
Naples, FL

Hotels and Resorts—

Edgewater Beach Hotel
1901 Gulf Shore Boulevard N.
Naples, FL

LA PLAYA Beach Resort
9891 Gulfshore Boulevard
Naples, FL

Marco Island Hilton Beach Resort
560 S. Collier Boulevard
Marco Island, FL

Naples Beach Hotel and Golf Club
851 Gulfshore Boulevard N.
Naples, FL

The REGISTRY Resort
475 Seagate Drive
Naples, FL

The Ritz–Carlton Naples
280 Vanderbilt Beach Road
Naples, FL

Vanderbilt Inn on the Gulf
1100 Gulf Shore Drive N.
Naples, FL

Private Clubs—

Bay Colony Club
8553 Bay Colony Drive
Naples, FL

Bear's Paw Country Club
2500 Golden Gate Parkway
Naples, FL

Bonita Bay Club
27598 Marina Point Drive
Bonita Springs, FL

Collier Athletic Club
710 Goodlette Road N.
Naples, FL

The Club Pelican Bay
707 Gulf Park Drive
Naples, FL

Collier's Reserve Country Club
11711 Collier's Reserve Drive
Naples, FL

Country Club of Naples
185 Burning Tree Drive
Naples, FL

Countryside Country Club
600 Countryside Drive
Naples, FL

Hole–in–the–Wall Golf Club Inc.
Frank Road
Naples, FL

Imperial Golf Club
1808 Imperial Golf Course Boulevard
Naples, FL

Lakewood Country Club
4235 Lakewood Boulevard
Naples, FL

The Moorings Country Club
2500 Crayton Road
Naples, FL

Naples Bath & Tennis Club
4995 Airport Road N.
Naples, FL

Naples Sailing & Yacht Club
896 River Point Drive
Naples, FL

The Naples Yacht Club
700 Fourteenth Avenue S.
Naples, FL

Quail Creek Country Club
13300 Valewood Drive
Naples, FL

Royal Poinciana Golf Club Inc.
Goodlette Road
Naples, FL

Vineyards Country Club
400 Vineyards Boulevard
Naples, FL

Wilderness Country Club
101 Clubhouse Drive
Naples, FL

Worthington Country Club
13500 Worthington Way
Bonita Springs, FL

Wyndemere Country Club
700 Wyndemere Way
Naples, FL

Retirement Resorts—

Bentley Village
561 Bentley Village Court
Naples, FL

Glenview at Pelican Bay
100 Glenview Place
Naples, FL

Moorings Park
120 Moorings Park Drive
Naples, FL

Compliments of the Chef Committees

Co-Chairmen
Clara Obern
Judy Keim

Executive Committee
Jinny Dean
Jody Glatt
Betty Lagay
Neena Lurvey
Bunny Pendleton
Rose Somogyi
Betty Steers
Pat Ware

Office Staff
Joan Hazlett
Sharyn Shubert

Recipe Collection Coordinator
Bunny Pendleton, Chair
Jody Glatt
Howard Kaufman
Neena Lurvey
Clara Obern
Judy Pearson
Pat Ware

Writer of Naples History
Jinny Dean

Design and Layout Consultants
Sherry Cabral
Lee Mills
of Sir Speedy/Digital Alternatives

Recipe Advisor/Home Economist
Neena Lurvey

Researchers for Page Fillers
Jinny Dean
Penny Graham-Yooll
Bunny Pendleton
Betty Steers

Typing
Clara Obern, Chair
Judy Keim

Recipe Review Committee
Clara Obern
Jody Glatt
Judy Keim
Peter Keim
Rose Somogyi

Recipe Tester Coordinator
Jody Glatt

Art Solicitation and Selection
Bunny Pendleton, Chair
Jody Glatt
Judy Keim
Clara Obern

Special Events
Dorothy Coakley
Pat O'Hara
Paula Robertson

Sales/Distribution
Sue Benson, Co-Chair
Judy Keim, Co-Chair
Betty Lagay, Off-site Sales
Betty Steers, On-site Sales
Dorothy Coakley
Pat O'Hara

Recipe Testers
Jody Glatt, Coordinator

Barbarita Arredondo
Doreen Austrevich
Elinor Bedell
Corinne Capor
Helen Caruso
Violet Church
Noreen Clesen
Mary–Lou K. Coyle
Joyce Derry
Joyce Doyle
Susan Eibel
Suzanne Fantucchio
Glenda Farlander
Mona Foulke
Muriel Girard
Jody Glatt
Florence Hiniker
Carol M. Hird
Lois Kaul
C. Kelly
Peter Keim
Edna Kley
Betty Lagay
Marie Lagnese
Lois Lange
Nancy Lewis
Mary Ann Lowenkron
Susie Lublin
Marilyn Matos
Sara McIntyre
Cindy Mihalic

Adelia Muir
Betty Mulder
Barbara Monroe
Mary Lou Munroe
Charles Nevaril
Maureen Nevaril
Clara Obern
Marcia Reff
Bernice Reisman
Barbara Rogers
Helen Ross
Marla J. Roulton
Kay Ruel
Darla Routson
Fritzi Ryan
Catherine Smith
Rose Somogyi
Kay Stopford
Ellie Thompson–Stephans
Christine Tilchen
Francine Tuite
Rena M. Walter
Mim Wedel
Jerry Weinstock
Frances Welch
Andi Whitney
Maxine Williamson
Heather Winsby
Barbara Wright
Madeline Yager
Liz Zoarski

Bibliography

Altschul, B. J. *Cracker Cookin' and Other Favorites*. Altamonte Springs, FL:
    Winner Enterprises, 1986.

Baum Earl L., M.D. *Early Naples and Collier County*. Naples, FL:
    Collier County Historical Society, 1973.

Brown, Robin C. *Florida's First People:-12,000 Years of Human History*. Sarasota, FL:
    Pineapple Press, Inc., 1994.

Dean, Virginia. *Naples-on-the-Gulf*. Chatsworth, CA:
    Windsor Publications, Inc., 1991.

Prop Roots Vol. I, *Recipes from the Mangrove Country of The Everglades*. Everglades City,
    FL: Courtesy of Everglades City High School, c. 1986.

Index

Compliments of the Chef
THE FRIENDS OF THE LIBRARY OF COLLIER COUNTY, INC.
P.O. BOX 2921
NAPLES, FL 34106
(941) 262-8135

Please send me_____copies of *Compliments of the Chef* at
$24.95 EACH, plus $3.50 handling and shipping. **(FLORIDA RESIDENTS
ADD 6% SALES TAX.)** Payable in U.S. funds. **Make checks payable to
The Friends of the Library of Collier County, Inc.**

Enclosed is my check or money order in the amount of $_____

Please charge my: (circle one) **MC VISA DISCOVER AMEX**

CARD # _____ EXP_____

SIGNATURE_____

NAME —————————————————

———————————————————

ADDRESS———————————————

———————————————————

CITY————————————————

STATE _____ ZIP _____

DAYTIME PHONE (____) _____

- -

Compliments of the Chef
THE FRIENDS OF THE LIBRARY OF COLLIER COUNTY, INC.
P.O. BOX 2921
NAPLES, FL 34106
(941) 262-8135

Please send me_____copies of *Compliments of the Chef* at
$24.95 EACH, plus $3.50 handling and shipping. **(FLORIDA RESIDENTS
ADD 6% SALES TAX.)** Payable in U.S. funds. **Make checks payable to
The Friends of the Library of Collier County, Inc.**

Enclosed is my check or money order in the amount of $_____

Please charge my: (circle one) **MC VISA DISCOVER AMEX**

CARD # _____ EXP_____

SIGNATURE_____

NAME —————————————————

———————————————————

ADDRESS———————————————

———————————————————

CITY————————————————

STATE _____ ZIP _____

DAYTIME PHONE (____) _____

- -

Compliments of the Chef
THE FRIENDS OF THE LIBRARY OF COLLIER COUNTY, INC.
P.O. BOX 2921
NAPLES, FL 34106
(941) 262-8135

Please send me_____copies of *Compliments of the Chef* at
$24.95 EACH, plus $3.50 handling and shipping. **(FLORIDA RESIDENTS
ADD 6% SALES TAX.)** Payable in U.S. funds. **Make checks payable to
The Friends of the Library of Collier County, Inc.**

Enclosed is my check or money order in the amount of $_____

Please charge my: (circle one) **MC VISA DISCOVER AMEX**

CARD # _____ EXP_____

SIGNATURE_____

NAME —————————————————

———————————————————

ADDRESS———————————————

———————————————————

CITY————————————————

STATE _____ ZIP _____

DAYTIME PHONE (____) _____